MW00762919

THE AMERICAN LANGUAGE OF RIGHTS

Richard A. Primus examines three crucial periods in American history (the late eighteenth century, the Civil War and the 1950s and 1960s) in order to demonstrate how the conceptions of rights prevailing at each of these times grew out of reactions to contemporary social and political crises. His innovative approach sees rights language as grounded more in opposition to concrete social and political practices than in the universalistic paradigms presented by many political philosophers. This study demonstrates the potency of the language of rights throughout American history and looks for the first time at the impact of modern totalitarianism (in Nazi Germany and the Soviet Union) on American conceptions of rights. *The American Language of Rights* is a major contribution to contemporary political theory, of interest to scholars and students in politics and government, constitutional law, and American history.

RICHARD A. PRIMUS studied political theory at Harvard and Oxford and law at Yale.

IDEAS IN CONTEXT

Edited by QUENTIN SKINNER (*General Editor*), LORRAINE DASTON
and JAMES TULLY

The books in this series will discuss the emergence of intellectual traditions
and of related new disciplines. The procedures, aims and vocabularies that
were generated will be set in the context of the alternatives available within
the contemporary frameworks of ideas and institutions. Through detailed
studies of the evolution of such traditions, and their modification by
different audiences, it is hoped that a new picture will form of the
development of ideas in their concrete contexts. By this means, artificial
distinctions between the history of philosophy, of the various sciences, of
society and politics, and of literature may be seen to dissolve.

The series is published with the support of the Exxon Foundation.

A list of books in the series will be found at the end of the volume.

THE AMERICAN LANGUAGE
OF RIGHTS

RICHARD A. PRIMUS

CAMBRIDGE
UNIVERSITY PRESS

PUBLISHED BY THE PRESS SYNDICATE OF THE UNIVERSITY OF CAMBRIDGE
The Pitt Building, Trumpington Street, Cambridge, United Kingdom

CAMBRIDGE UNIVERSITY PRESS
The Edinburgh Building, Cambridge, CB2 2RU, United Kingdom   http://www.cup.cam.ac.uk
40 West 20th Street, New York, NY 10011–4211, USA   http://www.cup.org
10 Stamford Road, Oakleigh, Melbourne 3166, Australia

© Richard A. Primus 1999

First published 1999

Printed in the United Kingdom at the University Press, Cambridge

Typeset in Baskerville 11/12.5 pt   [CE]

A catalogue record for this book is available from the British Library

Library of Congress cataloguing in publication data

ISBN 0 521 65250 2 hardback

for Sarah
like everything else

"All of us, grave or light, get our thoughts entangled in metaphors, and act fatally on the strength of them."

George Eliot, *Middlemarch*

Contents

Acknowledgments

My foremost thanks for help with the project that became this book go to Michael Freeden, who patiently inducted me into the discipline of political theory. I am also grateful for the assistance of a host of other fine teachers, including Bruce Ackerman, Bernard Bailyn, Peter Berkowitz, Eric Foner, Paul Kahn, Sanford Levinson, Mark Philp, and Adam Swift. Without the benefit of their skepticism and suggestions, the ideas in this book would be even less developed than they now are. I also thank three others who have touched the life of this book in more diffuse but not less important ways: Guido Calabresi, Owen Fiss, and Bob Gordon.

There are two other teachers without whom this book could never have been written. One is H. W. Perry. I have studied constitutional law with several distinguished scholars since the September morning when he required me to state the facts of *Marbury v. Madison*, but his course remains my image of what a course in that subject should be. Finally, it is my greatest regret in these acknowledgments that I cannot thank the teacher to whom, in some ways, I owe more than any other: Judith Shklar. I believe that she would have disapproved of much of this project, but I find some consolation in believing that she would have enjoyed fighting with me about it.

The friends who have helped me with and through this book, in one way or another, are so many that I would risk offending by omission if I tried to name them all. Nevertheless, the pleasure of naming names is so great that I accept the risk, hoping to do more good than ill. I thank Gary Bass, Michael Bloom, Jennifer Bradley, Niko Canner, Marilyn Cooper, Ariela Dubler, Jonah Edelman, Elie Fishman, Jesse Furman, Robert Gordon, Eric Gregory, Jay Koh, Niko Kolodny, Rachel Harmon, Dan Libenson, Sarah Levine, Meira Levinson, Jack Levy, Laura McGrane, Nader Mousavizadeh, Brian Reed, Kevin Stack, Jody Seim Timmins, and Rebecca

Thomas Tingle. I also thank three others who followed by progress so closely and participated in my thinking so intimately, that I sometimes wondered how they could have any time or mental energy left for their own work. They are Noah Feldman, Nien-he Hsieh, and Kurt Strovink. For their friendship and their intellectual comeradeship, I am deeply grateful.

Richard Fisher and Elizabeth Howard of the Cambridge University Press provided patient hand-holding as a rough manuscript became a presentable book. Alan Lord tirelessly accommodated my demands on his library. I also thank the editors of the *Duke Law Journal* and the *Yale Law Journal* for permission to publish here, albeit in expanded form, some of the same ideas that I have previously presented in their pages.

Finally, I thank Aryeh, Lisa, Roni, Ida, Dima, my parents, and my grandparents. They know why.

R.A.P.
New Haven, 1999

Introduction

This is a book about rights. It is, to be more specific, a book about the place of rights in American political debate. The language of rights has been central to American political culture for centuries, and nearly every major issue in American political history has been argued as an issue of rights. In some circles, however, rights have recently fallen upon hard times. It has become a familiar refrain in politics that America is a land of too many rights and too few responsibilities. In the academy, the concept of rights today attracts criticism that is both serious and diverse. The critical legal studies movement charges that a rights-based political order is intellectually incoherent and morally pernicious, the former because rights conflict with one another and the latter because a system of rights entrenches the power of the privileged classes. Communitarians contend that framing political debate in terms of rights leads to excessive individualism, unwillingness to compromise, and the decline of community spirit. These two schools of thought differ in many important ways, but their different critiques of rights share the idea that the substance of American politics is conditioned by the fact that it speaks the language of rights. To some extent, that observation must be valid. Because language is often a constituent element of thought, belief, and action, political activity from legislative drafting to electioneering to international diplomacy relies upon and is shaped by the language that mediates and helps constitute the political world. When communitarian and critical legal scholars argue that speaking the language of rights pushes a political culture toward some substantive outcomes and away from others, the reality that language plays a constituent role in politics lends intuitive appeal to their claim.

That claim, however, underplays two other elements of the relationship between politics and language. First, the constituent relationship between them is reciprocal. Precisely because language and politics are closely interconnected and therefore difficult to analyze sophisticatedly in isolation from each other, it is hard to imagine language as a separate and antecedent sphere that influences politics while remaining itself untouched.[1] Language does shape politics, but politics shapes language as well. Second, the influence of language upon politics is not always narrowly determined. Even if speaking the language of rights does distinctively condition political discourse in America, it does not follow that the language of rights shapes politics in the specific ways that prominent critics contend. The tendency of rights discourse to favor one set of political outcomes over another, I suggest, has been widely overstated. As a conceptual matter, people with all sorts of differing political views can use the language of rights to their advantage. Such diverse usage is a historical fact, not merely an abstract possibility: the history of American rights discourse shows that Americans of all political stripes have in fact used the language of rights to support their various causes, and all of the greatest political conflicts in American history have involved, and been spoken about as, conflicts of rights. That these political conflicts have been described as conflicts between opposing rights rather than as conflicts between rights on one side and something else on the other suggests that the language of rights does not attach to only one kind of political outcome. Instead, either side of an issue can and usually will use the language of rights in support of its position. Eighteenth-century Americans who advocated independence from Britain drew heavily on the language of rights in their political writings, but Americans who opposed independence were no more loath to use rights language in their anti-independence arguments. In the nineteenth century, when the issue of slavery split the United States, abolitionists and Republicans argued their cause in the name of a whole battery of rights, ranging from the natural rights of people to be free to the rights of free labor and free speech. Southerners and slaveholders, however, also marshaled arguments from rights, invoking the right to property and the rights of states. Later conflicts in American history featured the right to strike against the right to work, the right to dispose of one's property in whatever way one

---

[1] I explore these ideas in more detail in chapter 1, with reference to scholars such as W. V. O. Quine and Quentin Skinner.

chose against the right to regulate private property in the public interest, the right to equality against the right of association, the rights of the federal government against the rights of the states, and the "right to life" against the "right to choose." In short, the language of rights has not shown itself systematically partisan to any one political vision at the expense of all others. It has been a versatile tool, suitable for many different agendas.

It could, of course, be argued that both sides in all of those conflicts shared elements of the classical liberal framework and that the language of rights is useful to all those (but only those) who are within that political family. Whether all of American politics can be described as liberal is the subject of a venerable scholarly debate which cannot be satisfactorily resolved here. I suspect that significant currents in American political thought can indeed be described as illiberal and that those currents, like others, have managed to use the language of rights. For present purposes, however, it is enough to say that a liberalism broad enough to encompass all major currents in American politics necessarily encompasses everything, or almost everything, that is worth studying in American political discourse. Whether or not rights language can only support liberal ends, it can and has supported virtually every significant agenda that has been pursued in American politics.

If it is not true, as both the critical legal scholars and the communitarians allege, that rights discourse systematically privileges a certain kind of political outcome, it still might be true that arguing in terms of rights is not an intellectually coherent way of framing political or moral debate. After all, the critical scholar might point out, the litany of conflicts above suggests that we cannot resolve issues by reference to rights, because rights so often conflict with one another. There is a sense in which that critique is well made. It is true that rights conflict, so it is true that asking which side in a dispute is the possessor of applicable rights will not always yield a clear resolution to the dispute. It does not follow, however, that the language of rights is an incoherent way of talking about political issues, because conflicts among rights raise problems only if one believes that we should be able to settle substantive questions by reference to rights alone. In other words, the charge that rights language is an insufficiently good adjudicatory framework is significant only if one assumes that the sole or highest function of rights language is adjudicatory. That assumption is common, ironically, to the liberal theorists who would use rights as means of adjudication and the communitarian and critical legal scholars who object that rights discourse is inadequate as an adjudicatory framework.

The language of rights is, however, at least as much about rhetoric and reflection as it is about adjudication. Rhetoric is one of the obvious ways in which language and politics come together, and, considered as a species of political rhetoric, the practice of rights discourse is entirely coherent. As I argue throughout this book, analyzing rights discourse as a form of political rhetoric exposes patterns that leave the meanings of various rights claims more clear than they would otherwise be. There is a gap between the common literal understanding of statements like "I have a right to privacy" and a different set of meanings that the statement carries, meanings that say more about the political values of the speaker than about an objective moral or legal order and which may be all the better for the refocusing, given the real deficiencies of rights discourse as a means of describing such orders. Not all uses of rights language are merely rhetorical, of course: careful reflections of judges and scholars concerned with rights often differ in character from the assertions of agitators and political skirmishers. Accordingly, the rules governing the uses and best interpretations of rights language are not rigidly identical for all circles of discussion. But no sharp line divides jurisprudence or political philosophy from politics itself. Indeed, the best way to understand even the self-conscious rights philosophy of sophisticated liberal theory is not as abstract philosophy alone but also as political discourse.

Not only does liberal rights theory have a political aspect, but its uses of rights language are politically powerful. One reason why the liberal theorists who use the language of rights are likely to defeat their critics on the field that really matters – that is, the field of politics – is precisely that they use the language of rights rather than deconstructing it. In the world of American political discourse, a strong claim of rights, any rights, tends to overpower a subtle intellectual argument about the shortcomings of rights as a concept. When I say that the political field is the field that matters, I say nothing with which those critics should disagree. Critical legal studies has long insisted that philosophy is inescapably political, and communitarian thinkers generally argue, in an aspirational vein, that the philosopher should strive to bring philosophy and politics together. It is ironic that many of those who most explicitly argue for the nexus between academics and politics cannot or do not use the political value of academic discourse as effectively as the liberals whom they critique. That pattern is especially characteristic of the critical legal scholars. Some communitarians, in contrast, have shown themselves more able to use the language of rights when it is useful to advance their political arguments, irrespective of the fact that communitarianism also contains a strong strain critical of rights discourse.[2] Their willingness to use the language of rights greatly increases the possibility that their political arguments will be persuasive to American audiences, and indeed communitarian ideas are now ascendant in American political discourse. Using the language of rights may dilute communitarianism's intellectual distinctiveness, but it also contributes to the political potency of its platform.

Similarly, the recent critical race theory movement in American law schools tries to support its political agenda by adding an affirmative view of rights to the critical legal studies paradigm. It is not yet clear how, if at all, a legal theory can coherently merge the deconstructive posture of critical legal studies with the celebration of traditionally conceived notions of rights. My own suspicion is that it cannot be done, at least not from a purely philosophical perspective which judges theories by their intellectual consistency. Critical race theory, however, is avowedly political, measuring its success not just by those abstract philosophical standards but also by the concrete results it can achieve for its vision of society.[3] Just as the rights-affirming communitarians have helped make communitarianism a more significant political force, the use of rights language by critical race theorists may make them more powerful political players than their critical legal studies predecessors. In both cases, the uses of rights language raise questions about how much of a scholarly discourse should be understood as different from political rhetoric and how much should be interpreted in the ways appropriate for the analysis of everyday political claims.

This book, then, analyzes how politicians, lawyers, and philosophers in the United States have actually used the language of rights. Rights discourse, I argue, should be understood as a coherent social

---

[2] Compare, for example, the attitudes toward rights of more politically engaged communitarians like Amitai Etzioni with those of more philosophical communitarians like Michael Sandel.

[3] On critical race theory's framework and goals, see Angela Harris, "Foreword: The Jurisprudence of Reconstruction," *California Law Review* 82, 741 (1994).

practice, available to a wide range of political agendas and including within its scope the political argument of philosophers as well as politicians, though more sophisticated in some contexts than in others. At the crudest level, Americans often claim the satisfaction of any needs or interests they consider important and deserving of special protection as "rights." These claims are limited in only two ways. First, "rights" is an umbrella term encompassing entitlements, liberties, powers, and immunities, concepts that will be explicated in chapter 1. Second, "There is a right X" means approximately "X is important and should be protected." No other principle, formal or substantive, underlies all the claims of rights that Americans advance or even accept. This understanding of what it means for something to be a right might seem rough and permissive, but it does capture the way that the concept of rights actually operates in much of American politics.

In more disciplined rights philosophy, rights are often the conclusions or waystations of an argument rather than raw normative declarations. Theorists who think about rights in a justificatory way recognize that they must give arguments for why certain things should be rights and that those arguments should not be reducible to emotivism, and theorists who reason in what is now called "reflective equilibrium," revising in turn a set of tentative principles and tentative implications until a desirable system is found, can have "rights" stand in on either side of the ledger. Rights so conceived are revisable working constructs rather than ontological truths.[4] It is not the case, however, that these sophistications make the patterns of academic rights discourse wholly different from the cruder rights discourse of simple advocacy. More refined versions of the same two rules described above do in fact capture the way the concept operates in much of political philosophy. The four categories named in the first rule bound academic as well as non-academic rights discourse; one difference between the discourses is that many academics as well as judges are loath to use "rights" indiscriminately across the four analytic categories, preferring to restrict rights to one or two among the four. Many also try to narrow the second rule, developing theories ostensibly aimed at giving more specific content to rights than "X is important and should be protected." Both of those projects, however, have political undercurrents, because both

---

[4] The idea of reflective equilibrium is discussed further in chapter 1.

have the effect of limiting the rhetorically powerful category of rights to a subset of the propositions that it might be used to support. Theorists with different political commitments tend to produce different formal conceptions of rights which, in turn, support the different commitments that suffuse the formal theories. Deciding which formal conception of rights is best can therefore be much the same as deciding which set of substantive political commitments is best. In other words, even sophisticated arguments about rights are frequently surrogates for arguments about the substance of politics. To try to settle political questions by reference to theories of rights is problematic at best, because theories of rights do not supply evidence of an order prior to and regulative of politics. They are part of what is contested in political discourse, and the student of politics can learn a great deal about the commitments of political actors, including political philosophers, by analyzing how they use the language of rights.

Not only do formal conceptions of rights reflect substantive political commitments, but the substantive political commitments they reflect change in response to changing historical conditions. Characteristically, the change has been reactive, as people respond to a new set of problems by articulating a new set of rights. I say "reactive" rather than "adaptive" because the major pattern of development in American rights discourse has been one of concrete negation: innovations in conceptions of rights have chiefly occurred in opposition to new adversities, as people articulate new rights that would, if accepted, negate the crisis at hand. In the first years of the American republic, for example, conceptions of rights were frequently grounded in opposition to the British colonial administration. In the nineteenth century, political and judicial conceptions of rights in the American North were often framed in opposition to the slave-labor system of the South. During and after World War II, Americans participating in every kind of rights discourse from the crudest to the most refined rethought the content and form of rights in ways inspired by opposition to European totalitarianism and especially to Nazism. At the end of the twentieth century, the rights discourse of American law, politics, and political philosophy bears the mark of all of these influences. Thus, when the substantive aims of rights discourse change, new rights and sometimes new theories of rights arise to carry the content of the new political commitments. Moreover, the relationship between the substantive commitments and the formal, conceptual aspects of rights theory is reciprocal: after new crises shape new commitments and new commitments shape new approaches to rights, linguistic and conceptual elements of the new approaches to rights can in turn help shape substantive political commitments.

The language of rights, then, is a powerful and coherent method not just of reflecting but also of privileging substantive political commitments, a method suitable for an extremely wide variety of ends and regularly employed by academics, politicians, lawyers, and virtually everyone else who argues about political issues. And yet, rights discourse has failings. Notably, as the coming chapters will illustrate, it frequently permits obfuscation in political debate, because claims of rights often enable bare assertions to pass as reasoned arguments. Perhaps that very feature, clearly a short-coming from a rationalist point of view, explains part of the lasting appeal that rights discourse has held in American politics. Because rights language offers advocates the possibility of presenting asser-tion as argument, people more concerned to advance a substantive set of political ends than to illuminate a philosophical question are often well served by harnessing the language of rights. Such advocates sacrifice precision of thought, and they expose themselves to the charge that their arguments cannot, in the end, be grounded in anything outside their own political commitments. But that is no more than to say that their politics are rooted in their politics, which may be the case already.

There is here a temptation to say that this problem of circularity should be avoided by not permitting rights language to obfuscate debate and instead insisting that the true grounds underlying a claim of rights should be considered and argued about directly. If one theory of rights relies upon a strong notion of individualism and another on a normative conception of nature, perhaps it would be better to decide conflicts between them not by arguing about rights but by asking about individualism and nature directly. Unfortunately, it would then be necessary to look for the grounds of individualism and naturalism, and, having grounded those concepts in yet other concepts whose grounds would have to be sought in turn, we might soon question what we really meant when we said we were looking for the "true grounds" of the normative argument in the first place. Clifford Geertz told a now-famous story about being confronted by a man who denied the reigning scientific understanding of planetary orbits, insisting that the earth is in fact borne aloft on the back of an elephant. The elephant, he said, was standing on a turtle. When pressed as to what supported the turtle, he replied that it was another turtle; in fact, he explained, it was "turtles all the way down."[5] Rights are not rights all the way down, but they may not be standing a step or two from the bottom, either, perhaps because there is no bottom to stand upon and perhaps because it is unclear what a bottom would look like if we found one. That rights cannot be the ultimate justificatory ground of a normative argument is thus not a conclusive argument against using rights discourse in politics, because it may not be the nature of normative theory to yield that kind of ground. Knowing that rights are not themselves the grounds, however, does mean that we should be careful not to regard them as such. That caution is all the more important in a culture like America, where the language of rights carries substantial rhetorical power. And it should be applied to the discourse of philosophers and judges who think reflectively about rights as well as other kinds of political actors whose theories are thinner, because philosophers and judges are partly political rhetoricians, perhaps inescapably so. Language and politics come together for them as well as for others, shaping their theories of rights.

[5] Clifford Geertz, *The Interpretation of Cultures: Selected Essays* (Basic Books, 1973), pp. 28–29.

CHAPTER I

Rights theory and rights practice

When two people compete in a game of chess, they each try to win according to the same set of rules. The means of achieving victory are identical for both of them and known to both players in advance. They may find infinite ways of playing the game within the rules that set permissible moves and victory conditions, but those rules and conditions are prior to the game. Nothing that either player can do would suddenly increase the size of the board, or permit one player to move twice in a row, or let one player declare victory by, say, taking the other player's queen as opposed to the king. The rules of the game are static and defined outside the play of the game itself; playing the game consists in adhering to those rules rather than challenging or trying to reshape them.

Law and politics have their share of games or competitive situations like games. When a legislature or a court is going to decide a controversial issue, advocates for rival outcomes use power, rhetoric, argument, and whatever else they can muster to try to secure a favorable outcome. They compete with one another, trying to out-argue and outmaneuver their opponents, and the competition among them is a kind of game with certain patterns and restrictions that might be thought of as rules. There might be a rule specifying that nothing will be a law that does not receive the support of a majority of some legislature, or that one cannot secure someone's vote by promising to pay him or her millions of dollars, or that nobody may be convicted of treason without the testimony of two witnesses. One of the most important ways in which these games of law and politics differ from games like chess, however, concerns the relationship between the rules and the play of the game. In political and legal argument, part of the contest is over how the issue in dispute will be characterized and what kinds of arguments will count as valid or superior. When the same question could be presented as a matter of free speech or a matter of community decency, it matters which presentation prevails; if something is agreed to be a matter of free speech, it matters what the decision-makers take "free speech" to mean. The struggle to define the grounds and terms of an argument is a struggle to set the rules of the game for a particular contest. As such, it is often the most important element of the contest, because setting the rules can go a long way toward determining the outcome. In legal and political discourse, then, shaping the rules is not something that happens before the game is played but is itself the subject of a contest, and attempts to shape the rules are not preliminaries to the game but moves within the game itself.

In one of the most important books of recent legal theory, *Law's Empire*, Ronald Dworkin offers an account of law that recognizes this interconnection between conducting legal arguments and arguing about what the rules of legal argument should be.[1] Dworkin argues that legal interpretation, the activity required of judges, consists in making the law and the legal system the best that they can be, and deciding which construction of the law makes the law the best that it can be involves choosing some theory of how the law in general should be understood. That choice is inescapably normative, and, once the choice is made, the normative theory chosen is supposed to set the rules for legal argument and interpretation. Nevertheless, the choice of theory should not be understood as occurring outside of or prior to legal argument itself. Theorizing about law, Dworkin knows, is part of legal argument; interpretive legal theories are not descriptions that stand outside the game but rather moves within the game. The descriptive and the prescriptive collapse on this model, as theories about the law are seen as attempts to construct law in one way rather than another. Definitions of legal concepts or canons of interpretation therefore must be seen as part of, rather than prior to, the contest that is legal argument.

It is therefore ironic that Dworkin's leading contribution to the theory of rights is a definition of rights as a legal concept and that Dworkin sometimes treats that definition as regulating substantive argument rather than being part of what legal and political argument contests. His definition is that a right is a metaphorical trump card, held by an individual, that can prevent the government or

---

[1] Ronald Dworkin, *Law's Empire* (Harvard University Press, 1986).

society at large from doing a certain thing, even if doing that thing would be in society's general interest.[2] Thus, if I have the right to free speech, I cannot legitimately be silenced even if my keeping quiet would be better for society. My right to speak trumps society's interest in my silence. Some things simply cannot be done or denied to individuals, Dworkin says, and we call the guarantees of those imperatives "rights."

Dworkin's definition holds a central place in contemporary rights theory, perhaps because it so powerfully captures two prevailing intuitions about rights. First, it ties rights to individualism. Liberals like Dworkin have placed protection of individuals against the will of the community at the center of their concerns for centuries; John Stuart Mill's argument that there is a circle around every individual that society may never invade and Immanuel Kant's images of individual dignity and the kingdom of ends are two easy examples. Accordingly, liberal theory has long associated rights with individualism. That view of rights remains dominant today, both among liberals like John Rawls and Joseph Raz who approve of rights frameworks and critics of liberalism like Michael Sandel and Mary Ann Glendon who take more skeptical views.[3] Dworkin's definition of rights as individualist trumps admirably articulates this widely shared idea about the nature of rights. Second, the metaphor of the trump card subtly acknowledges that rights can conflict with each other. A trump card, as the term is used in card games like bridge, is a card that wins any round of play if no higher trump card is played, and so Dworkin means to say that possession of a right defeats any non-rights-based considerations in a legal or political conflict. But there is more to the metaphor. Sometimes, in cards, more than one trump card is played in a single round. In those cases, the trump with the highest value prevails and the others, although trump cards, lose. Dworkin's definition thus incorporates the legal realist and critical legal studies criticism that rights can conflict with one another, but it does so while preserving the idea that rights provide a coherent framework for settling disputes.

---

[2] Ronald Dworkin, *Taking Rights Seriously* (Duckworth, 1977 [1991]), pp. 91–93, 189–191, 269; Ronald Dworkin, *A Matter of Principle* (Oxford University Press, 1985), pp. 2–3.

[3] John Rawls, *A Theory of Justice* (Harvard University Press, 1971), pp. 3–4; Joseph Raz, *The Morality of Freedom* (Oxford University Press, 1986), p. 166; Michael Sandel, *Democracy's Discontent: America in Search of a Public Philosophy* (Harvard University Press, 1996), p. 33; Mary Ann Glendon, *Rights Talk: The Impoverishment of Political Discourse* (Free Press, 1991), pp. 47–48.

When Dworkin applies his definition to concrete cases, however, he sometimes argues that the substance of rights must be or not be certain ways simply because those consequences follow from his definition, as if the definition were evidence of the nature of rights rather than an attempt to construct rights in one of several possible ways. In so doing, he winks at *Law's Empire*'s insight about definitions and interpretations and presents his definition of rights as trumps as prior to the contest of rights discourse rather than a move within the discourse itself. Consider the argument that Dworkin makes about individualism and a contested concept called "the right to know." The "right to know," of course, is something that journalists claim on behalf of society in support of their quest to discover and publish guarded information. It is related to but not coextensive with the right of free press. One who invokes the right to know claims that the public is entitled to have access to government documents or courtroom records or whatever else the right is applied to, and the argument for the right to know is customarily advanced in terms of empowering citizens to monitor the activities of government. Dworkin argues against the existence of such a right to know, and his argument follows syllogistically from his definition. Recall that on Dworkin's definition, rights are things that only individuals can have.[4] It follows that no non-individual can use the language of rights to protect its interests and that society itself, the very opposite of the individual, cannot have any rights. This stance is not a substantive claim, Dworkin might say, but merely an analytic necessity. Nothing that is in society's interests can be a right, because rights are by definition things that stand *against* the general interest of society. It is thus analytically senseless to speak of the rights of society; indeed, Dworkin says that predicating rights of society is "incoherent" and "bizarre." The right to know, however, is alleged to be a right of society at large, and its application is alleged to be grounded in the general interest, not in protecting individuals against the general interest. Dworkin therefore concludes that those who believe in the right to know are committing a category mistake.

---

[4] Dworkin does grant that "individual" should not be limited only to actual human individuals, saying that "legal persons," such as corporations, may have rights as well (*Taking Rights Seriously*, p. 91n.). Why he and other theorists like Joseph Raz make this concession is discussed further in chapter 3; as I argue there, it may be due to their preference, when confronted with data that their theories do not map well, to redefine the data rather than change their definitions. This nuance does not, however, affect the current argument.

Given that rights attach to individuals and not to society, Dworkin easily concludes that there cannot possibly be such a thing as the right to know.[5]

The proof is entirely formal; the conclusion that the public has no right to know is entailed within Dworkin's definition of rights. His argument against a public right to know need not and does not weigh the substantive questions of public access to information. Dworkin does not, for example, make an argument about the merits and demerits of allowing television cameras inside courtrooms. But by arguing that there is no public right to know, Dworkin promotes a particular answer to the question of whether trials should be televised. The answer he promotes is "No." Technically, it is still possible for Dworkin to take either side on the substantive question. He could claim that television cameras should not be permitted in courtrooms and that there is no right to know that such a ban would violate, or he could claim that television cameras should be permitted in courtrooms, though on grounds other than that of a right to know. It would, however, be a mistake to give too much weight to this last possibility. In the context of American rights discourse, to declare that there is no such thing as the right to know is, at least presumptively, to take sides against having cameras in courtrooms. At the very least, it is to weaken the argument for televising trials by denying its articulators the use of a powerful rhetorical tool: the language of rights.

It may be that Dworkin opposes the uses to which the putative "right to know" is put, in which case his argument against the right to know is convenient to his purpose. It may even be that some of those uses, such as televising trials, are pernicious and deserve our opposition. Nevertheless, Dworkin's case against the right to know is not a good way to make the point. Doing nothing more than tracing the logical entailments of a definition, it neatly dismisses the possibility of a right to know and, because we know that the right to know means certain things about cameras and reporters, encourages us to infer conclusions about televising trials and printing govern-

---

[5] Dworkin, *A Matter of Principle*, pp. 387–388. When Dworkin and others use definitions of rights to "disprove" the existence of certain rights, they mean that those rights do not or cannot exist in a moral sense, prior to the law. Dworkin would not contest that a proposition codified into law as a right would be a right, e.g., that if a legislature enacted a "right to know statute," a right to know would then exist in that jurisdiction as provided in the law. None of the theorists I discuss denies that rights talk is sometimes simple legal positivism.

ment records. Furthermore, it does so without showing that such publicity would be against the general welfare, or unjustifiably harmful to particular people, or unjustifiable on any other substantive grounds. Instead, a purely formal definition of rights fosters a substantive position on issues of public access to information.

The formal definition, however, is not a rule that pre-exists the game of legal argument. It is a move within the game. As Dworkin's own theory of adjudication and interpretation explains, his "definition" of rights is not just descriptive or constitutive of some aspect of the game (like "the chessboard measures eight squares by eight squares") but an attempt to prescribe, as among multiple possibilities, how that aspect will function in the game. Dworkin's political commitments, including his commitment to individualism, are present in his definition of rights, as *Law's Empire* alerts us to expect. It would be ironic if Dworkin, when making his argument against the right to know, forgot that definitions and interpretations are moves within the game and always carry substantive commitments, such that it is dangerous to treat definitions of normative concepts as fixed truths – in a word, as definitive. It is more probable that Dworkin knows his definition to be a move within the game of legal discourse and that he does not bother to acknowledge it as such. He does not preface his argument by saying "This definition of rights is itself subject to challenge, because it is only my attempt to construct the category in the way that I, subjectively and normatively, believe makes rights the best that they can be." Instead, he simply offers his definition and winks at his theory of interpretation. He knows that what he presents as simply descriptive is actually normative, but he makes his move without calling our attention to the fact.

Insofar as Dworkin is a player in the game, concerned with establishing or refuting a specific right like the right to know, winking at the interpretive insights of *Law's Empire* and forging ahead with a definition of rights is an effective tactic. Because everyone agrees that rights have force, embedding political commitments within a definition of rights is an excellent way to tip arguments in their favor. If I argue that I should be permitted to do X, I may or may not win the argument and get to do X. If I argue that I should be permitted to do X and point out that I have a right to do X, my chances of winning the argument and getting to do X are greater than if I make the argument without reference to my rights. The same is true if I argue that respecting some other right Y necessarily entails my being allowed to do X. As part of what it means to be a right, each political commitment within a definition of rights (e.g., the commitment that people should be allowed to do X) travels under a privileged banner. Extra weight is given to the argument because it is an argument not just about X but about rights.

At the same time, however, something should give us pause about Dworkin's using his definition of rights as he does when he dismisses the right to know. Given his presumed awareness that definitions and interpretations of legal concepts contain normative judgments, it does not seem entirely right for Dworkin to argue from a definition that he presents as no more than descriptive. We might expect him instead to use the case of the right to know to test his definition, perhaps by asking whether dismissing the right to know makes the law the best that it can be. If it did, then both his definition and his argument about the right to know would be strengthened. That kind of analysis would require Dworkin to engage substantive questions such as whose interests are served and harmed by placing television cameras in courtrooms or prohibiting photographers from snooping on celebrities. Instead, however, Dworkin bypasses all such questions and rests his argument on the definition of rights alone. In so doing, he relieves himself of having to defend a set of normative commitments by cloaking them in the banner of rights, a category he has appropriated for the purpose. But it does not make sense to let the banner do the persuasive work if the commitments it contains could not do the same work on their own. Similarly, if certain propositions do not travel under the banner of rights, and if their not traveling under that banner is due only to the way that rights have been defined, then we have no reason to suppose that those propositions are less compelling than the commitments included within the going definition of rights.

Appropriating rights language for a particular set of substantive political commitments is a widespread feature of rights discourse, political as well as academic. Consider the rival approaches to rights found in "will theories" and "interest theories," each of which builds a distinct set of normative choices into its conception of rights and then argues for its positions based partly on the strength of definitions.[6] "Will theories" of rights, which are sometimes called "option

---

[6] For the early history of the rivalry between these two ways of seeing rights, see Richard Tuck, *Natural Rights Theories* (Cambridge University Press, 1979).

theories" or "choice theories," have roots in Hobbes and are expressed in the writings of Wesley Hohfeld and H. L. A. Hart.[7] Roughly, will theories define having a right as having an opportunity to make a choice. Interest theories of rights, which are sometimes called "welfare theories" or "benefit theories," promote a different definition, according to which one has a right if a condition of one's well-being is sufficiently important to place someone under a duty. Joseph Raz, Joel Feinberg, and Neil MacCormick are interest theorists.[8] Will theories elevate the value of autonomy, and interest theories elevate other aspects of well-being.

Sometimes, a theorist of one of these schools will attack the other by showing that some desirable right is not possible on its terms. For example, MacCormick attacks the will theory by arguing that children should be provided with basic care and nutrition for reasons having nothing to do with anyone's choices or autonomy, including that of the children. Because the imperative to care for a child does not derive from the child's autonomous choices, a theory that equated rights with opportunities for making autonomous choices would not include a right of children to basic care. MacCormick continues: "Either we abstain from ascribing to children a right to care and nurture, or we abandon the will theory. For my part, I have no inhibitions about abandoning the latter."[9] Even if this argument successfully shows that the will theory cannot account for all rights, the conclusion that the interest theory is thereby established is based on a false choice. There is no reason why all rights must be grounded only in autonomy or only in welfare; some rights can derive from respect for human choices, and others can derive from other kinds of needs. To define the ground of rights exclusively in either criterion is to load later arguments in favor of a set of substantive political commitments, either those prizing autonomy or those prizing other conditions of human well-being.[10]

---

[7] Wesley Hohfeld, *Fundamental Legal Conceptions as Applied in Judicial Reasoning* (Greenwood Press, 1978); H. L. A. Hart, "Are There Any Natural Rights?" in Jeremy Waldron, *Theories of Rights* (Oxford University Press, 1984), pp. 77–90. See also Michael Freeden, *Rights* (Open University Press, 1991), pp. 43–49.

[8] Raz, *The Morality of Freedom*, p. 166; Joel Feinberg, *Rights, Justice, and the Bounds of Liberty* (Princeton University Press, 1980), p. 209; Neil MacCormick, *Legal Right and Social Democracy* (Clarendon Press, 1982), pp. 143–160.

[9] MacCormick, *Legal Right*, p. 158.

[10] For an argument that is the mirror image of MacCormick's, presenting a dichotomous choice between will theories and interest theories and preferring the former, see Hillel Steiner, *An Essay on Rights* (Blackwell, 1994), pp. 62–73. Steiner applies his theory to the

Just as rights theorists sometimes attack one conception of rights in the attempt to establish another, theorists critical of rights in general sometimes try to attack the entire concept of rights by criticizing a single conception of rights and presenting the short-comings of the conception attacked as if they were problems with rights as a general category.[11] The conception of rights most commonly targeted in this kind of attack is probably the strong individualist-based notion of rights that Dworkin's theory exempli-fies. That conception is dominant in contemporary rights thinking, and it is often easy to pass that dominant conception off as the concept of rights itself rather than one version only. Attacking rights by attacking that conception of rights is a staple among some communitarian theorists. Being skeptical of individualism to begin with, they identify rights with excessive individualism and condemn rights accordingly.

Consider, for example, Michael Sandel's stance toward Dworkin-ian rights. In *Democracy's Discontent*, Sandel routinely merges "rights" with individual rights, discussing rights in American history as if rights had always and only been imagined in Dworkin's fashion, that is, as attaching only to individuals.[12] As a matter of history, that presentation is lacking: as I discuss in the coming chapters, American rights discourse has often predicated rights of entities other than individuals. Sandel's collapsing of all rights into individual rights, however, helps explain his hostility to rights as an outgrowth of his views on liberal individualism. Indeed, Sandel's attack on rights prominently features a self-conscious attack on the Dworkinian view. The idea that rights are trumps is the theme, Sandel charges, of one of the most infamous court decisions in American history: *Lochner v. New York*, the 1905 case in which the Supreme Court struck down a maximum-hours law for bakers on the ground that it violated every

question of children's rights, reaching conclusions directly opposite MacCormick's, at pp. 245f.

[11] A word is in order here on the difference, as I am using the terms, between concepts and conceptions. Following Dworkin and Hart, I use "concept" to refer to broad categories in political and legal thought generally, such as the concept of rights, or of equality, or of democracy. The meanings of those concepts, however, are contested by politicians and theorists; what rights or equality or democracy means to adherents of one political party or philosophy may differ from what it means to others. The rival meanings or interpretations of those concepts are what I refer to with the term "conceptions." Particular conceptions impart more specific meanings to capacious concepts. For example, we could say that equality is a concept of which liberals and Marxists hold different conceptions.

[12] Sandel, *Democracy's Discontent*, e.g., p. 33.

individual's right to freedom of contract.[13] The decision consigned bakers and untold numbers of other laborers to work seventy or eighty hours a week in unhealthy conditions, unable to seek regulation and relief through the political process. In the grand narrative of American constitutional development, *Lochner* symbolizes the law gone bad. For more than sixty years, lawyers and judges have known that "Lochnerizing" is a conceptual sin of the first order. When Sandel associates rights as trumps with *Lochner* – rather than with widely approved decisions on issues like free speech or privacy – he tars Dworkin's theory with a very large brush. And because he has merged rights as trumps with rights in general, his attack on Dworkin-style individual rights appears as an attack on rights as a whole.

It does not follow from Sandel's substantive views that he must attack rights as he does. Rather than confining rights to an individualist conception of which he disapproves and then denigrating the concept wholesale, he might have chosen to advance a different conception of rights, one that would incorporate normative commitments that he preferred. Sandel knows that theories of rights always embody some set of normative commitments, or, as he puts it, some vision of the good.[14] Republicans interpret rights according to republican principles, he correctly notes, and liberals interpret rights according to liberal principles. It is not clear, therefore, why Sandel seems not to think that he can interpret rights in light of his own conception of the good. Surely, it cannot be a good argumentative strategy to attack a popular idea like "rights" when one has the option of appropriating it instead. Nevertheless, Sandel declines that opportunity. He, like many other theorists, seizes on one strain in rights theory and treats it as rights theory in general, the only difference being that he does so not in order to establish that theory but to condemn rights as a whole.

FEINBERG, RAZ, AND THE RIGHTS OF HUMAN VEGETABLES

What Sandel sees correctly about rights, however, is that claims of rights are inescapably normative, because rights are always interpreted according to some vision of the good or set of substantive political commitments. Some theorists of rights refuse to see this

---

[13] Ibid., p. 42.   [14] Ibid., p. 321.

aspect of rights discourse, arguing as if the existence of rights could in some cases be a purely descriptive matter. Consider Joel Feinberg, who holds an "interest theory" of rights. Feinberg's theory reasons from formal definitions to substantive conclusions in a way similar to Dworkin's theory, but it shows a different face of that technique. "To have a right," says Feinberg, "is to have a claim *to* something and *against* someone."[15] Feinberg argues that claims are bound up with interests and further proposes that "only beings who have interests are conceptually suitable subjects for the attribution of rights."[16] Rocks, for example, cannot have rights, because rocks do not have interests. Animals, Feinberg says, do have interests and do have rights. The argument works like this: animals prefer to be treated some ways and not others, and their preferences are tantamount to interests. Given that animals have interests, they are "conceptually suitable" to be rights bearers. It is true that animals cannot assert claims in support of their interests, but that is just because they cannot speak. What they lack is the ability to assert, not the capacity for having claims in a moral sense. Feinberg therefore concludes that animals, as suitable rights bearers who have claims, have rights.[17]

In contrast, Feinberg argues that human vegetables have no rights at all. If assumed to be incurable, he says, human vegetables cannot be said to have interests. Under his definition, that makes them conceptually unsuitable to be rights bearers, so Feinberg concludes that they cannot have rights, but he balks at the normative implications of that conclusion.[18] He contends that the fact that human vegetables cannot and do not have rights is not a license to treat them in any malevolent or destructive way one might choose. He knows that people might interpret him as saying that human vegetables may be legitimately killed, warehoused, or who knows what else, and he is morally uncomfortable with that implication. He therefore explicitly denies that his arguments about rights-bearing have any kind of moral impact. According to Feinberg, whether human vegetables "are the kind of beings that can have rights [is] a conceptual, not a moral question, amenable only to what is called 'logical analysis,' and irrelevant to moral judgment."[19]

The claim that rights analysis is "conceptual" and not "moral" is quite comprehensible within the framework of analytic inquiry.

---

[15] Feinberg, *Rights*, p. 159. Emphasis in original.   [16] Ibid., p. 209.
[17] Ibid., pp. 159–267.   [18] Ibid., pp. 176–177.   [19] Ibid., pp. 180, 213.

Feinberg is claiming to do no more than show what consequences follow from a set of definitions. In a way, he is urging us not to reason from his formal definitions of rights to substantive conclusions about political morality, because that would confuse the conceptual with the moral. When he argues that animals have rights and human vegetables do not, Feinberg says, he is not telling us what to do when confronted with political or moral decisions. But in that case, it is hard to understand what the argument is about. If animals' having or not having rights entails no consequences for action or appraisal of action, whether or not they have rights is of little importance. Indeed, if the definitions Feinberg develops and analyzes bear no connection to the world of normative decisions, it is not clear why we should be interested in his arguments at all.

These last implications do not really need to be addressed, because Feinberg's arguments are, despite his protestation to the contrary, inescapably normative. Saying that some class of beings (animals, human vegetables, fetuses, "the public") can or cannot have rights is a political and a moral act, not just an analytic one. The concept of rights is one of the constituent concepts of politics in Feinberg's society, and proposals to prefer one or another understanding of such constitutive concepts are necessarily political acts.[20] On Dworkin's model, such proposals are about interpreting the constitutive concepts and therefore must be normative, because they involve deciding which understanding makes the constitutive concept the best that it can be. In a similar vein, Quentin Skinner has argued that a dispute over the applicability of an appraisive term cannot be only a linguistic or a semantic dispute. It is a political or moral dispute as well.[21] In America, "rights" is an appraisive term, among the most appraisive of all. To say that X has a right to Y is to make a normative statement about the relationship between X and Y, and only if the term could be divested of its normative meanings could its employment be non-normative. That divestment is probably not possible, and if theorists really could divest the term "rights" of its normative meaning, it is doubtful that we would discuss their use of the term at all. Other than to express normative

---

[20] On the political nature of contesting concepts, see William Connolly, *The Terms of Political Discourse* (Basil Blackwell, 3rd edn., 1993), pp. 39–40, 180.

[21] Quentin Skinner, "Language and Political Change," in Terence Ball, James Farr, and Russell L. Hanson, eds., *Political Innovation and Conceptual Change* (Cambridge University Press, 1989), pp. 6–23.

views of the kind that "X has the right to Y" expresses, we have little use for the term "a right." It is unlikely, then, that Feinberg is actually interested in divesting "rights" of normative meaning. What he is interested in, I suspect, is finding a way to mitigate the unpleasant conclusion that human vegetables do not have rights, a conclusion which seems to open the way to deliberate slaughter. Rather than defend that position, he ducks by denying the argument's relevance to morality.

It is here interesting to compare Feinberg's view of rights with that of Joseph Raz. Raz, like Feinberg, is an interest-based rights theorist, and their definitions of rights are almost the same. Raz argues that X has a right if some aspect of X's well-being, alternately formulated as X's interest, is a sufficient reason for holding someone else to be under a duty, and Feinberg defines rights as claims to something and against someone. Both definitions hold that rights are based on interests and that interests give rise to rights when they are important enough to justify imposing a duty on some other party. One key difference between them, however, is that where Feinberg says that only beings with interests can have rights, Raz says that a being can have rights if its well-being is of ultimate value.[22] This provision would let Raz argue that, contrary to Feinberg's conclusion, human vegetables can have rights. All he would have to say is that the well-being of humans is of ultimate value, which he certainly believes, and that human vegetables are human. It seems likely that Raz would be more comfortable with that conclusion than Feinberg is with his, because Raz could conclude that human vegetables do have rights and thereby avoid the implication that it is legitimate to kill or warehouse them. Raz can reach this preferred conclusion because he loaded his "formal" definition of rights and rights-bearing with more of his important substantive moral commitments than Feinberg embedded in his.

The problem that provokes Feinberg's unsuccessful attempt to escape from the normative implications of his argument is similar to the problem with Dworkin's argument against the right to know. In each case, a rights theorist analyzes possible rights by comparing them to a formal definition. In each case, the rights in question are incompatible with the definition and accordingly pronounced non-existent. Dworkin's argument reaches a desired conclusion by

---

[22] Raz, *The Morality of Freedom*, pp. 166–180.

building it into his premises, and Feinberg's pushes him into a conclusion that he would not have chosen. Both problems stem from the same source: the tendency to infer conclusions about the substance of rights from definitions of their form.

THREE KINDS OF DEFINITION

I suggest that these problems are unnecessary. They occur only if we believe that formal definitions of rights regulate particular rights, and that belief seems unwarranted more often than not. Consider that a political theorist who offers a definition of "rights" might be doing any of three different things. First, he might be asserting that there exists an ontological category of moral imperatives called "rights" and that the definition offered specifies the properties that all members of that category possess. This approach to definition is characteristic of Platonism. As a second alternative, he might be generalizing from a set of desirable normative abstractions, trying to identify principles that would support a worthy set of rights if adopted as definitive of the category. He could reason back and forth between the particular desirable norms and the general principles until he found a set of norms and principles that fit well with each other. This approach to definition resembles the notion of "reflective equilibrium" as pioneered by Nelson Goodman and made famous in the work of John Rawls.[23] A third possibility is that he is trying to explain how the language and the concept of rights functions in some political discourse, that is, what it means within some set of linguistic practices to call something a right. This approach is characteristic of the later work of Ludwig Wittgenstein.

A formal definition of rights that purported to regulate the possible content of particular rights would have to be a definition of the first or second kind. A definition of the first, ontological kind would regulate rights in the simplest possible way, stating un-wavering criteria for all rights. A definition offered in reflective equilibrium would regulate the category of rights less rigidly, because it would leave open the possibility that the definition could itself be revised, but the definition would still purport to define the category as nearly as possible and would be more successful the more it was

---

[23] Rawls, *A Theory of Justice*, pp. 48–50; Nelson Goodman, *Fact, Fiction, and Forecast* (Harvard University Press, 1955), pp. 65–68.

able confidently to deem propositions "rights" or "not rights." In contrast, a definition of the third kind could not exclude certain things from the category of "rights" on the basis of content, because the third kind of definition is attendant on actual uses of the term "rights." Whether definitions like Dworkin's and Feinberg's are of the first or second kind is not always clear. Feinberg sometimes gestures toward the ontological mode, as when he asserts that at the core of human dignity lies a set of "*facts* about the possession of rights,"[24] and both Feinberg and Dworkin treat their definitions as if they were ontological in their arguments about human vegetables and the right to know described above. Nevertheless, reflective equilibrium is perhaps the favorite mode of thought among sophisticated modern theorists, and it may be reasonable to presume that Dworkin and Feinberg mean their definitions to be so understood. If it is not clear whether their definitions are ontological or reflective, however, it is clear that they are one or the other, because their arguments reason from definitions to the conclusion that a certain kind of thing cannot be a right, even though people talk about it as if it were a right. I suggest that neither of those approaches to definition offers the best way to understand the nature of rights and rights claims. As I will discuss below, the first approach is conceptually problematic and the second systematically misses important aspects of rights discourse. In explicating rights in the context of American politics, I make use of the third approach.

Let us consider the ontological approach first. Moral and political theorists who view rights this way try to identify the formal attributes of all rights irrespective of the normative content of particular rights. "Rights," on this understanding, is the name of a pre-existing category of moral imperatives, and the quest to identify the properties of rights is the attempt to identify the criteria for inclusion in the category. That project presumes not only that certain moral imperatives exist *a priori* but also that they necessarily exist as "rights." Here the project becomes problematic. Perhaps some moral imperatives do exist *a priori*, but the categories with which we organize moral imperatives tend to be linguistically constructed. Indeed, it is a central insight of pragmatist philosophers from William James to W. V. O. Quine and Donald Davidson as well as social scientists like Max Weber that human construction rather than natural ordering

---

[24] Feinberg, *Rights*, p. 151. Emphasis in original.

underlies most of the categories with which we organize objects and abstractions.[25] Rights, I suggest, is such a category. In that case, moral imperatives cannot reside *a priori* in a category called "rights," because the category of "rights" is not an *a priori* feature of the conceptual universe. Whether or not a given moral imperative that we recognize as a right exists *a priori*, it does not exist *as a right* until we apply that categorization.

If, as this reading argues, the features of the category "rights" are not inherent, it does not make sense to try to determine which things the category inherently includes. Formal rights inquiry consists of arguments for different ways to construct the category, not better and worse attempts at discovering the ontological form of rights. This is an aspect of interpretation that Dworkin recognizes in his arguments about the normative decisions involved in making some concept the best it can be, and Sandel specifically recognizes the application of that idea to rights when he notes that rights are always defined in light of some moral or political conception of the good. An argument over the formal definition of rights, being an attempt to construct the category in a particular way, is an argument about which moral or political imperatives to endow with the status of "rights." The link between definition and status within the defined category is obvious; it is largely in order to declare particular propositions "rights" or "not rights" that theorists formulate formal definitions in the first place. But unless a formal definition has a better claim to authority than some other formal definition, the substantive inferences it supports have no more force than opposing inferences drawn from other definitions. If the category of "rights" is linguistically constructed, no definition can claim authority by virtue of its accordance with the *a priori* nature of rights.

Under the second kind of definition, as abstraction in reflective equilibrium rather than ontology, rights theorists could claim that their definitions deserved acceptance not because of their *a priori* truth but because they articulated a plausible principle that supported a desirable set of rights. If we believe that A, B, and C should be rights, and some principled definition D accommodates A, B, and

---

[25] William James, *Pragmatism* (Hackett, 1981), pp. 113–114; W. V. O. Quine, *From a Logical Point of View* (Harvard University Press, 2nd edn., 1980), pp. 61, 103; Donald Davidson, "On the Very Idea of a Conceptual Scheme," in his *Inquiries into Truth and Interpretation* (Oxford University Press, 1984), p. 189; Max Weber, *The Methodology of the Social Sciences* (The Free Press, 1949), pp. 104–112.

C, D might be a good definition. If D implies some other right E that seems like it should not be a right, perhaps D should be adjusted or perhaps our thinking about E should be revised. A great deal of modern political and legal theory works this way, and repeated reasonings back and forth between tentative definitions and sets of results that the definitions would entail often assists greatly in elucidating concepts and clarifying debates.

As a way of conducting political debate or examining rights discourse, however, reflective equilibrium also has limitations. First, in arguments about particular rights, definitions based in reflective equilibrium run the risk of circularity. In the illustration above, someone who disagreed about the value of A, B, and C as rights would have no reason to accept D. Let us give content to that example. If I endorsed rights to practice contraception, to have abortions, and to refuse life support, I might infer that rights protect individual choices on questions of one's own bodily processes. Confronted with someone who believed that individuals should not have the right to refuse life support, I could try to support my position with that inference. But my opponent could easily reject the inference by rejecting one or more of the specific rights from which it was inferred. If he denied rights to practice contraception and have abortions, an argument from individual choice on questions of bodily processes would not persuade him of a right to refuse life support. To try to persuade him with that argument would be to use an inference with rejected premises to try to establish one of those premises. Second, reflective equilibrium, like ontology, carries the idea that rights can be identified according to some common criteria of content or normative principle, and that idea should be questioned: the commonalities among rights, I suggest, have more to do with functional patterns of how people use the term "rights" than with elements of form or content. Reflective equilibrium and ontological definition do not pay attention to the role that the discourse of rights plays in the formation of normative opinions and legal and political truths. They therefore ignore some of the most important aspects of rights in American law and politics.

If we look to rights discourse as a social practice in American politics, we discover that whether a proposition is deemed a right has important consequences for whether it is honored and upheld. In other words, a need, interest, or conception of well-being has a better chance of being fulfilled if it is considered a right. This point is another on which rights theorists and rights critics agree, though in different tones of voice.[26] To deny the status of "right" to some substantive proposition on purely formal grounds is thus not only an analytically dubious move but also, if the proposition is morally or socially beneficial, a harmful move as well. I suggest, therefore, that we should not look to formal definitions for the reasons why certain propositions are regarded as rights. It makes little sense to settle questions about whether to televise trials or how to treat human vegetables by consulting the form of rights themselves, because no such inherent form exists. Rights are bound up with needs, interests, and well-being, the subject matter of political morality generally, and what propositions achieve recognition as rights grows largely from our opinions about which of those propositions are the most substantively deserving of the privileged status that the label "rights" bestows.

Furthermore, needs and interests and conceptions of well-being are not static. They change through time. Because rights are bound up with those changing concerns, the content of rights must also change as time passes and circumstances change. As I discuss throughout the next four chapters, a process of concrete negation of past evils is a leading dynamic of change in the content of rights. Many of the propositions we accept as rights today, or that have been accepted in the past, have been classified as rights because recent events convinced people of their substantive importance. If it is also true, as I think it is, that the most important aspect of classifying something as a right is precisely to guarantee its recognition as important and protected, that pattern of change in the set of rights people accept is a fitting one. I am, therefore, arguing against two mistakes in the analysis of rights. The first is the tendency to argue questions of rights as matters of form, abstracted from the needs, interests, and so on that give rights their content. The second is the practice of tying questions of rights to parameters inherited from earlier times when concepts of well-being, need, and so on were different.

---

[26] Compare Dworkin, e.g., *Taking Rights Seriously*, p. 191, and Feinberg, *Rights*, p. 151, with Glendon, *Rights Talk*, p. 31.

RIGHTS TALK AS SOCIAL PRACTICE

The notion that we need not abandon "rights talk" but that we should mute our interest in the formal properties of rights implies that we should reevaluate what kind of formal consistency rights possess. I do not claim that the conceptual category of "rights" has no formal consistency whatsoever; in that case, "rights" would not be a conceptual category at all. But the consistency among rights does not reside in a set of analytic properties that all rights share. To be sure, someone could produce a theory of rights that reasoned entirely from first principles and in which every right shared a given analytic trait. Such a theory, however, would be less illuminating of our political world than a different kind of theory, a theory that located the consistency among rights not in a set of analytic properties but in the way that the concept is used in a social practice.

I use the idea of a social practice in the sense described by Charles Taylor, who points out that some realities exist in a society whether or not there are vocabularies to describe them and that other realities rely upon particular vocabularies for their existence. The vocabulary-dependent realities are the ones for which he adopts the term "practice," or "social practice." Voting is a practice. Someone lacking the vocabulary and concept of voting could observe a room full of people and notice that half of them raised their hands at a given time, after which they put their hands down and the other half raised their hands. But to understand these movements as voting requires knowledge of a practice.[27]

The simplest practices are defined by constitutive rules, and John Searle has illustrated this kind of practice with examples from games. Kicking a ball into a net is not a practice, but scoring a goal is. Goals, in this sense, are scored because of certain rules that govern the meaning of certain actions in certain contexts; they do not exist independent of the vocabulary of the game. One who kicks a thousand balls into a thousand nets on some remote island where soccer is unknown scores no goals. Similarly, moving a piece of wood from one spot to another is not a practice, but moving a chess bishop is. Outside the practices of chess, I could move the same piece of wood diagonally or vertically. I cannot, however, move a chess

---

[27] Charles Taylor, "Interpretation and the Sciences of Man," in his *Philosophy and the Human Sciences, Philosophical Papers* (Cambridge University Press, 1985), vol. II, pp. 32–33.

bishop vertically, because a bishop is only a bishop by virtue of a practice according to which bishops only move diagonally. To take the piece of wood that chess players call "bishop" and move it vertically is not to move a bishop at all. In other words, the rules of chess are constitutive of the bishop *qua* bishop, and what it means to be a bishop is given by the way that the rules of chess permit the bishop to be used.[28]

Rights, like bishops and goals, are creatures of a practice. If I stood outside the town hall and castigated the mayor in a loud voice, any observer could understand that I was shouting and, assuming basic comprehension of English, that I was criticizing a government official. But those observers familiar with a certain practice could say something more: "He is exercising his right to free speech." I could shout the same words in the same place with or without the practice, but the existence of the practice gives a different aspect to what I am doing. That I exercise a right to free speech is a fact, as surely as it is a fact that I move a bishop or score a goal. Of course, identifying rights is more difficult than identifying bishops, because the constitutive-rules model is inadequate to explain practices outside of specially crafted situations like chess. In debates about political morality, where the practice of rights identification might obtain, the possible moves are not as strictly predetermined or rule-governed as the possible moves in a chess game. As Alisdair MacIntyre puts it, "The problem about real life is that moving one's knight to QB3 may always be replied to with a lob across the net."[29] Nevertheless, the range of possible moves even in real-life practices is not without limit. Speaking English is a practice, and the moves that an English speaker might make at a given point in conversation are virtually infinite, but not every utterance will count as a move within the practice, because some will simply not be English speech. When someone does speak English, someone who understands the English-speaking practice can understand what the speaker is doing, even though the rules of the practice are loose and the number of moves the speaker might make is very large. The same is true of real-life practices generally. To the extent that we understand a practice, we

[28] John Searle, *Speech Acts: An Essay in the Philosophy of Language* (Cambridge University Press, 1969), pp. 33–42. See also Stanley Cavell, *Must We Mean What We Say?* (Cambridge University Press, 1976), pp. 25–29.
[29] Alisdair MacIntyre, *After Virtue* (University of Notre Dame Press, 1981), p. 98.

can describe the meanings of its constituent actions, even if the practice is not one strictly governed by *a priori* rules.

Let us compare the identification of two practice-dependent phenomena, one born of a strictly rule-bound context and the other not. The two phenomena I have in mind are checkmates and rights. Within the game of chess, a checkmate is a game-ending situation, and the rules of chess specify exactly what shall be a checkmate. Someone who did not know the rules of chess would see chessboards and not grasp that the arrangement of pieces constituted a checkmate. Someone familiar with the practice could look at any conceivable arrangement of chess pieces and announce, factually, whether or not a checkmate was present. The concept of checkmate, however, sometimes transcends the game of chess and appears elsewhere. If the hero of a film, backed by the police, corners the fleeing villain and says "checkmate," we do not frantically search the screen for a chessboard. We know that the hero is using "checkmate" to mean "You have no escape, and the game is over." The hero has not, of course, achieved a checkmate within the game of chess, but the statement of "checkmate" is not false. We understand how it is being used, and its use seems appropriate. We could, of course, imagine other situations in which "checkmate" might be stretched beyond recognition or propriety. To hand three apples to a sales clerk in a fruit shop and say "checkmate" is not comprehensible.[30] If we were to try to determine the point at which alleged checkmates passed from the credible to the incredible, we could refer to the rules of chess and make arguments about whether a given situation sufficiently resembled a chess checkmate to warrant application of the checkmate concept.

The rules of the practice governing rights are far less clear than the rules of the practice governing checkmates. People familiar with the practice can call things "rights" and generally understand one another. But when they try to determine the point at which alleged rights are not credible, they are at a disadvantage relative to anyone trying to make the same determination about checkmates. They do not have an originating context to refer to, a context in which the meaning of "right" is fully given by constitutive rules. The possibility of such constitutive rules is what I opposed earlier when I argued

---

[30] I assume that other extraordinary circumstances that might make it comprehensible do not obtain (e.g., that the sales clerk is a secret agent and that "checkmate" is a coded instruction).

that rights, as a category of moral imperatives, is not susceptible of a single privileged definition based on form. And yet, people who speak English and are familiar with the practice of rights identification can use the concept of rights to convey meanings comprehensible to other such people.

Following a methodological tradition that derives from the later Wittgenstein, I suggest that the way those who participate in the practice use the concept of "rights" shows what it means for something to be a right. Rather than regarding "rights" as an *a priori* category with a formal essence, we can examine the relevant practice to see how rights discourse actually functions. If we can discover what people are doing when they say things like "X has a right to Y," we will understand what such utterances mean.[31] From that point, we should be able to determine when, in a particular context, it is appropriate to use the language of rights. What differentiates such determinations from definitions of rights like Dworkin's and Feinberg's is that the rules of use it will yield will be constantly open to revision. They are attendant on, not prior to, actual uses of language. They aim not to exclude uses of the term that fall outside given parameters but rather to explain many different uses of the term as part of a coherent practice.

Analyzing rights discourse as a social practice is a hermeneutic undertaking, by which I mean that the project tries to interpret an unclear, seemingly self-contradictory object of study, in this case American rights discourse, in such a way that underlying coherences come to light. To attempt a hermeneutic understanding of rights discourse presumes, as Taylor has pointed out about hermeneutics in general, that meaning and expression must admit of a distinction within the practice studied.[32] If meaning and expression were identical, no interpretation would be necessary. The full meaning of the object would already be explicit, leaving nothing for an inter-

---

[31] Wittgenstein put it this way: "When philosophers use a word – 'knowledge,' 'being,' 'object,' 'I,' 'proposition,' 'name' – and try to grasp the *essence* of the thing, one must always ask oneself: is the word ever actually used in this way in the language-game which is its original home?" (Ludwig Wittgenstein, *Philosophical Investigations* [Blackwell, English edition, 1958], p. 48.) The language-game with which I am concerned is the American argument about rights, and I will try to show how "rights" is actually used in that language-game.

[32] Taylor, "Interpretation," pp. 15–16. Paul Ricoeur makes a similar point, saying that understanding an object of hermeneutic study is the same as understanding a metaphor: that which is to be interpreted "says" one thing to "mean" another, and the task of the interpreter is to make this apparent contradiction intelligible. Ricoeur, *Hermeneutics and the Human Sciences* (Cambridge University Press, 1981), p. 175.

preter to do. In much of American rights discourse, it is certainly the case that meaning and expression are distinct. Indeed, the many unsuccessful attempts to define and elucidate the meaning of rights testify to the degree to which meaning in rights discourse is not readily apparent and stands in need of interpretation.

THE LIMITS OF THE PRACTICE

Analyzing rights discourse as a linguistic practice requires having some way of knowing what uses of language count as part of the practice and what uses of language do not. In line with the methods described above, the practice must be understood to include actual uses of the word "right" rather than only those uses which accord with some formal definition. It would be easy to say that I will consider all uses of the word "right" equally, but it would also be terribly misguided. Some uses of the word "right," such as by a geometer discussing a right angle, have nothing to do with the current topic.[33] We want to explore not just a word but a concept. Additionally, some attempts to employ the concept of rights may be incoherent, like the utterance of "checkmate" to the clerk at the fruit shop. We need some criteria to determine what uses of the term and the concept "rights" are part of the practice we are investigating. These criteria should tell us not the formal or objective essence of the concept but rather when we are seeing the concept at work.

In choosing the necessary criteria, I rely upon the patterns of use to which the term "rights" has been put throughout American history. The writings of Wesley Hohfeld provide an excellent framework for examining the ways in which Americans speak about rights, and, as discussed below, I draw upon his work partly for his analysis and partly for what his methods reveal about uses of rights language. I also rely upon historical patterns in rights language as presented in chapters 3, 4, and 5. The patterns present in Hohfeld's study and the patterns I explicate in the coming chapters match each other well, providing mutual support for the proposition that those patterns

---

[33] Richard Dagger has illustrated the range of uses of "right" as follows: "We may turn to the *right*, for instance, even when that is not the *right* way to turn; the Pythagorean theorem deals with *right*-angled triangles; governments sometimes shift to the *right*; straightforward people come *right* to the point when they seek to *right* matters; and we occasionally find that what someone is doing is not *right*, morally speaking, even though she has the *right* to do it." Richard Dagger, "Rights," in Ball, Farr, and Hanson, *Political Innovation*, p. 293. Emphases in the original.

really do typify the practice. Thus, the criteria that I have chosen as representative of the practice are conclusions I draw from the history of American rights discourse. Patterns in the use of the term suggest rules of the practice. This method bears some resemblance to reflective equilibrium, reasoning back and forth between a set of data and a set of criteria for what data to include. What keeps the reasoning from being circular is that not every use of the term is admitted as a legitimate use of the practice. Decisions about which uses are legitimate are contestable, of course, but they need not be arbitrary.

In determining the limits of the practice, I have used a hermeneutic principle adapted from W. V. O. Quine and William James and which I shall call "nonviolence." Given a system of actions, statements, or beliefs, the nonviolence principle directs an interpreter to "disturb the system as little as possible" in rendering it coherent.[34] In other words, unlike the limiting definitions of Dworkin, Feinberg, and similar rights theorists, the criteria I use for identifying instances of rights discourse should accommodate as many ostensible uses of the concept as it can. Criteria which explained more ostensible uses would be superior to criteria which explained fewer of the instances in which people claimed to be discussing "rights," assuming no disproportionate sacrifice of conceptual coherence. There is a point beyond which accounting for ostensible discussion of rights destroys coherent conceptual meaning, as for example if a single interpretation of "right" were proffered for "right angle" and "right away." But the choice of criteria should seek to encompass as many instances of seeming rights discussion as can be accommodated before coherence breaks down.

The sense of "right" relevant to this discussion, of course, is not that of "right angle" but that of "X has a right." It is not yet clear,

---

[34] W. V. O. Quine, "Two Dogmas of Empiricism," in Quine, *From a Logical Point of View,* pp. 42–44; and *Word and Object* (MIT Press, 1960), pp. 58–59. See also James, *Pragmatism,* p. 31.

[35] The issue here is not the meaning of the individual word "right" within "X has a right" but of the whole statement "X has a right," and even that only within a larger set of statements. H. L. A. Hart, following Bentham's *A Fragment on Government,* insisted on the first half of this point with respect to legal words in general and the word "right" in particular, writing "we should not, as does the traditional method of definition, abstract words like 'right' ... from the sentences in which alone their full function can be seen, and then demand of them so abstracted their genus and differentia." (H. L. A. Hart, "Definition and Theory in Jurisprudence," in his *Essays in Jurisprudence and Philosophy* [Oxford University Press, 1983], p. 31.) This recommendation is good so far as it goes, but it needs to be extended. Just as we

however, that that use of "right" has only one meaning.[35] If "X has
a right" is ambiguous, then perhaps we should not include all uses of
"X has a right" in the practice we study any more than we include
the use of "right" in "right angle." Hohfeld made such an argument
more than seventy years ago, and his analysis was precise and
influential. According to Hohfeld, "X has a right" as generally used
admits of four different conceptual meanings, only one of which
properly involves the concept of rights. Hohfeld's view of rights
proper is too restrictive, but his scheme of possible meanings for "X
has a right" admirably articulates the meanings of "right" that fall
within the practice I want to study.

HOHFELD'S TAXONOMY

Hohfeld argued that what Anglo-American political and legal
discourse calls "rights" is actually divisible into four categories:
rights, privileges, powers, and immunities.[36] A "right" in Hohfeld's
stricter sense might also be called an "entitlement" and is defined as
having a correlative duty.[37] Thus, X has a right to Y if there is some
agent Z who has a duty to provide Y to X. Note that this definition
of rights excludes certain things that Americans include among their
most prominent rights, such as the freedoms of speech and religion.
Hohfeld would classify those as "privileges," where a "privilege" is
defined as the absence of a duty to do or abstain from doing a given
thing.[38] Thus, a person who has no duty to speak or to refrain from
speaking has a privilege (not a right) of free speech. For Hohfeld, the
closest synonyms for "privilege" were "freedom" and "liberty."[39]
The third category, "powers," encompasses abilities to change legal
relationships. For example, a person may have the power to execute

---

should consider words with reference to the sentences in which they occur, we should
consider sentences with reference to the larger discourses in which they occur. To try to
determine the meaning of a single word or a single sentence in isolation is to practice a
linguistic reductionism that Quine has shown to be untenable (Quine, "Two Dogmas," esp.
p. 41; *Word and Object*, pp. 5–17).

[36] Hohfeld, *Fundamental Legal Conceptions*, p. 36.   [37] Ibid., pp. 36–37, 39, 71.

[38] Ibid., pp. 38–39. Given that rights are defined as the correlatives of duties, and that having
a privilege is defined as not being under a duty, some agent X has a privilege if no other
agent has a relevant right against X. Thus Hohfeld: "A right is an affirmative claim against
another, and a privilege is one's freedom from the right or claim of another" (ibid., p. 60).

[39] Ibid., pp. 42, 47.

[40] Ibid., pp. 50–60. Compare Hart's discussion of "enabling laws" in *The Concept of Law*
(Oxford University Press, 2nd edn., 1994), e.g., pp. 26–28.

a will, or to vote, or to make contracts.[40] Finally, to have an "immunity" is to be free of another's legal power. Immunities stand to powers as privileges stand to rights: if Jones has an immunity (or a privilege) with respect to Smith, then Smith lacks a power over (or right against) Jones.[41] A Hohfeldian analysis of the American Bill of Rights would show that an American accused of a crime has a *right* to legal counsel, a *privilege* against self-incrimination, a *power* to obtain witnesses in his favor, and an *immunity* against being tried twice for the same offense.

One of Hohfeld's main aims in offering this taxonomy was to prevent people from using a single term, "rights," to denote several analytically distinct relationships, thereby forfeiting precision of thought.[42] If his argument were correct, it would be a mistake to include instances of privileges, powers, and immunities in a study of rights, even if the parties discussing those relationships mistakenly used the word "rights" to describe them. There are, however, at least two problems with Hohfeld's argument. First, his four categories frequently overlap, suggesting that rights, privileges, powers, and immunities are not always inherently different from one another after all. Whether a particular relationship involves rights or powers, privileges or immunities, often depends only on how it is described. For example, the freedom of speech is a privilege if construed as the liberty to speak or refrain from speaking but an immunity if construed as the absence of a governmental power of censorship. The same ambiguity obtains with respect to the free exercise of religion, the freedom to travel, and so on. These challenges to the defined boundaries of Hohfeld's categories stem from the same problem with arranging normative abstractions into formal categories that I discussed at the beginning of this chapter, namely, that moral imperatives do not come into the world neatly labeled as "rights," or, for that matter, as "privileges," "powers," or "immunities." People group imperatives into such categories in different ways depending upon the linguistic apparatuses they bring to bear and, since none of the groupings captures an *a priori* scheme, whether a given abstraction is a member of one category or another depends largely upon how it is described.

The second problem with Hohfeld's argument is that it completely ignores the normative and performative features of American rights

<hr>

[41] Hohfeld, *Fundamental Legal Conceptions*, p. 60.   [42] Ibid., p. 38.

discourse. Calling something a right endows it with a sacred status, deeming it important and worthy of special protection. Many things that Hohfeld would call privileges, powers, or immunities, such as freedom of speech, have valid claims to that status, and the labels "privilege," "power," and "immunity" cannot confer that status in the way that the label "right" does. Like Dworkin and Feinberg three generations later, Hohfeld would limit the scope of "rights" on purely analytic grounds. He would say that American citizens do not have a right to vote or a right of free speech. Under his definitions, the former is a power, and the latter is a privilege. But these implications are seriously problematic when seen in light of the way that Americans, including politicians and judges, speak about rights. Any definition of rights in the American context must be dubious if it does not include free speech, free press, liberty of conscience, and participation in the franchise, because the overwhelming preponderance of informed Americans considers those items paradigmatic rights. A public official who announced that free speech was not actually a right would do so at great peril, because such an announcement would be interpreted as making a substantive political claim denigrating the value and protected status of free speech. It could hardly be argued that free speech is a privilege and just as sacred and secure as if it were a right, because "privilege" does not carry the same connotations as "right." A privilege sounds weaker than a right, as if it were granted on sufferance and could be revoked. Our Hohfeldian public official would attract less opprobrium by using one of Hohfeld's suggested synonyms for "privilege" and calling freedom of speech a "liberty," but would still be ill-advised to claim that freedom of speech is a liberty and not a right.

Hohfeld's central insight is correct: several analytically different concepts travel under the name "rights." His mistake is in the conclusion he draws from that insight. Hohfeld assumes that "rights" can exist in only one kind of relationship between parties, formally defined. Having distinguished four different relationships in which "right" is used, Hohfeld concludes that three of the uses must be incorrect and reserves "right" for the fourth. Keeping the nonviolence principle in mind, I suggest a different conclusion. The fact that people, including trained legal professionals, frequently see "rights" as applicable in several analytically distinguishable situations suggests that rights can obtain in more than one kind of relationship. It is not necessarily wrong to distinguish among the four different relationships that Hohfeld describes. From the standpoint of political discourse, however, it is problematic to limit the status of "rights" to only one of the four categories, because to do so is to devalue the other three.

Despite these problems, Hohfeld's analysis provides a framework for determining whether a question of political morality is a question of rights. It does not do so in the place where Hohfeld argued it would, in the definition of the first of the four categories, but rather with the totality of the four categories combined. In the process of explaining rights, privileges, powers, and immunities, Hohfeld catalogs numerous judicial uses of the term "rights" and classifies each use as falling within one of his four categories. What Hohfeld's catalog demonstrates, in spite of Hohfeld's own interpretation, is that "rights" is used to cover all four of the concepts he seeks to distinguish, a conclusion that the historical exploration of rights discourse in chapters 3, 4, and 5 readily confirms. In keeping with my methodological decision to regard use as meaning (assuming that some coherence of use can be identified), any question of Hohfeldian rights, privileges, powers, or immunities can be seen as a question of rights. After all, Hohfeld's encyclopedic catalog of uses of rights language demonstrates that "rights" is regularly used in all four ways. Taken together, Hohfeld's four categories encompass all of the major American rights that an adequate definition of rights must include. The typology requires some modification, of course, because "rights" cannot be used within the same argument to mean the first category exclusively and all four categories inclusively. I will therefore gloss Hohfeld's typology as follows: what he calls "rights," I will call "entitlements." What he calls "privileges," I will call "liberties." I adopt the terms "power" and "immunity" without change. Thus, when studying American rights discourse, I will consider any use of the term "rights" to fall within the practice studied if it pertains to entitlements, liberties, powers, or immunities.

This framework serves only to choose what data is analyzable as rights discourse, not to perform the analysis that aims to interpret the data. Accordingly, its work in the rest of this book will be largely invisible; its role is to filter out potential objects of analysis that actually do not belong, so the analysis I present takes place mostly after the Hohfeldian screen has done its work. It is also worth noting that this framework determines only whether a given argument is part of the practice of rights conversation, not whether any particular claim of rights within that conversation is normatively valid. The question of normative validity, of whether something that is conceptually suited to being a right actually is a right, is separate from, and follows after, the question of whether something is the kind of thing that could be a right. The normative question is not part of this project, and the present concern is only to delimit the scope of the linguistic practice within which people make the normative arguments. The scope of that practice, as suggested by Hohfeld's catalog of the uses of rights language, includes all uses of the term "rights" that involve entitlements, liberties, powers, or immunities.

FEATURES OF THE CONVERSATION: COHERENCE OF USE

The last point above could be expressed as follows: it is a (provisionally) constitutive rule of the practice of rights discourse that only entitlements, liberties, powers, and immunities can be rights. A second rule of the practice is that claims of rights are used to prioritize and protect whatever specific content is at issue. To claim "X has a right to Y" is, within American political and legal discourse, to make a special kind of prescriptive claim. Consider a hypothetical suffragette who in 1910, before the extension of the franchise to women, declared, "Women have the right to vote." Her statement should not be understood to mean that women were able or permitted to vote. She was not offering a false description of society but making a prescriptive statement about the way in which society should operate. If told that no such right existed in American law, she would respond that American law was in moral error. This kind of rights assertion flows from a view of rights as discovered rather than invented; in its simplest form, it makes a descriptive, ontological claim about the way rights are, independent of society's attitudes. In a more refined version, it might claim that the existing legal code of rights does not correctly instantiate the real values of society and that the law must be changed to incorporate a right which those social values imply. In either case, the suffragette is making a claim about the way rights truly are, irrespective of positive law. Women have the right to vote; the right of women to vote exists, and regulations preventing them from exercising that right are unjust. Of course, the 1910 suffragette could also have taken a different tack. Instead of "Women have the right to vote," she might have said "Women should have the right to vote." That formulation depicts the existence of a right as dependent upon the attitudes and enactments of society.[43] "Women should have the right to vote" is alternately rendered "Society should establish/create/institute a right of women to vote." Where this approach uses "establish," "create," or "institute," the approach that declared "Women have the right to vote" would use "recognize" or "guarantee." The right itself already exists, even if unrecognized, and society can only change its stance toward that right. It cannot change the right itself.

In actual political argument, the two kinds of rights claims – that the right exists and that the right should exist – are used side by side. The first kind has greater rhetorical force, because it appeals to a moral order that pre-exists and binds the polity that is being urged to change its ways. It is, or pretends to be, a descriptive claim about rights that requires no more from its audience than recognition of the true state of things. The second kind, by contrast, is explicitly a prescriptive claim about how things should be. But this difference is illusory. Both statements are prescriptive, because rights themselves are normative (i.e., prescriptive). Thus, the 1910 suffragette's statement "Women have the right to vote" is prescriptive, because what the statement does is express a normative view and attempt to get someone to do something.[44]

But to understand more fully how claims of rights operate in political debate, it is necessary to move beyond classifying statements as "descriptive" or "prescriptive." Rights claims do many things in politics which those terms do not capture. I want to suggest three general kinds of work for which political actors deploy claims of rights, whether consciously or unconsciously. People use rights claims (1) to claim general authority for specific propositions, (2) to attempt to entrench politically precarious practices, and (3) to declare particular practices or propositions to be of special importance.

---

[43] Bentham held this view and accordingly considered claims of non-positive rights to be underhanded renditions of prescriptive claims about what positive rights should exist. Thus, he would have interpreted the suffragette's statement "Women have the right to vote" as a less-than-honest way of saying "Women should have the right to vote."

[44] A more significant difference between the two kinds of rights claims occurs at a different level, namely, at the level of what they tell us about the people who make them. One who makes the ostensibly "descriptive" claim – "Women have the right to vote" – invokes a pre-existing structure of rights and endorses discovery. One who makes the other claim – "Women should have the right to vote" – may believe in discovery and pre-existing rights, but she does not make them relevant to women's right to vote.

THREE ASPECTS OF CLAIMING A RIGHT

The three aspects of claiming a right are elements of what a person *does* when saying "There is (or should be) a right to X." Let us return to the suffragette who says "Women (should) have the right to vote." Given the general patterns of American rights discourse that will be illustrated in chapters 3, 4, and 5, we can say that the speaker is implicitly arguing at least three different things beyond the simple proposition that women should be permitted or enabled to vote. She may not be intending all these aspects as functions of her claim, but all of them are present nevertheless.

First, she implies that the specific proposition that women should be permitted or enabled to vote is supported by some general normative authority. "Women have the right to vote" will be heard to mean that some morally binding force mandates the right claimed, even if that force is not specified. Indeed, the claim derives much of its strength from this implicit invocation, because it seems to give a reason why women's voting should be sanctioned: because it is a right. It is assumed that the right-claiming suffragette, if challenged, would argue that the right she claimed was conferred by, or inherent in, the Constitution or the values of society or natural law or some other entity with moral jurisdiction. This aspect of the claim has two varieties, one in which the speaker aims at instantiating a general principle and therefore argues for a specific application and another in which the speaker aims at establishing the specific application and therefore invokes a general principle. Formal rights theory sometimes implies that proper rights argument is only of the first kind, proceeding from a principle of rights to a specific right. Actual argument about rights, however, is more complicated: rights claims frequently originate when people wish to argue for specific outcomes in specific cases and seek principles that support those outcomes. Much sophisticated thinking about rights deals with general principles and specific applications in reflective equilibrium with one another, but there are times when a particular outcome is the *sine qua non* of an acceptable theory. Consider, for example, the current disagreement among pro-choice activists about whether the right to have an abortion is grounded in a right to privacy or a right to equality of the sexes. Both sides wish to establish a specific application of rights (i.e., the right to abortion), and the dispute over which principle grounds that right is a dispute about how best to legitimate that desired outcome. As chapters 3, 4, and 5 illustrate, that outcome-driven kind of argument has long been typical of American rights discourse.

Second, our suffragette is arguing that the question of whether women will vote should not be left to normal decision-making processes of politics such as popular voting and legislative bargaining. It should be entrenched, removed from politics, placed beyond the power of a hostile majority to undo. "I have a right to vote" means, among other things, "I should be able/permitted to vote whether other people want me to or not." Dworkin's metaphor of the individual's trump card against the will of the majority is an expression of this aspect of rights claims. This aspect is especially important when the right in question aims to protect something that is or could become politically unpopular. We claim the status of "right" for something that we wish to defend against that danger: as Mary Ann Glendon has written, "When we want to protect something, we try to get it characterized as a right."[45] That women have a right to vote is more important in a society in which the predominant sentiment among enfranchised persons is that women should not vote, and women's voting is therefore endangered, than in one where everyone believes that women should vote and there is no danger of disfranchisement. Part of the function of a right is to protect something against the threats of its opponents. One who claims a right argues that the practice protected by the right should not, even in a democratic system, be subject to the obstruction of a hostile majority. It is this aspect of rights claims that puts them in tension with majoritarianism and all other forms of democracy that see the popular will as the final arbiter of legitimacy.

Third, the suffragette declares that women's voting carries an importance that social and political practices that are not matters of rights do not share.[46] Given the moral authority that rights command in American political discourse, to claim rights status for some practice is to argue that that practice should command assent, if not reverence. To argue for a right of women to vote is to argue that women's voting is not only desirable or necessary but somehow untouchable. Far from being a contested point, or even an unfortunate circumstance over which one might grumble, women's voting, if

---

[45] Glendon, *Rights Talk*, p. 31.
[46] See Freeden, *Rights*, on the assignation of priority (e.g., p. 7).

it is a right, should be a secure point. Claiming the status of "right" thus implies that the associated practice or proposition inhabits the higher realms of normative significance. Conversely, if something is sufficiently important, it is likely to be discussed as a right no matter what its substance.

Claims of rights articulated persuasively can bring about, or make more secure, whatever the rights claimed are designed to protect. The claim "Women have the right to vote," in the context of political argument in the early twentieth century, helped to create the conditions under which the statement became true in the simple descriptive sense. In 1910, American society did not recognize a right of adult women to vote. In 1930, it did. Part of the change was due to the pressure brought by people who made relevant rights claims, including those who claimed that women should have the right to vote as well as those who claimed that the right was already in existence. As more people became persuaded by the rights claims of the suffragettes, the right that the suffragettes claimed approached establishment or recognition. Thus, when rights claims are made in political debate, statements which purport to describe a state of affairs sometimes function as causal forces helping to call that state of affairs into existence.

SUMMARY

Many rights theorists conduct their arguments either as if some formal category of rights existed ontologically prior to our discussions about rights or, more sophisticatedly and perhaps more commonly, as if it were the role of definitions of rights, even definitions offered in reflective equilibrium, to restrict the scope of propositions that could be called "rights" on the basis of form or content. These arguments have many different permutations. Sometimes theorists infer substantive positions about rights from the definitions they propose; others attack theories of rights by showing that some normatively desirable conclusion cannot be reached on their definitions; theorists hostile to the concept of rights in general sometimes identify and attack particular conceptions of rights as if those conceptions were definitive of the concept as a whole. Each of these forms of argument presumes that what rights have in common is a set of formal or content-based characteristics. I suggest, however, that the fundamental commonalities among rights are neither of form nor of content but of function, having to do with how claims of rights are used and understood within the discourses of law and politics. Whether or not any of the normative propositions that Americans call "rights" are *a priori* moral truths, the category "rights" itself is a linguistic construct whose coherence has little to do with an analytic similarity among the propositions it includes. Calling moral imperatives rights is a practice, in the sense described by Taylor and by Searle, whereby people declare those imperatives to be important and deserving of special protection. The boundaries of the practice are given by long historical usage and captured in Hohfeld's four categories, which I have glossed as entitlements, liberties, powers, and immunities; any question involving one or more of those concepts can be a question of rights. When people discuss such a question and invoke the concept of rights to do so, they are participating in the practice of rights discourse, and that practice is, in principle, available for the use of a very wide range of political agendas.

To call something a right within that practice is not to give a reason why it is important or deserving of special protection but simply to make those claims on its behalf.[47] Giving reasons would entail a different kind of argument, an argument about the desirability or importance of the proposition claimed to be a right. The question of whether the proposition is a right is often a surrogate for that substantive argument. Moreover, the relationship between people's substantive positions on the desirability of certain rights and their use of rights language works in both directions. Those who have strong incentives to establish and protect particular propositions are more likely to produce theories that describe those propositions as rights, and, at the same time, those who can be persuaded that the concept of rights encompasses a set of propositions are more likely to afford those propositions substantial respect. Indeed, it is precisely the power of rights language to win special status for a proposition that makes it an attractive language for those who would enthrone those propositions in the first place.

Sometimes, the interplay between "rights" as a functional discursive label and the substantive arguments in which rights are invoked obfuscates important questions or misleads the participants.

---

[47] Hart characterizes Bentham as having held that people often speak of rights "when they wish to get their way without having to argue for it" (*Essays in Jurisprudence*, p. 186).

Someone who took Dworkin's argument about the right to know at face value, for example, might be persuaded not to allow certain kinds of reporting activities without ever having considered the content of the issue. Sometimes, it does make sense to avoid trying to settle normative questions by asking whether the propositions debated have the formal properties of rights, preferring to discuss the substance directly. If we conclude that some entitlement, liberty, power, or immunity is indeed important and deserving of special protection, we may call it a right – and in doing so announce our attitude toward it, not some inherent property within it that makes it worthy of our respect and protection.

It would be a mistake, however, to believe that the elimination of rights language in favor of some truer ground of political morality could solve the problem once and for all. Rights are not final grounds for normative arguments, because conceptions of rights must rest on other normative theories, theories that articulate conceptions of goodness or justice or some other binding vision. But if rights stand on other normative theories, those theories also need something to stand on. Arguments about rights are waystations and placeholders, and clarity of argument requires us to remember that they are not final resting places. If, however, they are waystations on the way only to other waystations, resting on rights is not inherently worse than resting on the next turtle down.

CHAPTER 2

History and the development of rights

A generation ago, in an essay on how history can serve political theory, Samuel Beer distinguished between history as past behavior and history as development. Political theorists can use history as past behavior to expand their scope of knowledge, to have a larger range of human experience available when they generalize about politics and morality. That the behavior studied occurred in the past is not relevant to the theorist who uses history strictly in this way; it is simply more data. When a theorist uses history as development, however, the temporal element is crucial. History as development tries to explain some state of affairs as having grown out of some previous state of affairs, under the influence of whatever forces might be relevant.[1]

To examine the American practice of rights discourse, I use history both as past behavior and as development. Using history as past behavior, I draw on many uses of rights discourse in order to infer the rules and patterns of the practice. My aim with this use of history is to show that rights language in American politics is often a placeholder for substantive moral argument. It asserts that something is important and should be protected, but it does not give reasons why. Beyond showing this pattern, however, I aim also to show that Americans regularly use rights language to express their opposition to concrete problems or crises. Because different times pose different problems and crises, this process of concrete negation repeatedly alters American conceptions of rights. To show how this concrete negation has changed the corpus of American rights through time, I use history as development, illustrating how each

---

[1] Samuel Beer, in Melvin Richter, ed., *Essays in Theory and History* (Harvard University Press, 1970), pp. 58–73.

period's system of rights grows from the system of a previous period under the influence of new crises and new commitments.

The process of development occurs differently in different conversational circles; most ordinary citizens, many politicians, and some judges may be quicker than other judges or academic philosophers to discard old theories of rights or to entertain contradictory theories of rights simultaneously. Even if it is true, as I believe it is, that both uses of history indicate that rights at a given time derive less from any formal nature of rights than from people's attitudes about which normative propositions are most important and most in need of protection, it does not follow that all claims about rights are crass and untheorized. Some are. Others, however, are part of subtle and reflective theories, marked by considered judgment and a striving for intellectual consistency. Something can be learned, however, from examining the historicity and the causal influences of even the most careful justificatory arguments, for although these arguments express more than crude reaction to historical circumstance, the concrete negation that permeates rights discourse in general plays a role here as well. Cass Sunstein, Ian Shapiro, Akhil Amar, and Bruce Ackerman have all recently offered developmental accounts of conceptions of rights, sometimes giving attention entirely to high theorists and sometimes taking in political and judicial conceptions as well. Drawing methodological guidance from Richard Rorty and Cornel West, the history of rights I offer here supplements or corrects those accounts.

THE PARTIAL CONSTITUTION

In his recent book *The Partial Constitution*, Cass Sunstein presents a general theory of American constitutionalism, and he places neutrality and deliberation at the center of his story. It has always been a guiding principle of constitutional debate in America, he argues, that the Constitution prohibits government from acting in purely partisan ways to vindicate the naked preferences of the powerholders. Instead, government must abide by some kind of neutrality among competing interests.[2] The other value he emphasizes is deliberativism, which he presents as a constitutional value of the longest standing and the highest order. The two values are con-

---

[2] Cass Sunstein, *The Partial Constitution* (Harvard University Press, 1993), p. 3.

nected: both neutrality and deliberativism support a republican vision of politics in which members of a community talk about what would be best for everyone rather than voting as separate interest groups, each group or individual taking what spoils it can.[3] Sunstein actually seems to like deliberativism even more than neutrality, but he likes neutrality insofar as it opposes the liberal or pluralist model of interest-group politics. According to Sunstein, the members of the Founding generation were strong supporters of deliberativism over interest-advocacy, and the project of Reconstruction was to fortify that original republican commitment.[4]

In presenting American constitutional history as a story of the opposition between liberal-pluralist and republican models of government, Sunstein's *The Partial Constitution* resembles Sandel's *Democracy's Discontent*, and the preference of both books for the republican model strengthens the tie. Also like Sandel, Sunstein recognizes that rights are constructed and interpreted against some background normative theory. Unlike Sandel, however, Sunstein sets about interpreting the canon of American rights from a republican point of view, trying to harness the power of rights for his perspective rather than denigrating the rights framework. Many communitarian and republican theorists, Sandel included, are wary of traditional constitutional rights because of the strong commitment to individualism that those rights contain; Sunstein acknowledges that these rights look individualistic but argues that they are actually republican. "Many of the original individual rights," he claims, "can be understood as part of the idea of deliberative democracy." Even the right to individual property, he says, frequently considered the most absolute and liberal-individualist of constitutional rights, was designed to prevent not any governmental power over individuals' private possessions but to prevent such public interference unless it was preceded by adequate political deliberation.[5]

Sunstein certainly understands the importance of a background normative theory in giving content to rights, but the way he employs background theory makes his account of American rights thinking far too limited, at least as an account of conceptual development. The theory he presents as background to the American rights tradition is only one theory, and that theory is his own republican deliberativism. Instead of exploring the many diverse theories that

---

[3] Ibid., pp. 25–26, 38–39.   [4] Ibid., pp. 22–23, 136.   [5] Ibid., p. 23.

have shaped conceptions of rights, he tries to explain the whole system in terms of one. Sunstein knows that his is not an exhaustive historical account, saying that he aims only to discuss certain ideas that have been prominent in American constitutional history. He even goes so far as to say that the ideas he is interested in are those "suited to those of us now in search of a usable past."[6] Usability, however, depends upon goals. His narrative is not usable for people who would learn about the development of political conceptions on their own terms, nor is it usable for people whose normative commitments are different from his own. His past is usable only from the republican perspective through which that past is invented.

Moreover, because Sunstein always foregrounds the deliberative theory, his methods are ill suited for seeing that conceptions of rights have changed through time. In selecting which issues and concepts to analyze, he says, he looked for material that speaks powerfully to "recurrent dilemmas."[7] That is sometimes a good method of analysis, but it is not a good way to notice or evaluate change. It selects for continuity, and ideas or issues that appear in or disappear from the political discourse are systematically screened out. Because the method does not easily see change, it has limited ability to see the role of extra-theoretic causal factors in making different theories attractive at different times. It cannot, for example, find or explain patterns like the repeated concrete negation of new crises that I suggest pervades the development of rights thinking. An account that does not understand patterns of change in how people deploy political concepts misses a vital element in understanding their conceptions and the function of the concepts generally. Because finding those patterns requires theorists to use history not just as past behavior but also as development, theorists seeking to understand the nature of rights must analyze diversity and change in rights thinking as well as continuity.

CHANGING CONCEPTIONS OF RIGHTS

Other scholars, however, have directed more attention to the processes of change and development in conceptions of rights. Ian Shapiro, for example, has analyzed conceptions of rights through time in a mode specifically geared to monitor change. In his book

---

[6] Ibid., p. 18.   [7] Ibid.

The Evolution of Rights in Liberal Theory, Shapiro offers a developmental account of liberal rights through the work of Rawls and Nozick, whose views he identifies as the two dominant ideologies of contemporary America.[8] He presents the "evolution" of liberal rights as having had four "moments." The first two moments, which Shapiro calls "transitional" and "classical," are identified respectively with Hobbes and Locke, and the last two moments, the "neo-classical" and the "Keynesian," with Nozick and Rawls.[9] The book has four major sections, one devoted to each of those four thinkers, and thus is the story of liberal rights told. Shapiro makes an interesting case about the relationship of the two later thinkers to the two earlier ones, arguing that the major twentieth-century theories of rights are less coherent than their seventeenth-century predecessors in part because the later theorists' desire to take the earlier theorists seriously leads them to try to combine contradictory principles. For example, Shapiro claims that modern rights theorists combine a substantive appeal to British philosophers and a methodological appeal to Kant, and he suggests that the synthesis never entirely works.[10] He similarly argues that Nozick's theory of acquisition in the state of nature suffers from its attempt to combine "private conception" acquisition theories like that of Grotius with the "common conception" acquisition theory of Locke.[11] These analyses cast considerable light on subtleties and tensions within liberal theories of rights.

Nevertheless, Shapiro's analysis is not an adequate account of a theoretical "evolution," because it pays almost no attention to the three hundred years between Locke and Rawls. It seems unlikely that a concept as important as "rights" in a field of ideas as broad and deep as "liberal theory" could have had an "evolution" of only four stages in three hundred years, with the first two stages occurring in seventeenth-century England and then a period of quiescence until the last two stages followed in 1970s America. It is certainly revealing to interpret contemporary rights theorists in terms of their intellectual predecessors, and Shapiro is correct that earlier theorists influence Rawls and Nozick. But Hobbes and Locke are not the beginning and end of that influence, nor are related figures like Grotius and Kant. Other thinkers also shape Rawls and Nozick, as

---

[8] Ian Shapiro, *The Evolution of Rights in Liberal Theory* (Cambridge University Press, 1986), pp. 154–155.

[9] Ibid., p. 15.   [10] Ibid.   [11] Ibid., p. 166.

do the political conditions that changed the discourse of rights in different ways from the eighteenth century to the late twentieth.

One might try to rescue Shapiro's analysis by arguing that his book is not about the evolution of liberal rights but about the evolution of rights in liberal *theory*, where "theory" means just this kind of abstract philosophy. If so, paying attention only to two settings three hundred years and three thousand miles apart might be defended on the grounds that those are the settings in which "liberal theory," or the most important liberal theory, occurred. This interpretation, however, must confront the reality that many highly relevant and influential liberal theorists made their contributions between 1700 and 1970. Jefferson, Paine, Mill, Hohfeld and many others have shaped the development of rights theory, and their influences continue to inform modern conceptions. If Shapiro aimed simply to compare and analyze a few first-rank philosophers, comparing their theories in a relatively ahistoricized way, his paying less attention to important intervening developments would be less problematic. The concept of evolution, however, is necessarily historical. Once historicity is part of the analysis, it is necessary to address the relevant history adequately.

Perhaps more importantly, it would be a mistake to construe "theory" in a way that implies that nineteenth- and twentieth-century Americans who did not write in the genre of the *Second Treatise* had no theory of rights or of liberal politics. On the contrary, any society that has a practice of rights discourse has a theory of rights, even if that theory is not articulated in the systematic manner of a Rawls or a Nozick, because some implicit theory shapes and animates the practice. Rorty distinguishes between what he somewhat polemically calls "philosophical theories," which attempt to find external grounds for elements of social practices, and "real theories," which are the systems of rules that guide the actual operation of the practices.[12] The implication that "philosophical theories" are unreal seems unsubtle and unsound, and Rorty's claim that the part of an argument that attempts to ground a practice is, in a good pragmatist image, "a wheel that plays no part in the mechanism" may not do justice to the real contributions of certain philosophical theories.[13] Indeed, there may no longer be many

---

[12] Richard Rorty, *Consequences of Pragmatism* (University of Minnesota Press, 1982), pp. 167–168.
[13] Ibid., p. 167.

philosophical theories around to malign, if philosophical theories are only those that really purport to find ultimate normative grounds. Aware of how many turtles lie between here and there, many sophisticated theorists offer their ideas reflectively rather than deductively from a final normative ground. "Philosophical theories" and "real theories" thus may define a continuum rather than a dichotomy. Even on that understanding, however, the four figures Shapiro examines do lie toward the philosophical end, and his analysis neglects the implicit or "real" theories that suffuse conceptions of rights.

Rorty is correct to think that consistent use of a social practice entails application of a theory, a "real theory." That theory is what specifies what moves are possible within the practice and what those moves mean. Thus, people who participate coherently in the practice of rights discourse have a theory of rights, whether or not that theory aims at grounding the practice in something external. Once it is clear that many people other than self-conscious philosophers have and employ theories of rights, it must also be clear that understanding the evolution of rights theory requires more than analyzing the rights discourse of self-conscious philosophers. It requires analysis of a broader conversation, a conversation that does include philosophers but that includes political, legal, and perhaps other actors as well. By narrating and analyzing their conversation about rights, we can understand the concept of rights as they employ it. And if we understand rights as the creatures of a discursive practice, then understanding how the concept of rights is employed in their conversation is tantamount to understanding the nature of rights.

The idea of narrating conversations to understand political ideas brings us once again to Rorty. Rorty sees shifts in political and moral attitudes as shifts in language, as changes in the vocabulary used to describe given situations, and he is more interested in the vocabularies themselves than in extra-linguistic entities that the vocabularies try to map.[14] The world may be "out there" beyond human language, he says, but truth about the world cannot be, because truth is a property of sentences and language games. So when one vocabulary of description replaces another, it cannot be because the new vocabulary is true and the old one is newly discovered to be

[14] Richard Rorty, *Contingency, Irony, and Solidarity* (Cambridge University Press, 1989), pp. 3–22.

false. Instead, people gradually acquire the habit of using a new set of terms in place of an older set.[15] Why a vocabulary shifts is a question about causality, Rorty says, and therefore a better subject for empirical disciplines like history than for the kind of philosophy that would ask, fruitlessly, which vocabulary was correct. It is more fitting to ask what the rules of the relevant language games are and how intellectuals of a given time might have been led to drop one language game and begin playing another one.[16]

Rorty's recommendations are compelling, but there are three important limitations to the case he presents. First, he undersells the role that self-conscious theory, including reflective and even ontological normative theory, can play in the process of altering vocabularies. When Rorty looks at changes in philosophical conversations, he sees only causal forces at work, and he underestimates the force of justificatory arguments themselves as among the causes of conversational change. It would be better to see justificatory and other philosophical arguments as among the causes of change in how people employ political conceptions. Although the rationality or philosophical cogency of a given position is not necessarily a sufficient explanation for how people came to hold that position, it is also not the case that such rationality and cogency never contribute to forming people's views. These influences will not operate with equal power on all audiences: again, academic theorists may be the most likely to be affected, though they too are also influenced by other causal forces. Given that academics are Rorty's prime specimens, his lack of interest in justificatory theory as a causal force is a significant gap in his account.

Second, Rorty never actually analyzes a changing vocabulary in the way he recommends. He presents provocative and sometimes persuasive accounts of our conceptions of things like selfhood, liberal community, and the Mirror of Nature, but none of these accounts turns on demonstrating that one set of terms replaced another, much less on determining the causal reasons behind certain terms arising and others falling away. Rorty tells us to look at language games

---

[15] Rorty is here following in the path of Thomas Kuhn (*The Structure of Scientific Revolutions* [University of Chicago Press, 1962]) and Quine (e.g., "Two Dogmas," esp. pp. 42–46) but stopping short of the more radical view urged by, say, Nelson Goodman (*Ways of Worldmaking* [Hackett, 1978]), according to which there is no world beyond language and social construction.

[16] Richard Rorty, *Philosophy and the Mirror of Nature* (Blackwell, 1980), pp. 170–174, 270–273.

historically, but he does not show us how it is done. In the next three chapters, I apply the approach that Rorty articulates but does not execute to the practice of American rights discourse. I show how different arguments have been made at different times within the relevant language game, and I suggest reasons why Americans adopted different terms at different times. For example, chapter 4 illustrates how Northern Republicans during Reconstruction used the terms "political rights," "civil rights," and "social rights" to reconcile emancipation and black suffrage with their continuing opposition to full black equality. Chapter 5 illustrates how a later generation committed to racial nondiscrimination abandoned the Reconstruction vocabulary. A new term, "human rights," then arose to express and support that generation's new political commitment.

The third limitation to Rorty's method concerns the scope of the language games in which he is interested. As Cornel West has argued, the stories Rorty wants to tell tend to emphasize intellectuals and exclude politics. According to West, Rorty views the "conversation" on which he comments as only the explicit philosophical conversation, and he thereby repeats the ahistoricism of the people he criticizes by not paying sufficient attention to political and social conditions. Thus West: "To tell a tale about the historical character of philosophy while eschewing the political content, role, and function of philosophies in various historical periods is to promote an ahistorical approach in the name of history."[17] Furthermore, because Rorty's version of history is narrowly intellectual, even academic, the conclusions he draws are mostly about the world of the university. As regards the non-academic world, West plays on a Rortian phrase and charges Rorty with promoting a "pragmatism without consequences." Rorty's recommended analysis, West argues, should be extended to incorporate factors outside the academy and voices other than those of professional intellectuals. What we need, says West, are detailed accounts of the rise and fall of vocabularies and practices in light of their attendant economic, political, and cultural conditions.[18]

Ironically, West largely fails to heed his own advice. West's critique of Rorty's method is part of a "genealogy of pragmatism" that focuses almost exclusively on the thought of prominent intellectuals:

---

[17] Cornel West, *The American Evasion of Philosophy: A Genealogy of Pragmatism* (University of Wisconsin Press, 1989), p. 208.
[18] Ibid., pp. 206–208.

Emerson, Pierce, James, Dewey, Hook, Mills, DuBois, Niebuhr,
Trilling, Quine, Rorty. Just as Rorty advocates narrating historical
conversations but fails to deliver adequately historical narratives,
West advocates political and heterogeneous analysis but seems to
have settled for intellectual history. Nevertheless, for the theorist
whose aim is to understand a social practice like rights discourse, at
least part of West's challenge to Rorty is well taken. Legal and
political philosophy are legal and political as well as philosophical,
and the account of American rights that I present in the next three
chapters gives a central place to legal and political forces. The
language games of law, politics, and philosophy overlap, and each
influences the way that the others conceive of rights. That is why this
analysis of rights discourse examines political and legal developments as well as philosophical ones.

Although I follow West's recommendation to include non-academic sources, I do not follow all of his other prescriptions. Notably,
West urges that special prominence be given to relations of domination and to the histories of certain oppressed peoples. It is not my
intention to write a "history from below" of American rights:
indeed, my analysis concentrates on the most powerful members of
society. This focus is probably justifiable on the grounds that the
people to whom I pay the most attention were among the most
influential shapers of the wider discourse of their day, but even if that
point were to be doubted, it would not be necessary to write a
history from below in order to support the main arguments of this
book. I hope to show that rights discourse is a practice through
which people prioritize and protect their most important normative
commitments and that the content of the commitments that rights
embody has regularly been given by a process of concrete negation,
as Americans have reacted to specific traumas by codifying rights.
Because these patterns are present in well-known sources, reinterpreting those sources is sufficient for present purposes. A work of
scholarship that would add to my interpretation through a history of
rights from below would be welcome, but for now, the task is to
render rights discourse in its already-familiar locales a coherent
practice along the lines I have described. Thus, my analysis is
neither as high and abstract as Shapiro's nor as ground-level as West
would like to see.[19] It is a middle-level account that examines the

[19] It is, however, less rarefied than the work in which West makes his plea for diverse and

reasons for rights through the historical discourses of politics and law as well as that of the academy.

TWO KINDS OF REASONS

When I say that my account tries to discover the reasons for rights, I use the word "reasons" primarily in the sense of "causes" rather than that of "justifications." Recall Rorty's point that the question of why one vocabulary replaces another is a question that calls for causal answers.[20] Nevertheless, the current analysis of rights cannot examine causes to the exclusion of justifications, because the two kinds of reasons cannot be wholly separated, at least not as regards the political development of rights. Especially where philosophers and some kinds of judges are concerned, arguments about justification are among the causal forces guiding the nature of rights at any given time. It is therefore necessary to say something more about the differences and relationships between these two kinds of reasons.

If "reason" means "justification," then the reason for a thing, action, or belief is some normative principle by virtue of which the thing, action, or belief is legitimate. If "reason" means "cause," then the reason for a thing, action, or belief is the circumstance or set of circumstances that brought it about.[21] Questions of "why" ask for reasons, but it is not always clear which kind of reasons they ask for. Some call for answers specifically in terms of cause (Why is the sky

---

ground-level studies: *The American Evasion of Philosophy* is not only intellectual history but elite intellectual history.

[20] Rorty, *Mirror*, pp. 270–273.

[21] The differences between reasons as causes and reasons as justifications are the subject of a large and complex body of philosophical literature. My presentation of the issue here largely follows Wittgenstein's in *The Blue Book*, with the key difference that I use the word "reasons" to denote a category including both justifications and causes. Wittgenstein used "reasons" to mean only what I have called "justifications." Thus, I have called "cause" and "justification" two kinds of "reasons"; Wittgenstein wrote that "cause" and "reason" were two kinds of answers to questions of "why." To read Wittgenstein's comments on this subject in terms compatible with my present argument, it is therefore necessary to read "justification" for "reason" when "reason" appears in his text. (See Wittgenstein, *The Blue and Brown Books* [Basil Blackwell, 2nd edn., 1969], esp. *Blue Book* p. 15; echoed at *Blue Book* p. 88 and again at *Brown Book* pp. 110–111.) I do not propose to settle the more subtle riddles that the relationship between justification and cause presents. What is necessary for my purposes is to note the basic distinction and to point out the importance of causal reasons to an understanding of the structure of rights in a given culture. The more intricate philosophical questions raised by the contrast between cause and justification are beyond the scope of this study.

blue?) or in terms of justification (Why should I tell the truth rather than lie?). The question "Why do Americans have right X?" can usually be answered with either kind of reason. Rights theorists like Dworkin focus on justifications. When they investigate why Americans have a particular right, they seek to identify the moral or philosophical grounds that make that right legitimate. On their model, "Why do Americans have right X?" means "Why is it a good thing that Americans have right X?" If asked, for example, why Americans have a right against arbitrary searches of their private property, a justificatory theorist might begin an answer by asserting the pre-political nature of privacy or the need to limit the power of government over individuals. A logical edifice could then be erected on that foundation, abstract proposition following abstract proposition, until the conclusion that there was a right against arbitrary searches was established.

It is also possible, however, to answer the question of why Americans have a right against arbitrary searches with a causal reason. This kind of answer deals less in normative abstractions and more in historical analysis. The causal answer might run this way: Americans have the right in question because the Fourth Amendment to the federal Constitution prohibits unreasonable searches and seizures. The Fourth Amendment was written and adopted because American colonists were upset at the measures the British government took to combat smuggling in the years preceding independence. Particularly unpopular was the practice of issuing generalized search warrants that empowered British officials to search private homes at will. If, hypothetically, there had been no smuggling and no generalized search warrants, the Fourth Amendment as we know it would not have been written. Why do Americans have rights against arbitrary searches? Because the British used generalized search warrants to enforce unpopular taxes, and the colonists, when they had the power to do so, abolished the practice.[22]

---

[22] On the limitations of using reasons as causes to explain social action, including belief systems, see James Bohman, *New Philosophy of Social Science* (Polity Press, 1991), pp. 18–53. Making reference to social theorists such as Carl Hempel and Talcott Parsons, Bohman argues that causal analysis is too indeterminate to yield definitive accounts of behavior and belief. Of course, this would seem to be a limitation of social science generally.

The story of the Fourth Amendment growing out of American distaste for the British practice of issuing generalized search warrants (called "Writs of Assistance") is canonical in legal circles, and I have provided only a thumbnail sketch of it here. Some scholars have recently challenged this story, claiming that the Writs of Assistance played less of a role in shaping American attitudes toward searches and warrants than did other affairs of the time.

Causal and justificatory reasons for rights are not wholly separate. Ideas about justification are part of the history of cause, and causes affect what people believe to be adequate justifications. It is true, causally, that the reason for Fourth Amendment rights lies in British anti-smuggling measures and the reactions they provoked, but the Americans who reacted believed themselves to be acting justifiably when they banned generalized search warrants. Their attitudes about justification are part of the causal reasons for Fourth Amendment rights. Conversely, the experience of having their homes invaded by hostile customs officials may have persuaded some American colonists that generalized search warrants should be prohibited, an opinion which they might not have held or might not have held as strongly but for the experience. In this way, causal factors help shape the attitudes that underlie justificatory arguments, just as justificatory attitudes are embedded within the causal processes. Generations after the Fourth Amendment was codified, when Americans who disagree about contraception and abortion argue about rights of privacy, the precepts of the Fourth Amendment stand ready to be invoked as legitimate justifications in the argument. Those justifications would not be so readily available to modern disputants, and the contemporary discussion about justifying rights of privacy would be differently structured, if the causal events behind the Fourth Amendment had never occurred.

Where I use history as past behavior to explicate rights discourse as a practice, the justificatory attitudes of the agents described are critically important.[23] Where I use history as development, however, the reasons I emphasize are often less justificatory than causal. The aim there is to show how the current content of American rights theory grew out of some previous content as influenced by inter-

---

A chief rival for the role of causal force is the English case of *Wilkes v. Wood*, 98 Eng. Rep. 489 (CP 1763), in which John Wilkes, a member of Parliament and a vocal critic of George III and his government, successfully challenged the legality of politically motivated searches of his house and papers. See Akhil Amar, *The Bill of Rights: Creation and Reconstruction* (Yale University Press, 1998), pp. 66–67. For present purposes, of course, it does not matter whether the causal sources of the Fourth Amendment lie in the Wilkes affair or in the Writs of Assistance; each is a story about cause rather than justification, and either story, if true, is an example of how the question "Why do Americans have a certain right?" can be answered with a causal rather than a justificatory reason.

[23] I distinguish their attitudes from my own. When exploring the justificatory reasons behind rights argument in American history, I am analyzing whether and how people at the time believed certain rights to be justified, not whether I consider those rights justifiable independent of their opinions.

vening historical circumstances. Many rights originally gained moral or legal recognition for reasons, justificatory and causal, other than the leading justificatory reasons advanced in defense of those rights today. To be sure, justificatory arguments often played roles in the political struggles that established particular rights in the first place, but even in cases where that kind of continuity is surely present, those justificatory arguments are usually only part of the reason why, causally, the rights in question originally gained acceptance. To assume that rights gain acceptance simply because of the force of justificatory arguments is, in short, the inverse of the naturalistic fallacy: instead of making empirical causality into a justification, it makes justification into empirical cause, as if the good sense behind a given right completely explained why people respect that right. When searching for the causal reasons why certain rights have gained credence in American law and politics, it is therefore important to remember that many propositions have gained rights status at earlier times partly or even largely for reasons – causal or justificatory – other than those that modern justificatory arguments advanced on behalf of those rights would suggest. Accordingly, in the context of development, the question I mean to pose when I ask why Americans have some right X is not "Why is it a good thing that Americans have right X?" but "How did it come to pass that Americans identify and respect X as a right?" Because attitudes about justification are part of any adequate answer to that question, I consider their role as well, but I do so to produce a fuller account of cause.

WHICH RIGHTS?

Any claim of rights within the rules of the American practice of rights discourse is fair game for inclusion in this historical analysis. Those rules, as specified earlier, are that the term "right" must be used and that the thing alleged to be a right must be comprehensible as an entitlement, liberty, power, or immunity. In explaining the causes underlying different rights claims within the practice, I adopt an attitude that some theorists have labeled "symmetry."[24] Sym-

---

[24] Martin Hollis, "The Social Destruction of Reality," in Martin Hollis and Steven Lukes, eds., *Rationality and Relativism* (Blackwell, 1982), p. 75. Hollis opposes symmetry and uses the term pejoratively, but I believe that others who consider symmetry a sound methodological perspective can use the term without fear of taint. For a strong version of the argument for

metry as a methodological commitment means that all beliefs stand in need of explanation, whether they seem true and rational or false and irrational. In other words, an account of rights discourse as a social practice should cover claims of rights that strike us as reasonable (e.g., "Every adult citizen has the right to vote") as well as claims of rights that strike us as unreasonable (e.g., "All six-year-olds have the right to two helpings of dessert"). A non-symmetrical approach would hold that there is no need to explain why people would articulate the first belief, because the belief is entirely rational. Attempts to explain why people would hold that belief would be attempts to explain the obvious, that is, to explain things that required no explanation. To be sure, the rationality of a belief often plays a role in that belief's acceptance, and that role may be more and more substantial as the community of acceptors is more and more theoretically minded. That it is rational to believe that the earth is round was not the exclusive reason why people came to believe that the earth is round, but the rationality of the belief did play a role in the causal process by which that belief became conventional, inasmuch as some people were brought to that belief by, or partly by, weighing competing arguments and evaluating their rationality. With that proviso, however, I adopt the "symmetrical" approach to explaining beliefs, and I do so for three reasons. First, what a person considers to be rational is itself likely to be influenced by non-rational factors. Second, as Jon Elster has noted, the content of a belief is not always the same as the reason for holding that belief. If we want to know why a belief is held, we need to know about the conditions in which it was adopted, not just whether or not it is rational.[25] Accordingly, my examination of rights discourse evaluates all claims of rights with the same method, regardless of whether those claims seem rational or irrational, beneficial or harmful, grounded or groundless. Finally, explanations of how rights discourse functions with regard to seemingly irrational or counter-

symmetry, see Barry Barnes and David Bloor, "Relativism, Rationalism, and the Sociology of Knowledge," in Hollis and Lukes, *Rationality and Relativism*, esp. pp. 25–28. The symmetry I adopt is more moderate than the one Barnes and Bloor advocate in that it recognizes that the rationality of a belief may be among the factors that cause someone to hold a belief.

[25] Jon Elster, "Bias, Belief, and Ideology," in Hollis and Lukes, *Rationality and Relativism*, pp. 147–148. This position is linked to my decision to emphasize reasons as causes, because reasons as causes address not whether a belief is rational but rather why the belief is held. To the extent that the rationality of a belief is a reason for holding it, then causal analysis should include that rationality among the factors it considers.

intuitive rights claims often cast more light on the practice than do more rational, familiar rights claims. To explain rights claims that seem manifestly sensible or even unremarkable may be a helpful exercise, but it is unlikely to change the way that we understand the nature of rights. In contrast, to examine seemingly nonsensical or outlandish claims of rights and make those claims intelligible might indeed advance our understanding.

Just as I decline for the purposes of this study to distinguish between rational and irrational claims of rights, I avoid making normative judgments about the political issues that are contested within the discourse I analyze. In the historical sections that follow, when I say that Americans had or did not have a certain right at a certain time, I mean to make a descriptive statement about the presence or absence of that right among the rights generally accepted by Americans at that time.[26] I distinguish this meaning from a different meaning which I do not intend, a meaning whereby saying that Americans have or do not have a certain right at a certain time is a prescriptive claim about what ought or ought not to have been included in the consensus or codified in law. Thus, when I say that American women over the age of eighteen have the right to vote in public elections, I mean that there is a general consensus within American rights discourse on the existence of such a right. I can point to the Nineteenth and Twenty-Sixth Amendments to the federal Constitution for support, and I make no comment on the justice or injustice of the existing structure of rights.

RIGHTS AND AMERICAN HISTORY

Throughout American history, people have used the language of rights to respond to pressing political issues. Frequently, specific events or conditions have prompted the creation (recognition, establishment) of new rights, most notably when people suffer some adversity and then establish rights against that particular adversity in hopes of preventing its return. Different people – and different peoples – react differently to similar historical circumstances; that Americans reacted to events in their history by producing certain rights does not mean that people of some other culture should have produced the same rights in response to similar historical experi-

---

[26] Legal codification is one way to gauge whether a right enjoys such acceptance.

ences. Indeed, it does not even mean that the response of another culture should have come in terms of rights at all. In the United States, however, factors including the influence of English common law and Enlightenment philosophy on early Americans made rights discourse the dominant mode of normative politics.[27] Of course, it is the people who live in particular circumstances and not the historical circumstances themselves that create rights. Only people can create normative meaning, and rights, being normative meanings, are finally the creations of those people and not of some impersonal force called "History." But if people make their rights, they do not make them just as they please. Rights are made within the parameters of a social practice, and that practice is historically conditioned.

A description of the process by which historical events affect rights and rights discourse would have to use flexible terms. History is full of diverse contingencies, and any proposal for a tight reductionist model that precisely describes, let alone predicts, all aspects of a political process as complex as this one is bound to fail. Accordingly, the following discussion seeks not to deduce a general rule governing every instance of the historical transformation of rights discourse but rather to illuminate common characteristics of the interaction between history and conceptions of rights.[28] Below, I describe three features of such transformations, features for which I adopt the terms adversity, reaction, and synthesis. In varying forms, those three features are present in each period of rights transformation that this book explores. Familiarity with each of them and with the relationships among them provides tools for analyzing the specific transformations discussed in chapters 3, 4, and 5.

Consider, as a preliminary example of a rights transformation marked by those three features, a sketch of the account of the American Founding that the next chapter treats in more depth. Eighteenth-century British colonists in North America had certain conceptions of what their rights were. During the period of the American Revolution, they experienced a collection of adverse

---

[27] I will discuss these factors in more detail in the next chapter, when I examine the rights of the American Founding.

[28] See Hans-Georg Gadamer, *Truth and Method* (Sheed and Ward, 2nd edn., 1993), p. 5; John Dewey, *Reconstruction in Philosophy* (Beacon Press, 1948), pp. 168–169. The reductionist or rule-deducing approach to political science that I am rejecting can be found in Carl Hempel, "The Function of General Laws in History," *Journal of Philosophy*, 39 (1942), at 35.

conditions related to policies of the colonial administration and the circumstances of a war of rebellion. Subsequently, the rebels reacted against those practices and circumstances by creating rights that would prevent their recurrence. Those rights were then added to the pre-revolutionary rights. Lawyers, philosophers, and other people then tried to articulate synthesizing principles explaining how all the rights in the nascent combination aligned with analytically true and normatively desirable propositions about the nature of persons and politics. Conceptions of rights were thus transformed from their pre-revolutionary to their post-revolutionary condition, where they remained until another set of adverse conditions triggered a repetition of the process.[29] Later reactions to other adversities caused new rights to accrue as a new layer on an existing system, changing the catalog of rights and soliciting a new burst of principled rationalization. Each new layer of rights alters the way Americans view earlier layers but usually without erasing the earlier layers altogether: one might think of the layers as translucent.[30]

ADVERSITY, REACTION, SYNTHESIS

The first feature of the process is adversity. Adversity can come in the form of war, poverty, political repression, or virtually anything else that people perceive as substantially undesirable. Adversity is a property of perceptions rather than of events. The actual experience of war, poverty, and so on is not essential to the process I am describing; the perceived threat of adverse conditions is often sufficient. Accordingly, although unmediated experience of adverse conditions is the most direct mode of delivery, the adversity I refer to

[29] This account of changes is similar to the paradigm shifts that Thomas Kuhn describes in *The Structure of Scientific Revolutions*. One important shared idea is that only significant crises can provoke the creation of new paradigms.

[30] Although this study is not comparative, it is appropriate at this point to note that the reactive pattern described is not unique to the United States. For example, Jürgen Habermas has recently noted that the fundamental rights codified in the constitutions of the German federal states in 1945 tend to address specific suffered injustices and negate them word for word. The same is true, he adds, of a proposed outline for a unified Germany in 1990. Jürgen Habermas, *Between Facts and Norms: Contributions to a Discourse Theory of Law and Democracy* (MIT Press, 1996), pp. 389, 558. Neither is the process unique to the topic of rights. Probably every society reacts to adversities and later rationalizes those reactions with previously existing practices and ideas. That reaction does not always occur in terms of rights, because rights do not hold the place in every political culture that they hold in the political culture of the United States. Why different political cultures speak the language of rights to greater and lesser degrees is beyond the scope of this study.

can also be imagined or narrated. The significance of adversity is that it persuades people that the prevailing arrangements for the regulation of political, social, or economic life are inadequate. An adequate set of arrangements, the implicit reasoning goes, would prevent the rise or threat of significantly adverse conditions.[31]

The second feature of the process is reaction. Reaction attempts to correct the adverse conditions and to prevent their recurrence, and it may involve sweeping social reform in accordance with an overriding principle or piecemeal rejection of particular things associated with the given adverse conditions. It usually involves both. In rejecting whatever is associated with recent adversity, reaction picks its targets with reference to the full description of the adverse conditions, not just the elements logically connected to the adversity itself: a town ravaged at night by bands of arsonists wearing masks would be likely to take measures against arson and might rationally ban certain nighttime congregations, but it might also ban the wearing of masks, even though masks are in no way necessary to arson. At issue is what is associated with the adversity in the minds of those who react.[32] Adversity calls for reactions, and reactions are articulated within existing cultural matrices. In America, if the adversity is sufficiently important, the cultural matrices for articulating reactions have usually involved the language of rights. Reaction to a set of adversities involves establishing rights that will block those adversities from recurring and that will give people a moral basis on which to condemn those adversities that have already occurred. That the reaction should come in terms of rights is largely due to the role that common law tradition and Enlightenment philosophy played in forming the language of American political discourse, as I will discuss in greater depth in the next chapter.

That reactions are articulated within existing cultural matrices

---

[31] In the scheme I am suggesting, adversity plays a role similar to that of "crisis" in Kuhn's model of scientific revolutions. In Kuhn's terms, "Retooling is an extravagance to be reserved for the occasion that demands it. The significance of crises is the indication they provide that an occasion for retooling has arrived" (*Scientific Revolutions*, p. 76).

[32] The example is not as far fetched as it might seem. Consider the prohibitions on disguise promulgated as anti-Ku Klux Klan measures in the American South during Reconstruction (see Eric Foner, *Reconstruction: America's Unfinished Revolution, 1863–1877* [Harper & Row, 1988], p. 438). On a more general level, Michael Freeden describes the phenomenon of associating political phenomena on the grounds of their "cultural adjacency" as well as their "logical adjacency." Michael Freeden, "Political Concepts and Ideological Morphology," *Journal of Political Philosophy* 2(2) (1994), at 151–154.

means, in part, that new rights articulated at a given time must reach accommodation with some substantial part of the previously existing system of rights. Successive adversities create successive layers of reactive rights, each of which may partially obscure previous layers without eliminating them. Rights created at different times in the past thus exercise contemporaneous influence over the rights discourse of the present; experience of the past involves many layers of time simultaneously.[33] Moreover, the influences of different past times operate not just concurrently but interconnectedly. Gadamer notes that what an artifact of the past means in the present is partly a function of how its original conceptual "horizon" – that is, the historical perspective within which it operated – has fused with the horizons of intervening times as well as how various horizons can fuse with those of the present.[34] Americans in 1997 have rights that were born as reactions to different sets of conditions at different times over a period of more than two hundred years. Indeed, the true period is centuries longer than that, because the conceptions of rights that Americans held before independence already contained layers of rights compiled during centuries of British history. When new rights are created, they become part of a system already populated by these many layers of older rights.

The third feature of the process, which attempts to rationalize the most recently accrued layer of rights with the rights that came before, is synthesis. Synthesis takes place on the level of theory. Successful synthesis articulates principles that unite new rights with old rights. All of these rights are integrally linked, says the synthesizer, and our heroic ancestors who fought for rights A and B were fighting for these rights C and D as well, or at least would have done so, had they stood in our shoes, for the same (justificatory) reasons that they fought for A and B in the first place. Abraham Lincoln engaged in synthesis in his Gettysburg Address when he identified "all men are created equal" as the proposition to which the United

---

[33] Moreover, we do not necessarily experience those layers of experience in chronological order. We can sometimes, if we choose, match experiences with dates, but the experience itself is non-sequential. Borrowing an image from Christian Meier, Reinhart Koselleck writes that experience is "like the glass front of a washing machine, behind which various bits of the wash appear now and then, but are all contained within the drum." The drum represents what Koselleck calls the "space of experience," where bits of laundry appear in no particular order. Reinhart Koselleck, *Futures Past: On the Semantics of Historical Time* (MIT Press, 1985), p. 273.

[34] Gadamer, *Truth and Method*, pp. 302–307, 395.

States had been dedicated at its founding, giving a nineteenth-century application to an eighteenth-century slogan.[35] Martin Luther King, Jr., engaged in another synthesis a hundred years later when he gave the phrase another resonance in a twentieth-century struggle. Both synthesizers drew substantially on the meaning of their predecessor or predecessors, but each also fused that meaning with a new meaning suggested by contemporary circumstances. Many announcements of principles or sets of principles said to express enduring tenets of American political morality, past and present, are attempts at synthesis. Not every attempted synthesis is historically ingenuous, but not every one is historically disingenuous, either. Historical credibility is not the uppermost criterion for a successful synthesis, because synthesis aims to create rational principles in the minds of a present generation. It is usually a project for philosophers, lawyers, or politicians rather than one for historians, although the claims that non-historians make in their attempts to synthesize are sometimes constrained by the facts of history. Moreover, not every attempt at synthesis is successful, and the elements of a transformation are not always successfully synthesized with what came before. In many cases, the structure or discourse of rights contains multiple and even contradictory elements which coexist more or less easily without being rationalized into a coherent theory. Indeed, identifying which elements of the rights discourse of a given time do not work easily with which other elements can provide starting points for historical investigations into the causal reasons for the adoption of rights, because sets of rights that cannot be successfully synthesized cannot have arisen as the simple entailments of a unified justificatory philosophy of rights.

THE TRANSFORMATIONS

To explore how American rights and rights discourse came to their present states, I will sketch an initial condition and then chart the changes that the reactive process worked in three major periods of transformation. The initial condition, of course, is not truly initial, because it, too, has a history. No matter when this story began, it would begin *in medias res*. Some starting point must be chosen, and,

---

[35] For one now-prominent view of that synthesis, see Gary Wills, *Lincoln at Gettysburg: The Words that Remade America* (Simon & Schuster, 1992).

given the impossibility of a true time zero, the rights of the British colonists before the American Revolution are a reasonable starting point: their continuity with earlier British and European development is mitigated by geographic discontinuity and by the political rupture that soon followed. The three periods of transformation that I will explore are the period of the American Revolution and Founding in the eighteenth century, the period of the struggle against the Southern "slave power" in the nineteenth, and the period immediately following World War II in the twentieth. The farthest-reaching changes in the history of American rights took place during those times. Rights discourse was not wholly static at other times, of course, because there is a level at which change is gradual and continuous. But there are also times of upheaval in which thoughts and practices regarding rights are transformed farther, deeper, and faster than in the normal course of gradual change.

The Founding and Reconstruction are obvious choices as periods to analyze. The Founding institutionalized a new political order that had come into existence as a result of a rebellion fought significantly, though not entirely, over questions of rights. The Founders produced a constitutional Bill of Rights that remains the textual touchstone for American rights, and they also crafted political and philosophical defenses of their rights-based system that Americans still study and invoke as the most important writings on American politics. Reconstruction was the next major burst of rights activity. Rights of property and personal freedom were irrevocably altered. Three constitutional amendments expanding the domain and extending the scope of rights were adopted within five years. One of those amendments, the Fourteenth, contains the clauses to which constitutional lawyers today appeal more frequently than to any other clauses in the entire Constitution, those that guarantee the rights of due process and equal protection of the laws. Moreover, a process of synthesis between Reconstruction and the Founding altered the significance that certain elements of the Founding would hold for later generations of Americans, as Founding statements of rights came to be seen through the lens of Reconstruction. The Founding and Reconstruction have remained fundamental to American conceptions of rights ever since.

It is my choice of a third period, and of the post-war, anti-totalitarian period as that third period, that departs from present convention and stands in need of explanation. Much of the leading scholarship among constitutional scholars, for example, has tended to regard the Founding and Reconstruction as unrivaled for importance. Thus, Akhil Amar's recent book *The Bill of Rights* argues that Reconstruction is more important to what American rights are and mean today than the Founding is, but it does not take seriously the possibility that some third period might be as or more important than Reconstruction. The leading theorist to argue that other periods might be as seminal as Reconstruction and the Founding is, of course, Bruce Ackerman, for whom the New Deal was a third constitutional revolution on par with the earlier two. With Ackerman, and against Amar, I argue that transformations indigenous to the twentieth century are as indispensable to modern American conceptions of rights as the influences of Reconstruction and the Founding. Against Ackerman, however, I offer not the New Deal but the confrontation with European totalitarianism, Nazi and Soviet, as the most important twentieth-century influence.

AKHIL AMAR AND THE BILL OF RIGHTS: A STORY IN TWO PARTS

Akhil Amar's *The Bill of Rights: Creation and Reconstruction* offers a provocative account of changing conceptions of certain rights in two of the three transformative periods that I analyze in this book. The central concern of Amar's book is the way that Reconstruction reshaped the Bill of Rights. Through analyses of several rights contained in the Bill, Amar argues that what a given right meant to the Founders was frequently different from what it meant to the Reconstruction generation. Moreover, the revision of constitutional rights that Reconstruction worked was so profound that what the Bill of Rights means today is more a function of what it meant after the Civil War than what it meant after the Revolution. Instead of searching for the meanings and scopes of basic constitutional rights in the thought of James Madison and his peers, we should therefore turn our attention to John Bingham, the drafter of the Fourteenth Amendment, and his Reconstruction contemporaries. Thus Amar: "When we 'apply' the Bill of Rights against the states today, we must first and foremost reflect upon the meaning and the spirit of the amendment of 1866, not the Bill of 1789."[36]

---

[36] Amar, *Bill of Rights*, p. 223.

To show how Reconstruction rewrote American constitutional rights, Amar's book centers on what constitutional lawyers know as the "incorporation" of the Bill of Rights against the states. Before the Civil War and Reconstruction, the Bill of Rights bound the federal government but not the states. State governments could establish religions, or abridge the freedom of speech, or take private property without just compensation, and not be in violation of the Constitution. Today, most provisions of the Bill apply to the states as well: an unreasonable search or seizure is just as unconstitutional if undertaken by the state police as if undertaken by a federal officer. According to Supreme Court doctrine, this "incorporation" of the Bill of Rights against the states was worked by the Fourteenth Amendment. Passage of the Fourteenth Amendment, of course, was one of the central events of Reconstruction, and the phenomenon of incorporation is a natural lens through which to assess the relationship between conceptions of rights in Reconstruction and conceptions of rights at the Founding.

The proper theory and operation of incorporation have been heavily contested. One school, led by Justice Hugo Black, holds that the Fourteenth Amendment incorporates everything in the first ten amendments – or at least the first eight or nine – against the states. Another school, led by Black's rival Justice Felix Frankfurter, holds that only those provisions of the Bill of Rights that involve "fundamental fairness" or "the very concept of ordered liberty" are incorporated. The official position of the Court for well over a generation has been "selective incorporation" as engineered by yet a third Justice, William Brennan. Selective incorporation considers the rights in the Bill individually, as Frankfurter would have, but in practice has led to the incorporation against the states of almost the whole Bill. Amar now argues for an interpretive strategy he calls "refined incorporation," an approach that tries to combine the insightful parts of Black, Frankfurter, and Brennan into a single method.[37]

Refined incorporation is a thoughtful contribution, and many of Amar's accounts of how conceptions of particular rights changed from 1791 to 1868 are valuable and illuminating. Moreover, the idea that what American constitutional rights are and mean today is heavily influenced by events later than the Founding is well worth

---

[37] Ibid., p. xiv.

emphasizing. In an important way, however, Amar does not pursue that idea far enough. The eighteenth century did not have the last word in shaping American rights – but neither did the nineteenth. In claiming that understanding what the Bill of Rights means today requires us to reflect first and foremost on the meaning and spirit of 1866 rather than 1789, Amar implies a false choice. Certainly we should reflect on 1866 as well as 1789, but we should also reflect on other, later dates. A lot has happened in the last hundred and thirty years, enough to make a theory of rights pegged to 1866 almost as moss-covered as one pegged to 1789 would be. In presenting a developmental story with three major turning points instead of two, I hope to show that changes in conceptions of rights in the twentieth century have been at least as consequential as the changes Amar points to in Reconstruction. As I argue in chapter 5, the most important of the twentieth-century changes stemmed from reaction to European totalitarianism in the years after World War II.

It is in some ways ironic that Amar slights the twentieth century and the post-war transformation in particular,[38] because the judicial battle over incorporation doctrine is a distinctly twentieth-century and post-war phenomenon. Amar pays careful attention to Brennan, Frankfurter, and Black, critiquing and rearranging their theories, but he does not stop to inquire why those three Justices should have wrestled so mightily over incorporation at the moment in history when they did. After all, their debate was no immediate outgrowth of Reconstruction. By the time Black and Frankfurter sat on the Supreme Court, the Fourteenth Amendment had been law for seventy years. At the start of their tenures, most of the Bill of Rights had not yet been incorporated. Indeed, Black first set forth his "total incorporation" theory when dissenting *Adamson v. California*, a 1947 decision in which the Court refused to apply the Fifth Amendment right against self-incrimination against the states.[39] But between 1948 and 1969, the Court handed down no fewer than eleven decisions incorporating provisions of the Bill of Rights against the states.[40] The timing was not coincidental. Most of those decisions

---

[38] I do not mean to imply that Amar should have written a book about the twentieth century; one can perfectly well write a fine book limited to the relationship between Reconstruction and the Founding. I merely mean that Amar errs, having written such a book, in claiming that the topics and periods covered in his book are the topics and periods most important to an understanding of modern constitutional rights.

[39] *Adamson v. California*, 332 U.S. 46 (1947).

[40] The Court incorporated the right to public trial in *In Re Oliver*, 333 U.S. 257 (1948), the right

thickened individual rights against the police and prosecutors, concerns that resonated with the anti-Nazi and anti-Soviet preoccupations of American rights discourse in those years. Amar carefully considers the incorporationist theories at work in those years but without connecting them to their proximate causes. Rather than seeing Black, Frankfurter, and Brennan in their rival theories of incorporation as simply propounding theories about the relationship between two earlier transformative periods in the history of American rights, I suggest that we should see them as living through a third transformation. Part of what went on during that third transformation, predictably enough, was a struggle over the meaning of the first two. But that struggle occurred under the influence of the particular historical adversities of its own time, and understanding modern conceptions of rights requires us to take that time seriously as a transformative period in its own right.

BRUCE ACKERMAN AND THE NEW DEAL MOMENT

The theorist who has done the most to show that the twentieth century included transformative periods on par with Reconstruction and the Founding is Bruce Ackerman, and the twentieth-century transformation that he sees as paramount is that of the New Deal. According to Ackerman, the political order that the Federalists of the Founding period built after the American Revolution was the first of not two but three American constitutional regimes. The Reconstruction Republicans worked a second revolution in the 1860s, changing the way that the government operated under the Constitution. In the 1930s, New Deal Democrats conducted the third revolution, and the United States at present is in its third constitutional regime. After each revolution, Ackerman explains, new ways must be found to reconcile the principles of the new regime with the legacies of older ones, most notably by reading

to Fourth Amendment privacy from police intrusion in *Wolf v. Colorado*, 338 U.S. 25 (1949), the right against unreasonable search and seizure in *Mapp v. Ohio*, 367 U.S. 463 (1961), the right against cruel and unusual punishment in *Robinson v. California*, 370 U.S. 660 (1962), the right to counsel in *Gideon v. Wainwright*, 372 U.S. 335 (1963), the right against self-incrimination in *Malloy v. Hogan*, 378 U.S. 1 (1964), the right of a criminal defendant to confront the witnesses against him in *Pointer v. Texas*, 380 U.S. 400 (1965), the right to a speedy trial in *Klopfer v. North Carolina*, 386 U.S. 213 (1967), the right to compulsory process for obtaining witnesses in *Washington v. Texas*, 388 U.S. 14 (1967), the right to trial by jury in *Duncan v. Louisiana*, 391 U.S. 145 (1968), and the right against double jeopardy in *Benton v. Maryland*, 395 U.S. 784 (1969).

provisions of the Constitution written in earlier regimes in ways that are consistent with the principles of the new one.[41] Ackerman describes two different kinds of change which occur in his transformative periods. One is a changed relationship among the major institutions of government, and the other is a changed understanding of the rights of American citizens.[42]

The changing relationship among the institutions of American government is not the focus of this book, and I see in any case no reason to dispute Ackerman's choice of periods when those relationships were transformed. With regard to changing views of rights, however, which is very much the topic at hand, the last of Ackerman's choices seems questionable. His first two chosen periods, the Founding and Reconstruction, seem correct, as does his view that those two periods are not the alpha and omega of this developmental story – i.e., that there must also be a third period. I depart from his scheme, however, when deciding what that third period is. The rewriting of rights principles that has had such great consequences in the last two generations is less a product of the New Deal than of World War II and the years following. To be sure, the New Deal involved far-reaching changes in American conceptions of rights, and much of the structure and theory of American politics is still heavily influenced by the New Deal era. Nevertheless, the ideas that made possible the success of the civil rights movement of the 1950s and 1960s are better understood as reactions against adversities of World War II and the years that followed, namely the confrontation with totalitarianism in its Nazi and Soviet forms.

Consider, for example, that the signature rights of the 1950s and 1960s were less concerned with the economic issues that were central to the New Deal than with rights against racial discrimination, abusive police practices, censorship, and government regulation of personal privacy. Those issues correspond more closely to the threats of Nazism and Soviet communism than to the problems of the Great Depression and the New Deal. Similarly, the New Deal required the judiciary to become more relaxed about enforcing rights once thought fundamental, notably the absolute property right, so that

---

[41] Amar acknowledges that much of his recent book "is an effort to try to do the kind of detailed interpretive work that Ackerman at a more abstract level has called for" with respect to the synthesis of the first two transformative periods, Founding and Reconstruction, with which Ackerman is concerned. Amar, *Bill of Rights*, p. 299.

[42] Bruce Ackerman, *We The People: Foundations* (Harvard University Press, 1991).

Congress could legislate economic reforms. That passivism contrasts sharply with the judicial activism on behalf of fundamental rights that marked the post-war era. The trend toward judicial activism on behalf of fundamental and even unenumerated rights was part of a larger mid-century intellectual shift, as legal and political philosophers shifted their allegiances from legal positivism to *a priori* universal rights. That shift had to do not with the New Deal but with the problem of foreign totalitarianism. As I argue in chapter 5, Nazi Germany and the Soviet Union could both have been legitimate polities under positivist theory, and post-war theorists searching for theoretical grounds on which to condemn those regimes had to replace positivism with some other framework. A doctrine of universal individual rights served the purpose. Prevailing features of American normative theory at the end of the twentieth century, including ideas of notable theorists like Dworkin and Ackerman, still derive from reactions against that mid-century trauma, both in the tendency to consider rights inherent and universal and in the choice of which rights are most important. Having developed new readings of rights in the generation after World War II, Americans have subsequently prized principles that synthesize those rights with the rights of the earlier two transformations.

The chapters that follow examine those three transformative periods. Each chapter shows how reactions against adverse conditions during the time period in question generated new rights which were then appended to the rights structure inherited from a previous stage of history. Important differences among the rights discourse of the different historical periods considered require corresponding variations in analytic approach. For example, it would be tempting but unsound to select a few specific rights, such as the right of free speech or the right to vote, and to trace the development of those rights through history, letting patterns in the development of those rights stand for patterns in rights discourse. The temptation of that approach lies in its simple consistency. To adopt that approach, however, would be to confuse particular rights with the general discourse of rights. One of the most important features of the discourse of rights is that different rights are prominent within it at different times. Seeing the behavior of the discourse entails seeing not only how conceptions of particular rights change but also when and how different rights enter and exit. Examining the same rights in every time period would necessarily forfeit that part of the analysis, just as Sunstein's selecting for material that speaks to *recurrent* dilemmas cannot yield a full picture of a changing agenda's development. Accordingly, each chapter examines conceptions of the rights that were most important to the discourse of the relevant time period. The choice of those rights in each case requires justifications, and those justifications are left to the chapters in question.

As an example of the perils involved in following particular rights through history rather than keeping the focus on the more general level of discourse, consider a thumbnail sketch of the development of the right to free speech. Free speech, and more generally free expression, is a central concern of modern American politics. If the choice of a few key rights through which to see American rights discourse were made with reference to contemporary conditions, the right to free speech would be a strong candidate. But "the right to free speech" has sometimes meant something so different from what it currently means that examining free speech across historical eras might address different things under the same name. According to eighteenth-century understandings, free speech referred not to a general right of free expression but to a specific right of legislators to speak freely in the legislature. That was the conception of free speech handed down from seventeenth-century England, and it survived the Founding more or less unchanged.[43] The link between free speech and free press in the First Amendment, which seems to imply a free speech right broader than that pertaining to legislators, was an anomaly in its time; with only one exception, state constitutions that guaranteed free speech did so with specific reference to speech in their legislatures.[44] The right of free speech continued to

---

[43] Leonard Levy, *Constitutional Opinions* (Oxford University Press, 1986), p. 4.

[44] See, e.g., Massachusetts Constitution of 1780, Article XXI. Only Pennsylvania took the extraordinary step of making free speech a right of "the people" and linking it with the right of free press. Pennsylvania Constitution of 1776, section XII. Viewing the free speech right as a right of legislators, as all the other states did, was consistent with both common-law history and the original United States Constitution: the English Bill of Rights of 1689 provided "That the freedom of speech, and debates or proceedings in Parliament, ought not to be impeached or questioned in any court or place out of Parliament" (section 9) and the American Constitution echoed the principle with the guarantee that "for any Speech or Debate in either House, [Senators and Representatives] shall not be questioned in any other place" (Article I, section 6). The causal reasons why free speech and free press were linked in the First Amendment are obscure. James Madison, the drafter of what became the First Amendment, worked from a copy of resolutions passed by the Virginia ratifying convention, and that convention in turn had largely copied the Pennsylvania Constitution. Why the Virginia convention copied Pennsylvania's Constitution instead of its own on this

be associated with legislators into the nineteenth century, as chapter 4's discussion of the Congressional "gag rule" controversy illustrates. Construed as a right of legislators, free speech never had the importance within rights discourse that it has come to have in the twentieth century as a general right of free expression. No Supreme Court opinion contained the broad reading of free speech as the individual right we know today until Oliver Wendell Holmes's dissent in *Abrams v. United States* in 1919, and no Supreme Court decision made that theory of free speech the law of the land until *Brandenburg v. Ohio* was handed down fifty years later.[45] Thus, examining conceptions of the right of free speech goes much farther toward understanding the rights discourse of America in the twentieth century than in the eighteenth or nineteenth – and examining free speech in all three contexts would in any case not satisfy the desire for analytic consistency, because what was called "the right of free speech" in 1789 was substantively different from the right of free speech two centuries later.

WHOSE DISCOURSE?

Other ways in which this analysis must cope with differences among the discourses of different periods regard the selection of particular people within society on whose arguments to concentrate and the selection of sources taken to be representative of their views. Given the decision to reinterpret the rights discourse of familiar sources, the focus throughout is on elites. The pattern in rights discourse that I wish to analyze can be seen without having to write a new history from below, and, for the purposes of this project, sources already familiar are sufficient. Indeed, showing a new way to read well-known sources might do more to make us rethink our understanding of rights discourse than a reading of less-familiar sources would. The shape and composition of the elite classes whose discourse composes

matter is a mystery. It is at least possible that had the Virginia convention used its own state constitution as a model in this case, as it often did when proposing constitutional amendments, there would be no free speech clause in the First Amendment. David Anderson, "The Origins of the Press Clause," *UCLA Law Review* 30, 455, 473 (1983).

[45] *Abrams v. United States*, 250 U.S. 616 (1919); *Brandenburg v. Ohio*, 395 U.S. 444 (1969). Two articles by David Rabban present an excellent account of the rise of modern free speech doctrines. They are "Free Speech in Progressive Social Thought," *Texas Law Review* 74, 951 (1996), and "The Emergence of Modern First Amendment Doctrine," *University of Chicago Law Review* 50, 1205 (1983).

the familiar sources, however, has varied from time to time. In the late eighteenth century, the population of British North America was roughly one percent of what the population of the United States became by the middle of the twentieth. Moreover, the political leadership of the Founding generation largely overlapped with the intellectual and journalistic elites of the same era. Franklin was a printer, a politician, a philosopher, a scientist, a diplomat, a journalist, and the founder of a major university. With minor variations, Jefferson had the same credentials, and examples could be multiplied with little effort. Whether a study of Founding rights discourse concentrates on politicians or philosophers or newspaper editorialists, it studies more or less the same people. Studying later time periods is different. Many leading thinkers about rights in 1950 or 1970 neither sat in Congress nor published their arguments in general-circulation newspapers. Magnifying the distinction is the sheer increase in the number of people participating in the nation-wide argument about rights. The possibility of covering all facets of a discourse recedes as more voices enter the discussion, and one must instead strive to identify a few representative voices.

Accordingly, chapter 3, Rights of the Founding, deals with the rights discourse of the small Founding elite across many forums, most notably in public political debate but also in the side conversations that informed that debate; chapter 4, Rights and Reconstruction, relies a little more heavily on the official forums of political rights discourse, such as the debates of Congress and the decisions of courts; and chapter 5, Rights after World War II, similarly makes use of court decisions, but it also considers the academic discussion of rights, something that did not exist in the modern professional sense during the Founding and Reconstruction. In each case, the analysis rests mostly on interpreting documents well known to mainstream scholarship of the periods. One advantage of this approach is that it reduces the risk of reaching unwarranted conclusions by overestimating the representativity of obscure materials. Another is that it emphasizes that the dynamics of rights discourse as a social practice are present and prominent even in the acknowledged core of American rights discourse, in sources that have been studied many times but whose employment of rights language in the ways shown here has not been adequately recognized.

The elite conversation that the coming chapters analyze includes philosophical elites as well as those of law and politics narrowly construed. Given that the chapters on the Founding and Reconstruction eras do not treat academic philosophers, it might be thought that including academics in the analysis of post-World War II rights discourse poses a methodological problem. Given the aims of this book, however, it would in fact be the *exclusion* of academic philosophers that would raise a methodological problem. The distinct category of professional scholars barely existed in the United States until the late nineteenth century. To exclude academics from the analysis of twentieth-century rights discourse on the grounds that professional philosophical discussion was not a feature of rights discourse in earlier generations would be to allow a desire for the appearance of investigative consistency to obscure the complexity of the subject. Excluding legal and political philosophers from the analysis of twentieth-century rights discourse would be a methodological error analogous to excluding consideration of the right to free speech from that analysis on the grounds that it was little discussed during the previous two historical periods. At issue is the scope and composition of the practice of rights discourse. There are, of course, differences in how academics and non-academics discuss questions of rights, and those differences suggest that their discussions do not follow all of the same rules and patterns. It is easier and more common for politicians and ordinary citizens acting politically to make claims about rights without worrying about niceties like theoretical underpinnings or systematic consistency than it is for judges and philosophers to do the same. On some readings of politics, including some forms of interest-based liberalism, it may even be appropriate for elected representatives to use the rhetorical power of rights as an instrumental tool in advancing the interests of their constituents, without regard to the ultimate philosophical integrity of the claims they make. Like attorneys with private clients, they see their office as the vindication of interests, not the pursuit of truth. Judges are held to different standards, insofar as higher courts require them to maintain the consistency of a set of rules. Even among judges, of course, there are many opportunities for departing from or undermining an existing system of thought, but the premise of thoughtful consistency is nonetheless present and usually quite powerful.

Finally, most academic rights discourse sees itself as very different from the clumsy shouting of politics, and that self-image is frequently

justified. Some theorists actually do choose first principles from
which to derive rights and strive to hold to those principles rather
than finding ways to make other, contradictory arguments in order
to justify specific desired outcomes. Other theorists develop good-
faith, reflective arguments aimed at justifying or questioning particular understandings of rights, and the best of these theories
provide important insights for people who would understand and
perhaps re-order their normative commitments. Good scholars
know that they cannot provide naked support for a set of commitments they happen to prefer without offering justificatory reasons for
their preferences. Nevertheless, rights discourse among academics is
not wholly different from the rights discourse of lawyers and
politicians, and the similarities among these subconversations are
enough to see them all as a common social practice, or at least as
overlapping variations of a practice. As the next three chapters
demonstrate, all three circles of conversation use the language of
rights to prioritize and protect the normative commitments that
their members value most highly. All three use rights language
across the four categories of entitlements, privileges, powers, and
immunities. The concrete negation of recent or historical traumas is
common to all three, and the crises to which the different subdis-
courses respond are largely the same. Accordingly, the practice of
rights discourse in academic philosophy is not wholly different from
the practice of rights discourse outside the academy. Exploring the
operation of that practice throughout American history can therefore illuminate not just what politicians or lawyers are doing when
they make arguments about rights but what professional academics
are doing as well. What they are doing, it seems, often resembles
what everyone else does by invoking rights. As the examples of
Dworkin and Feinberg illustrate, academic rights discourse, like
rights discourse generally, is frequently about using a powerful
discursive tool to privilege substantive political commitments. The
content of those commitments is largely given by reaction against
and concrete negation of adversities, and the adversities and negations are largely the same among academics as they are among
others.

CHAPTER 3

Rights of the Founding

America has a fascination with its origins. Lawyers, politicians, and others who want to find truths about political morality or constitutional law regularly consult the thoughts and writings of the small group of men who are known collectively, if roughly, as the Founders of the Republic or the Framers of the Constitution. Founding codifications of rights in federal and state constitutions, as well as the Founders' arguments about the rights they claimed, continue to affect what rights modern Americans have and how they conceive of rights in general. For all of the attention that modern political and legal theorists pay to the Founding era, however, many differences between how the Founders thought and spoke about rights and how leading modern theorists think and speak about rights have not been noticed or sufficiently understood. There are differences as well as similarities between political and academic rights discourse, and although many of the Founders can legitimately be regarded as self-conscious political theorists, their major projects were more political than academic. Indeed, the category of professional academic philosophers hardly existed in America at the Founding. Perhaps not coincidentally, Founding rights discourse was relatively unconcerned with many of the analytic strictures that concern modern rights theorists and which some modern theorists try to read into the discourse of the Founding.

For example, much modern rights theory is concerned with defining what kinds of beings can have rights, or what the sources of rights are, or what kinds of content rights can be given. In contrast, analytic criteria specifying the possible bearers, sources, and contents of rights exercised little constraint on the Founders' conceptions of rights. The Founders did not classify normative propositions as rights on the basis of whether those propositions fit into formal categories like those discussed in chapter 1, such as the protection of individuals against the demands of general social utility or the securing of autonomous choice-making or of human welfare. Instead, whether the Founders claimed something as a right was largely a function of how important they believed it to be and whether it was in need of protection; in short, any entitlement, liberty, power, or immunity that they considered important and threatened could be claimed or defended in the language of rights. The major source of threats with which the Founders were concerned was the British colonial administration, and many rights of the Founding arose in reaction to specific British policies of the time.

For the purposes of this discussion, I will consider the Founding period to span the years 1764 to 1791. In 1764, Parliament passed the Sugar Act and began issuing general search warrants to customs officers in the American colonies; in response, James Otis published his essay *Rights of the British Colonies Asserted and Proved*. I will take these to be the opening moves in the dialectic of British administration and American protest that continued through American independence. At the other end of the period, ratification of the first ten amendments to the United States Constitution in 1791 is a logical resting point. The law codes and declarations of rights that Americans wrote during the intervening years illustrate the practice of rights discourse during the Founding, as do key essays, propaganda pamphlets, and other forums for political discussion.

TWO KINDS OF ATTEMPTED SYNTHESIS

Other societies have experienced some of the same conditions that Americans experienced at the Founding without producing a system of rights identical to that of revolutionary America. American reactions arranged themselves within a framework of rights partly because the language and concept of political rights was already strong in colonial America. As Jack Rakove puts it, the language of rights was the colonists' "mother tongue," present in their culture since their earliest consciousness.[1] The long tradition of English common law and the newer vogue of Enlightenment philosophy both spoke the language of rights, and, under those influences, Americans and especially American elites were disposed to under-

---

[1] Jack N. Rakove, *Original Meanings: Politics and Ideas in the Making of the Constitution* (Vintage Books, 1996), p. 290.

stand political questions in terms of rights. Reactions against eighteenth-century events could attach themselves to that conceptual framework.

The impulse to reject and prevent the recurrence of specific adversities incident to British rule guided much of rights discourse at the Founding, but that impulse was filtered through pre-existing ideas about rights that were already familiar to the Founders. Accordingly, Founding rights discourse displayed the influence of theory as well as of experience and, within the category of experience, of history as well as of contemporary conditions. Whether the Founders synthesized these various influences into one coherent concept of rights or merely agglomerated their effects into an unrationalized patchwork is a question without a systematic answer. Sometimes particular actors or documents successfully merged multiple sources; sometimes they did not. Almost always, however, more than one of these influences colored people's conceptions of a given right. The interactions among these different influences on conceptions of rights were not, of course, unique to the Founding. They are present in rights discourse generally. Illustrating the interactions at the Founding helps explicate the pattern and perhaps makes it easier to see similar competing influences in other areas of rights discourse, including the discourse of modern theorists like Dworkin, Sunstein, and Feinberg.

Past and present experience

As Rakove notes, the Founders' notion of the "experience" from which they drew political lessons included not only what they themselves lived through but also the experience of previous generations.[2] The Founders' ideas of what adversities they needed rights to protect against were thus informed not just by contemporary events but also by events from English history and even classical antiquity, and they produced conceptions of rights that incorporated both the concrete negation of adversities they experienced in their own lifetimes and the negation of adversities which they "remembered" from the history of earlier times. Not every historical experience, however, carried equal weight. The Founders' attitudes about which experiences were most significant were joint products of the histor-

---

[2] Ibid., p. 18.

ical importance of those events and the Founders' own needs and values, two factors that influenced each other in a kind of equilibrium rather than existing independently. Thus, many of the rights espoused or codified at the Founding had deep roots in colonial or English history, and history as well as contemporary conditions could underlie their codifications.

The pattern of inheriting historical rights appears prominently in many official lists of rights in revolutionary America that descend, in part, from dozens of early colonial documents. Some but not all of these documents bore traces of Magna Carta or English common law. Some used a blanket guarantee that residents of a given colony would have all the same rights as Englishmen in England.[3] Frequently, new documents would be piled upon old, announcing rights different from those articulated in earlier texts without instructions as to which version was to govern in case of conflict. Successful synthesis would have called on the Founders to perform what Gadamer would call a fusing of historical horizons, merging different and unequal layers of the past with present concerns in order to form a coherent worldview.[4] In some ways, that fusion followed in the spirit of the unwritten English constitution, in which murky historical patterns become synthetic and normative through a process with no recognized algorithm. Sometimes, however, the synthesis was never achieved, and disparate theories of rights simply coexisted without becoming reconciled.

Perhaps the best example of the Founders inheriting rights from earlier periods in history is the following set of immunities: "Excessive bail ought not to be required, nor excessive fines imposed, nor cruel and unusual punishments inflicted." That sentence entered English law as a declaration of the House of Lords in 1316, and, word for word, became the Eighth Amendment to the United States Constitution four hundred seventy-five years later. In the interim, it had appeared in English common law decisions, the English Bill of Rights, and the laws of most of the American states.[5] Bails and fines

---

[3] E.g., first Charter of Virginia, 1606, in Francis Newton Thorpe, ed., *Federal and State Constitutions* . . . (US Government Printing Office, 1909), vol. VII, p. 3788.

[4] Gadamer, *Truth and Method*, pp. 302–307, 374–375.

[5] See, e.g., the Virginia Bill of Rights, 1776; the Massachusetts Constitution of 1780. The textual formula does not use the word "right" and is therefore not itself an instance of rights discourse as I have defined it, but the large literature of comment on the propositions that the formula announces does use the language of rights and is part of that discourse. When the Founders used the language of rights with reference to the substantive immunities that

and unusual punishments were not unique complaints of the Founders' generation, but the Founders established immunities against them anyway, because the sentence guaranteeing those immunities was already embedded in their culture.[6]

Thus, codifications long past, once fixed in a legal or political tradition, can exert influence on conceptions of rights centuries later, even when other transformative periods have intervened. Rights born in the American Revolution affect today's American rights discourse in some of the same ways that these older rights affected Americans at the Founding. American perceptions of rights have undergone transformative periods since 1791, including those during Reconstruction and after World War II, but some rights of the Founding remain in the discussion. The process of change could be described as an aggregation of layered and translucent transformations, layered because each succeeding transformation covers, in whole or in part, the accumulated previous discourse and translucent in that it does not wholly obscure what lies underneath. Some parts are still visible as they were before; some parts are visible but in changed ways; some parts have disappeared.

Experience and theory

Inherited philosophy as well as previous history filtered the Founders' attitudes toward specific adversities of their time. Those two filters, of course, are not entirely separate, because philosophical abstractions and historical conditions are often interrelated. The philosophy of John Locke, for example, was partly conditioned by the historical circumstances of seventeenth-century England. In turn, his ideas provided a general theoretical framework for Amer-

---

the traditional formula guaranteed, they followed in an established tradition of regarding those immunities as rights. That the textual formula does not itself make use of the rhetorical power of rights language is not a cause for concern, because the present purpose is not to analyze the function of rights discourse in Eighth Amendment argument but merely to illustrate the influence of deeper history on Founding conceptions of rights.

[6] This is not to say that the sentence has had a fixed meaning. Jefferson, who in 1776 had written a letter to a friend expressing a desire to "restrain the sanguinary hue of our penal laws," drafted a criminal punishments bill for Virginia in 1778 that included not only ducking and whipping (for attempted witchcraft) but also maiming, disfiguration, castration, gibbeting, and dissection. Thomas Jefferson to Edmund Pendleton, 26 August 1776, in *Papers of Thomas Jefferson*, ed. Julian P. Boyd (Princeton University Press, 1950), vol. I, p. 505; "A Bill for Proportioning Crimes and Punishments" (1778), ibid., vol. II, pp. 492–504. Those measures would not pass muster under the Eighth Amendment today.

ican claims of rights, many of which would be specifically precipitated by concrete eighteenth-century events. The same is true for the philosophies of Montesquieu, Grotius, Harrington, and other thinkers whose ideas helped frame American political thought during and after the revolution. Accordingly, claims of rights that the Founders advanced are best explained by interrelated philosophical and political factors, not by only one or the other, and even the theoretical background to which American reactions attached was partly a product of reactions against earlier circumstances.

American revolutionary literature was densely littered with references to prominent European political thinkers of the previous century. Hamilton implied that no respectable argument about rights could ignore "Grotious [sic], Puffendorf [sic], Locke, Montesquieu, and Burlemaqui."[7] Otis distrusted Grotius and Pufendorf, but he believed ". . . the purer fountains of one or two of our *English* writers, particularly . . . Mr. *Locke*" to be indispensable.[8] Richard Bland defended colonial rights with the Lockean account of free men constituting states to protect their natural rights and retaining the right of secession if those natural rights are violated.[9] Other European philosophers of rights were also influential. In his *Summary View of the Rights of British America*, in which Thomas Jefferson described violations of the "natural right" to "free trade with all parts of the world," the argument Jefferson made about free trade as a natural right was very similar to the argument that Grotius had made a hundred and fifty years earlier.[10] Jefferson happened to write the paper, however, just after passage of the Boston Port Bill, the Act of Parliament that suspended all trade in and out of the port of Boston in retaliation for that city's Tea Party. Jefferson may have subscribed to the Grotian view of trading rights before the port of Boston was blockaded, but the timing of his essay suggests that the Boston Port Bill precipitated his writing. It may not be possible to determine whether one influence was dominant and if so which

---

[7] Alexander Hamilton, "The Farmer Refuted" (23 February 1775), in *The Papers of Alexander Hamilton*, ed. Harold C. Syrett and Jacob E. Cooke (Columbia University Press, 1961), vol. I, pp. 81–165, at p. 86.

[8] James Otis, *Rights of the British Colonies Asserted and Proved* (Boston: Edes and Gill, 1764), pp. 25–26. Emphasis in the original.

[9] Richard Bland, *An Inquiry into the Rights of the British Colonies* (Williamsburg: Alexander Purdie & Co., 1766), pp. 10–11.

[10] Thomas Jefferson, *A Summary View of the Rights of British America* (Williamsburg: Clementina Rind, 1774), p. 8.

one.[11] We cannot even be certain whether Jefferson's primary intention was to articulate a Grotian theory of trade rights or to protest the Boston Port Bill. But even if we knew that the former case obtained, we would know something only about Jefferson's own justificatory reasons for writing. We would know neither the causal reasons for his writing nor even the causal reasons for his holding Grotian views; recall Elster's point that the content of a belief is not necessarily coextensive with the causal reasons for holding that belief.[12] Jefferson held a belief with Grotian content, and conditions like the passage of the Boston Port Bill may have helped bring him to that belief. This pattern of specific political conditions and general philosophical theories merging in the assertion of rights recurred throughout the Founding era.

FOUNDING AND MODERN ANALYTIC RIGHTS DISCOURSES: FORMAL DISSIMILARITIES

That philosophical theories helped shape Founding conceptions of rights does not collapse the differences between the Founders and modern philosophers of rights. The Founders were primarily political rather than philosophical or academic actors, and even their explicit uses of abstract theories of rights did not partake of many of the distinctive characteristics of academic rights philosophy. For example, the Founders tended not to limit their claims of rights on the basis of formal criteria. As described in chapter 1, formal theories of rights tend to specify and thereby restrict the contents, bearers, and sources of rights. Most of the Founders, in contrast, used rights language freely across such categories. They did not restrict themselves to interest-theory or to will-theory conceptions of rights. Neither did they invoke rights deriving from only one source (e.g., nature) or borne only by one kind of rights-bearer (e.g., the individual). The same people would argue for the rights of individuals on one occasion, the rights of communities on another, and the rights of institutions or governments on a third. To be sure, some individuals maintained higher levels of philosophical consistency than others, but the most common patterns of argument paid little

---

[11] Ronald Dworkin makes a strong argument about the problems of determining whether "concrete" or "abstract" intentions dominate in situations like these in *A Matter of Principle*, pp. 48–56. Jefferson, for his part, did not explicitly acknowledge either influence.
[12] Elster, "Bias, Belief, and Ideology," pp. 147–148.

regard to such niceties. These aspects of Founding rights discourse suggest that the categories of modern analytic rights philosophy do not provide an adequate framework for historically reconstructing conceptions of rights at the Founding.

Bearers of rights

Many modern theories of rights entail formal limits on what kind of being can be a bearer of rights. Theorists like Raz hold that only beings of "ultimate value" can have rights; others, like Feinberg, hold that only beings with interests can have rights; others, like Hohfeld and Dworkin, hold that only individual humans can have rights. Sandel sometimes attributes the Hohfeld/Dworkin position to the Founders, describing the rights of the Founding as conceived on an individualist model.[13] Sandel means to attack rights, including Founding rights, as unhealthily individualistic, but the content of the Founders' conceptions of rights does not compel Sandel to count them among his adversaries. Unlike Hohfeld, Dworkin, and a host of other modern theorists, the Founders did not predicate rights of only one kind of bearer. Indeed, they attributed rights to a much wider range of subjects. Bearers of rights included legislatures, governments, cities, colonies, countries, specific communities, and "the people" as a collective entity distinct from individuals. The Maryland Constitution of 1776 declared "That the city of Annapolis ought to have all its rights."[14] Otis wrote in defense of the "Rights of the British Colonies," and John Dickinson referred to "the right of colonies to tax themselves."[15] Jefferson, John Adams, Thomas Paine, and many others discussed the rights of government and in particular of Parliament.[16] Nor were rebels alone in believing that non-individuals could have rights: on the Tory side, John Dalrymple wrote a pamphlet called "The Rights of Great Britain Asserted

---

[13] Sandel, *Democracy's Discontent*, p. 33.
[14] Maryland Constitution of 1776, section 37, in Thorpe, *Constitutions*, vol. III, p. 1686.
[15] Otis, *Rights of the British Colonies*; John Dickinson, "Letters from a Farmer, no. 5," in *Writings of John Dickinson*, ed. Paul L. Ford (The Historical Society of Pennsylvania, 1895), p. 335.
[16] Jefferson on the rights of legislatures in *Summary View*, p. 19; Adams on "the right of Parliament to tax us" (letter no. 4 of Novanglus [John Adams], 13 February 1775), in *Papers of John Adams*, ed. Robert J. Taylor (Harvard University Press, 1977), vol. II, p. 261. Paine held that a religiously intolerant government "assumes to itself the right of withholding Liberty of Conscience." Thomas Paine, *Rights of Man*, ed. Henry Collin (Penguin, 1969), p. 107.

against the Claims of America."[17] Notably, the pamphlet's title used the term "Rights" selectively in order to advance a substantive political agenda. By attributing "rights" to Great Britain while America had only "claims," Dalrymple loaded the argument in favor of the loyalist cause. This rhetorical effect of restricting the definition of rights is one of the important blind spots of theories like Hohfeld's, in which "rights" and "claims" are synonymous. Dalrymple's title illustrates an important way in which they are not.

Some rights were held to belong to "the people" as a collective body rather than to people as individuals. Constitutions in Georgia and North Carolina delineated state borders under the heading of "the essential rights of a free people," and a state border is less comprehensible as the right of a particular North Carolinian than as the right of North Carolinians as a whole.[18] Another example was the right to an independent judiciary. Modern political scientists treat the existence of an independent judiciary not as a right but as part of a structural principle of American constitutional government, but the Founders frequently discussed a right of the people to have judiciaries be independent.[19] Like state borders, independent judiciaries are institutions of a political community, and it is easier to make sense of a right to such an institution at the collective level than at the level of individuals.

The most prominent communal right of the Founding was the right to self-government. Guarantees that the people had the right to govern themselves, or the right to change or abolish government, did not mean that each individual was his or her own highest authority.[20] They certainly did not mean that any individual who so

---

[17] Sir John Dalrymple, *The Rights of Great Britain Asserted against the Claims of America* (Philadelphia, 1776).

[18] Georgia Constitution of 1798, Article I, section 23, in Thorpe, *Constitutions*, vol. II, p. 794; North Carolina Constitution of 1776, Declaration of Rights, section 24.

[19] See Samuel Adams, "Proceedings of the Town of Boston," in *The Writings of Samuel Adams*, ed. Harry Alonzo Cushing (G. P. Putnam's Sons, 1904–1908), vol. II, pp. 359–369; Delaware Declaration of Rights, 1776, #21; Virginia Bill of Rights, section 5. For discussion of the political fight over royal payment of judges, out of which the passion for independent judiciaries grew, see Bernard Bailyn, *Pamphlets of the American Revolution* (Harvard University Press, 1965), pp. 249–255. For the views of a modern theorist who sees structural constitutional provisions as part of a system of rights, and who also understands the Founders to have predicated rights of the people collectively and not only individually, see Amar, *Bill of Rights*.

[20] See, *inter alia*, the Declaration of Independence; Delaware Constitution of 1776, section 5, in Thorpe, *Constitutions*, vol. I, p. 562; An Act concerning the Rights of the Citizens [of New York], 1787.

desired could alter the form of government of Delaware or New York. They referred, rather, to rights retained by the people collectively. It might be possible to construe these rights as rights of individuals, along the lines of "The right to change government is the right of each individual person to have $1/n$ of the power necessary to change government, where n represents the number of persons comprising a majority, or some other proportion, of the political community," but such constructions seem unnecessarily tortuous. It is unlikely that the authors of the many declarations of the right to self-government bothered to contemplate $1/n$. They thought of the people bearing and exercising rights as a community. That one need not, and perhaps should not, try to read collective rights as if they were aggregations of individual rights is an important caveat when reading certain clauses of Founding texts, such as the First Amendment guarantee of "the right of the people peaceably to assemble." Assembly is an activity of the people, plural.[21] Understood that way, many rights of the Founding are more compatible with Sandel's critique of individualism than he sometimes admits, and, to the extent that the Founders' views carry weight in American political argument, Sandel might better help his own cause by claiming those Founding conceptions of rights for his own theory rather than opposing rights in general as individualistic. After all, many Founding rights were genuinely collective.

This reading of the colonists' attitude toward rights should be

---

[21] This point raises questions about highly contested rights in the Bill of Rights that refer to "the people." The Second Amendment, for example, guarantees "the right of the people to keep and bear arms." One could easily argue that it is the people, plural (or perhaps the people collectively) who go out to war and therefore that the Amendment confers no right of private armament upon individuals. Lawrence Cress makes such an argument in "An Armed Community: The Origins and Meaning of the Right to Bear Arms," *Journal of American History* 71 (1984), 22–40, esp. 23–24. Against this position, Sanford Levinson argues that "the people" cannot be a strictly collective term in the Bill of Rights because its appearances in the First, Fourth, Ninth, and Tenth Amendments do not admit of collective meanings. He concludes that the Second Amendment must confer a right of individual armament ("The Embarrassing Second Amendment," *Yale Law Journal* 99, 637, at 645 [1989]). This argument, however, is not conclusive. The term "the people," I believe, admits of collective readings in the First, Second, Ninth, and Tenth Amendments. Only the Fourth poses a real conceptual problem for this interpretation. Conversely, the phrase admits of an individualist interpretation in the Second, Fourth, and Ninth Amendments and perhaps also in the petition clause of the First. I do not think, however, that the Tenth Amendment or the assembly clause of the First admits of an individualist reading. Thus, neither a collective nor an individualist reading can account for every use of the phrase. To insist that no Founding rights assigned to "the people" can apply at the level of individuals is thus an interpretative error; to insist that all rights so assigned are rights of individuals is equally mistaken.

distinguished from an element of Raz's and Dworkin's theories that it resembles. The American Founders believed individuals, institutions, and communities all to have the capacity for possessing rights. Raz says that an entity can possess rights if it is an actual individual person or "an 'artificial person' (e.g., a corporation)."[22] Similarly, Dworkin says that his definition of the "persons" to whom rights can belong includes "legal persons," such as corporations, as well as natural ones.[23] These two positions are not identical with the Founders' view. Like the Founders, Raz and Dworkin recognize individuals and corporate groups as valid subjects of rights. Raz and Dworkin, however, achieve that recognition by attributing personhood to the corporate group. It is still only persons, conceptually, that can bear rights; Raz and Dworkin simply expand the idea of "person." That move would have been unnecessary for the Founders. They did not need to imagine a legislature or a religious sect to be a person in order to believe it to have rights. In their view, nonpersons could have rights and still not be persons.

Sources of rights

Just as the Founders predicated rights of many kinds of bearers, they invoked rights that supposedly derived from a wide variety of sources. The Declaration of Independence, several state constitutions, and innumerable revolutionary tracts followed the Lockean path and rested heavily on natural rights.[24] The image of the Founders as natural rights theorists has become dominant. Sandel, for example, claims that the move away from positive or local rights and toward natural rights was a hallmark of the Founders' thinking.[25] Nevertheless, the natural rights approach was only one among many. Few Founders rested their rights on nature alone, and some found natural rights claims dubious. Prominent thinkers explicitly rejected claims of natural rights that they thought misplaced:

---

[22] Raz, *The Morality of Freedom*, p. 166.   [23] Dworkin, *Taking Rights Seriously*, p. 91n.

[24] See the Pennsylvania Constitution of 1776, section II; Virginia Statute of Religious Liberty, 1785; Samuel Adams, "Rights of the Colonists"; Hamilton, "The Farmer Refuted," pp. 104, 122.

[25] Sandel, *Democracy's Discontent*, p. 31. Sandel also uses "human rights" as a synonym for "natural rights" in this context. As I discuss in chapter 5, that use is anachronistic: the term "human rights" did not come into common use for more than a hundred and fifty years after the Founding, when it arose in response to a distinct set of crises that called for solutions in terms of universal humanism.

Madison, for example, argued that trial by jury, though "as essential to secure the liberty of the people" as any right known, simply "cannot be considered as a natural right."[26] In the whole of the *Federalist Papers*, totaling eighty-five essays and more than two hundred thousand words, only *Federalist #2* by John Jay refers to natural rights, and that on only one occasion. Rather than relying on natural rights, many colonial writers grounded their rights in traditional English liberties, real or imagined. They claimed protection of the common law, the constitution, Magna Carta, and sometimes the rights of Englishmen generally, without bothering to specify a particular source. Other alleged sources included reason, benefit, and, of course, God.[27] The style of argument that I illustrated in chapter 1 with MacCormick's attempt to establish the benefit theory ("interest theory," "welfare theory") of rights by showing that the rival will theory ("choice theory," "option theory") could not account for children's rights to basic nutrition – that is, the tactic of attacking an alleged source of rights as illegitimate – was notably absent from rights discourse at the Founding. Simply put, Americans of the Founding era felt that rights came from many different sources, human, natural, and divine, and no source was accepted to the exclusion of the others.

This willingness to tolerate many different theories and sources of rights simultaneously may have signaled a failure of theoretical synthesis, because the Founders' eclecticism regarding the sources of rights contained large potential contradictions. As Bailyn points out,

---

[26] James Madison, *The Papers of James Madison*, ed. Charles F. Hobson and Robert A. Rutland (University Press of Virginia, 1984), vol. XII, p. 204.

[27] *Federalist Papers*, ed. Clinton Rossiter (Penguin, 1961). For reason as a source, see Dickinson, "An Address to the Committee of Correspondence in Barbados," in *Writings*, vol. I, pp. 251–276; Philip Livingston, *The Other Side of the Question: or, A Defense of the Liberties of North America* (Rivington, 1774), p. 9. Oxenbridge Thacher and James Wilson both argued that the rights of Americans derived from the benefit they brought to the British Empire and its king. Because the colonies brought wealth, power, and glory to Great Britain, this argument ran, Great Britain owed the colonies something in return, and that something included rights to life, liberty, and property. Oxenbridge Thacher, *The Sentiments of a British American*, (Edes and Gill, 1764); James Wilson, "Considerations on the Authority of Parliament," in Samuel Eliot Morrison, *Sources and Documents Illustrating the American Revolution 1764–1788* (Oxford University Press, 1965). God appeared as a source of rights in the writings of virtually every author of the period, from preachers like Moses Mather to bare deists like Jefferson. To be sure, some of the Founders drew few distinctions between God and nature, and some claims of the divine right against kings may legitimately be seen as interchangeable with natural rights. Not all claims of God-given right are so reducible, however: Jefferson may have had a naturalized view of God, but Mather had a different one.

the colonists' common practice of citing common-law authorities and appealing to centuries of legal precedent was "alien to the Enlightenment rationalists whom the colonists also quoted – and with equal enthusiasm." Enlightenment thinkers generally regarded precedent and common law as irrational and oppressive, and it was precisely those traditions that the natural lawyers sought to destroy. According to Bailyn, however, the influence of writers like Milton, Harrington, Neville, and Algernon Sidney helped mediate those poles in the minds of the Founders. Understood in light of those writers, Bailyn claims, the Founders' view of rights did not actually proceed from conflicting premises.[28] This proposed solution seems too easy; one wonders about the extent to which an entire political class can have reconciled the stark conflict between the Enlightenment's law of nature and the common law tradition. Instead of demanding a successful and thoroughgoing theoretical synthesis, the Founders may have tolerated different and even contradictory ideas within their discourse. If Founding rights discourse were primarily concerned with philosophic rigor and the deduction of rights from first principles, or even the approximation of the best ideas of rights in reflective equilibrium, those contradictions would represent failures. If, however, we understand Founding rights discourse as a political practice that was driven more by substantive commitments than by philosophical principles, the inconsistencies Bailyn notes become less important. They are not resolved, but they are not particularly troublesome, either, because what gives coherence to the discourse is not cogent argument from first principles but the rules of the practice, notably the need to reject specific adversities of colonial rule.

The choice of source was often immaterial to the substance of the Founders' arguments. Whether an American rebel argued from nature, reason, or the English constitution often made little difference to which rights he thought his arguments established. Claimed sources of rights did not even divide those who supported the revolution from those who opposed it. Just as rebels used varied bases of rights to press the American claim, loyalists used God, nature, and positive law alike to show that the colonies had no

---

[28] Bernard Bailyn, *The Ideological Origins of the American Revolution* (Harvard University Press, 1967), pp. 33–34.

legitimate grievances against Britain. Tories and revolutionaries who concurred in the theoretical source of rights did not reach compatible political conclusions: Dalrymple, for example, rested the claims of his loyalist pamphlet *The Rights of Great Britain Asserted* on the authority of God and nature, the same sources that the Declaration of Independence invoked.[29] Similarly, philosophical differences about the source of rights did not prevent people within a given camp from agreeing in the substance of their political claims. An American committed to the rebel cause was likely to endorse rights to freedom of conscience, freedom from military imposition, security of property, trial by jury, and representative government, no matter how he imagined the philosophical roots of rights.[30] We should accordingly be skeptical about the extent to which Founding claims of rights actually followed from their alleged sources; arguments about rights were regularly driven more by the need to reject hostile British colonial practices than by a set of philosophical premises. The Founders were not systematically and self-consciously using rights language in the underhanded way that Bentham derided, knowingly refusing to say more than that the things they claimed were important and should be protected. Most members of the Founding generation took seriously the sources of rights that they claimed and the arguments for rights that they made. Implicit in studying political argument as social practice, however, is that the self-understandings of the arguing parties are not always sufficient to explain their discourse. Consciously or not, the Founders' arguments about rights were driven at least as much by substantive commitments to particular propositions as by philosophical abstractions. And the reasons that certain propositions were considered important and in need of protection were bound up with the desire to reject specific adversities the Founders had recently suffered.

---

[29] Dalrymple, *Rights of Great Britain*, p. 88. See also Thomas Chandler, *A Friendly Address to all Reasonable Americans, on the Subject of our Political Confusions* (Rivington, 1774), p. 6.

[30] The set of rights that American Founders commonly agreed upon can be thought of as "culturally adjacent" to one another rather than as being "logically adjacent." Even if no single analytic argument dictated that those rights should go together, the historical circumstances of the revolution encouraged Americans to affirm these prospects as a bundle. On the difference between cultural adjacency and logical adjacency of political concepts, see Freeden, "Political Concepts," pp. 151–154.

THE SUBSTANTIVE COMMITMENTS: RIGHTS AND
OPPOSITIONAL POLITICS

Recognition and non-recognition of oppositionality

Americans of the Founding generation commonly saw their rebellion
as a rights-oriented rejection of the reigning political order. Richard
Henry Lee, for example, wrote in 1787 that the people of the United
States had fought a war to free themselves from the abuses of British
despotism and that a federal Bill of Rights should solidify that
rejection.[31] People like Lee understood that negative experiences
underlay their ideas about which propositions must be secured as
rights, and they deliberately shaped their arguments about rights to
support the specific rights they required. Among other Founders, the
nexus was not so explicitly theorized. Even in discussions of rights
where the reactive pattern is clearly present, the Founders often
stopped short of recognizing that the proposed ideas about rights
had roots in the adversities themselves. The most obvious example is
the Declaration of Independence, which recited a long list of the
king's offenses against the colonists and implicitly argued that those
offenses justified the revolution. Nevertheless, the rights claimed in
the Declaration are said to derive not from historical experience but
from "Nature" and "Nature's God." There is no explicit recognition
that Americans deemed certain entitlements, liberties, powers, and
immunities "rights" in part because those entitlements, liberties,
powers, and immunities were the ones threatened by the policies
that the Declaration protested against. Thus, the role of concrete
oppositionality in the Founders' ideas toward rights was more fully
theorized in some instances than in others.

Similarly, concrete oppositionality could play greater or lesser
roles in directing claims of rights at different times: Lee's approach
was directly outcome-driven, but a more abstract thinker like
Jefferson was more likely to operate in something like reflective
equilibrium, feeling the combined influences of theory and experience. His philosophical temperament could easily lead him to hold
that the rights he asserted derived from first principles like nature
rather than mere empirical experience, but just as his argument

---

[31] Richard Henry Lee to Sam Adams, 5 October 1787, in *The Letters of Richard Henry Lee*, ed.
James Curtis Ballagh (Macmillan, 1914), vol. II, pp. 444–445.

about the Grotian right of free trade was precipitated and perhaps even shaped by the Boston Port Bill, his argument in the Declaration was partly a product of events that even he thought significant enough to enumerate when setting forth his manifesto. He may not have deliberately constructed his arguments for the limited instrumental purposes of the revolution, but his concrete opposition to certain British practices certainly influenced his arguments. If his theories of rights were not outcome-driven in the bald way that Lee exemplified in his letter to Adams, they were also not outcome-insensitive. Those among his contemporaries who were more basic politicians and less abstract thinkers than he were yet more likely to tailor their claims of rights, whether more or less consciously, to effect the concrete negations they sought.

Nevertheless, even sophisticated analysts of American history sometimes neglect the rejectionist context of early American rights discourse. Oscar and Lillian Handlin, for example, criticize the Founders for "important omissions" that "revealed the erratic nature of the enumerations [of rights in the various bills and declarations at the Founding. N]o one bothered to affirm the widely recognized rights of individuals to move from one place to another or to practice the occupations of their choice."[32] Similarly, Gordon Wood describes five state bills of rights from 1776 and says that the colonists "prefaced these rights to their constitutions in a jarring but exciting combination of ringing declarations of universal principles with a motley collection of common law procedures."[33] Both Wood and the Handlins here commit what Skinner calls "the characteristic sin of the 'whig' intellectual historian: that of imputing incoherence or irrationality where we have merely failed to identify some local canon of rational acceptability."[34] The absence of a right to free movement is only an "omission" if, for some reason, that right should be present. That would be the case if the bills were intended as comprehensive lists of the rights that people possessed but not if they were specific reactions to specific abuses. Restricted movement did not belong to the category of "grievances against the British."

---

[32] Oscar and Lillian Handlin, *Liberty in America: 1600 to the Present*, vol. ii, *Liberty in Expansion, 1760–1850* (Harper & Row, 1989), p. 337.

[33] Gordon S. Wood, *The Creation of the American Republic, 1776–1787* (Norton, 1972), p. 271.

[34] In James Tully, ed., *Meaning and Context: Quentin Skinner and his Critics* (Polity Press, 1988), p. 244.

That was the category, the "local canon of acceptability," that made
bills of rights coherent.

Executive power and legislative representation

The reactive theme in the rights of the Founding appeared not only
in the selection of content for rights but also in the identification of
the institutional source of the threats against which entitlements,
liberties, powers and immunities had to be secured. As both Wood
and Rakove note, bills of rights in English history had traditionally
delineated the people's rights against the king or some other
executive power, not against the legislature. The legislature, after all,
represented the people and was not supposed to be hostile to their
rights. The articulation of rights against the abuse of legislative
power was thus an innovation of the Founding.[35] That change was
largely due to the reactive or oppositional nature of rights discourse:
Sugar Acts, Townsend Acts, Stamp Acts, Tea Acts and other
measures that had impelled the colonists to revolt had been Acts of
Parliament, and the impulse to negate and prevent the recurrence of
such abuses naturally addressed itself to legislatures. At the same
time, it would be a mistake to underestimate the continued prevalence of rights against the executive. The Founders also wanted to
reject abusive practices of the king and his officers, and they
articulated rights against the executive accordingly.

Many rights in the federal and state constitutions that are now
customarily considered protections against an individual's suffering a
given harm originated merely as rights against the executive's being
the agent to administer that harm. For example, the Third Amendment to the federal Constitution, which provides a right against the
quartering of soldiers in private homes, forbids such quartering
except when undertaken "... in a manner to be prescribed by
law."[36] Individual citizens could still have soldiers forced upon them

---

[35] Wood, *Creation*, p. 272; Rakove, *Original Meanings*, pp. 289, 313.

[36] US Constitution, Third Amendment. Other codifications of the anti-quartering right were
also subject to legislative override. See, e.g., Pennsylvania Constitution of 1790, section 23.
The text of the Third Amendment, like that of the Eighth discussed earlier, does not use the
word "right," and if the amendment's text were the whole of Founding discussion of the
subject, ideas about forced quartering would be outside the practice as I have defined it.
Quartering is within the practice not because of the text of the Third Amendment but
because the Founders frequently discussed the subject as a matter of rights. For example,
the Delaware and Massachusetts guarantees discussed next in the paragraph were both
listed as "rights" in their respective constitutions. See also Federal Farmer, letter #6, 25

in their homes, as long as their legislatures approved. Similarly, the 1776 Delaware Declaration of Rights and Fundamental Rules listed as a right "That no Soldier ought to be quartered in any House in Time of Peace without the Consent of the Owner; and in Time or War in such Manner only as the Legislature shall direct," and the Massachusetts Declaration of Rights of 1780 provided that "No person can in any case be subjected to law-martial [except those in the army and navy] but by authority of the legislature."[37] In other words, a civilian had a right not to be prosecuted in military courts unless the legislature decided to try him or her there.

To a modern American, or on the Dworkinian view of rights as trumps against the majority will, a right so simply overridden by the legislature is hardly a right at all. In 1780, however, erecting a legislative barrier to abuses of the executive was a meaningful institution of rights. The drafters of these constitutions were not engaged in drawing Millean circles around individuals, defining an absolutely inviolable space, as much as they were providing against particular evils experienced under British rule. What seemed important and in need of protection – that is, what qualified as a right – was popular control over these policies, not individual immunity from them. Quartering and military law had been imposed by a power not electorally responsible; the chosen solution was to establish a right against quartering and military law unless those measures had been approved by the legislature.

As the Founders' experience with Parliament suggested, a legislature not subject to popular control would be little better than an arbitrary executive, so establishing legislative barriers to executive abuse made sense only if the legislature in question was responsive to the people. Accordingly, they articulated a system of rights to ensure that legislators would reflect the will of their constituents. The first requirement, of course, was that legislatures must be chosen by the people, and the First Continental Congress proclaimed "a right in the people to participate in their legislative council."[38] Many state

December 1787, reprinted in Herbert J. Storing, *The Complete Anti-Federalist* (University of Chicago Press, 1981), vol. II, bk. 8, p. 86, and An Act concerning the Rights of the Citizens of [New York], 1787, section 13, both of which describe the immunity from quartering as a right.

[37] Delaware Declaration of Rights and Fundamental Rules, 11 September 1776, clause 21; Massachusetts Constitution of 1780, Declaration of Rights, Article 28.

[38] Declaration and Resolves of the First Continental Congress, 14 October 1774, in Morrison, *Sources and Documents*, pp. 119–122.

bills of rights, as well as parts of the federal Constitution and the
federal Bill of Rights, were intended to strengthen popular control of
and protection against legislatures. That is the shift that Wood and
Rakove know to be innovative. The North Carolina and Pennsylvania Constitutions of 1776, for example, established a right of the
people to instruct their representatives, meaning that a delegate to
the legislature would be bound to vote as specifically directed by his
constituents.[39] A right of instruction would make the legislature a
ratifier of public opinion, not a deliberative body capable of
opposing the popular will. The specific provision conferring the right
to instruct representatives declared, in full, "That the people have a
right to assemble together, to consult for their common good, to
instruct their representatives, and to apply to the legislature for
redress of grievances, by address, petition, or remonstrance." All
these rights were aspects of an overarching right, a right not to be
subject to the power of a hostile legislature.

It is important to remember the Founders' suspicion of legislatures
when evaluating Sunstein's attempt to ally Founding ideas of rights
with his theory of deliberative democracy. The right to instruct is
unfriendly to deliberativism, because a legislature cannot be a
deliberative body if the public issues binding instructions to its
representatives. In such a legislature, each representative votes for
the interests of his constituency without being willing to change his
views when confronted with another representative's ideas. Sunstein,
who would like to present all manner of Founding-era rights as tied
to deliberativism, therefore sees the fact that Congress refused to
approve a constitutional right to instruct as the most important fact
about early American attitudes toward that right.[40] That approach
underplays the strength of support for a right to instruct during the
Founding. Although the federal Constitution never contained a right
to instruct, the idea was often popular, codified into more than one
state constitution, and required serious debate in Congress, the body
whose institutional interests were most opposed to establishing such
a right.[41] The central project of Madisonian federalism was to
protect the people's rights by checking the power of legislatures, not

---

[39] North Carolina Constitution of 1776, section 17; Pennsylvania Constitution of 1776, section
16.

[40] Sunstein, *The Partial Constitution*, p. 22.

[41] *Annals of the Congress of the United States, 1789–1824* (Gales & Seaton, 1834–54), vol. I, pp.
731–740.

by giving legislatures more room to maneuver. The right to instruct and other projects for preventing abuses of legislative power thus had a serious career at the Founding, more serious that Sunstein sometimes allows. Given the oppositional development of rights discourse, the popularity of rights against legislatures immediately after a rebellion precipitated largely by a hostile Parliament should come as no surprise.

Oppositionality and specific rights of the Founding

Just as we can examine the reactive pattern with reference to specific categories of the British administration like unrepresentative executive and legislative power, we can examine it with reference to specific categories of Founding rights. In determining which categories of rights should be selected, I look to the best-known and most influential list of early American rights: the Bill of Rights in the federal Constitution. As the analysis below illustrates, the most prominent rights of the Founding were substantially conditioned by contemporary opposition to specific British practices. Investigating only the immediate discussions of the Bill of Rights, however, would yield a stunted view of Founding rights discourse, because the Bill of Rights was only one document among many to set forth rights that the Founders considered important. Between 1776 and 1792, newly independent states adopted nineteen separate constitutions and as many official lists of rights. All of those lists emerged from backgrounds of yet other lists of rights. Written colonial protests against specific British measures like the Stamp Act and the Boston Port Bill characteristically listed the rights that the offending measures violated, and these lists were widely circulated. Later, these protest-inspired lists were part of the background from which codifiers of rights worked. None of these lists was supreme, and none can be taken to embody the rights of the Founding completely.[42] Analyzing

---

[42] When many Americans wanted a Bill of Rights to accompany the new Constitution, some in the First Congress charged that an attempted enumeration of rights must degenerate into absurdity, because rights are virtually innumerable. Thus, after one representative said that the list should contain those rights that belonged inherently to the people, "... Mr. Sedgwick [of Massachusetts] replied, that if the committee were governed by that general principle, they might have gone into a very lengthy enumeration of rights; they might have declared that a man should have a right to wear his hat if he pleased; that he might get up when he pleased, and go to bed when he thought proper" (*Annals of Congress*, vol. I, pp. 731–732 (15 August 1789)). Sedgwick was not alone. In the same spirit, Noah Webster during the ratification debates facetiously proposed "That Congress shall never restrain any inhabitant

Founding rights discourse calls for attention to the whole range of these documents and the discussions around them. It is impossible, however, to investigate every single right that anyone claimed during the Founding; selecting a group of rights central to the discourse and investigating them is a more sensible approach. Therefore, when I take the Bill of Rights as a guide to which rights are worthy of investigation, the goal is not only to understand the origins of the rights that one central text specifies but to use the Bill of Rights as an organizing prism through which to examine the fuller discourse that underlay it. Inclusion in the federal Bill of Rights suggests that particular rights were important to Founding rights discourse and thus worthy of investigation, but the investigation is concerned with Founding attitudes toward those rights generally.

The Bill of Rights includes ten amendments to the Constitution, but only the first eight announce specific rights. Two categories of rights account for five of those eight amendments: rights of civilians against the military account for the Second and Third Amendments, and rights regarding the conduct of trials account for the Fifth, Sixth, and Seventh. Those two categories of rights clearly merit attention. Of the remaining three amendments, two have already been discussed and do not require further exploration here. The Eighth Amendment, as discussed above, simply reproduced verbatim a centuries-old formula of the common law. It is an example of inherited rights. Conversely, the Fourth Amendment is so obviously reactive to events of the Founding as not to require explanation beyond that offered in chapter 2.[43] We are left, then, with the First Amendment. As discussed in chapter 2, the central position of

---

of America from eating and drinking, *at seasonable times*, or prevent his lying on his *left side*, in a long winter's night, or even on his back, when he is fatigued by lying on his *right*" (quoted in Rakove, *Original Meanings*, p. 330). Moreover, many thinkers of the Revolution opposed the very idea of enumerating rights in authoritative lists. Otis thought such lists reminiscent of papal decrees and therefore against the dignity of England (Bailyn, *Ideological Origins*, p. 189). Hamilton argued against the adoption of a constitutional Bill of Rights on the grounds that anything not specifically mentioned would be implicitly denied the status of a right (Federalist #84). Even the constitutional amendments that came to be called a Bill of Rights explicitly denied being an exhaustive catalog, declaring in the Ninth Amendment that "The enumeration in the Constitution, of certain rights, shall not be construed to deny or disparage others retained by the people."

[43] One could argue that the Third Amendment is as obviously reactive as the Fourth, but I include it anyway because of its substantive connection with the Second, which does merit explanation here. In any case, examining a right whose reactive origins are easily seen can cause little damage; the important error would be ignoring discussion of a right whose origins were obscure.

freedom of speech is a twentieth-century innovation in interpretations of that amendment. I will focus on the element of the First Amendment that was most important to the founders: that pertaining to establishment and exercise of religion. Accordingly, the analysis below explores the substantive commitments guiding Founding assertions of rights regarding military affairs, religion, and trials.

In addition, and to show that the same processes were at work in fringe as well as mainstream areas of Founding rights discourse, I include one example of the reactive process with reference to a less famous right. For the purpose, I have chosen an obscure and seemingly inscrutable right in the Maryland Constitution of 1776, the rights of the City of Annapolis. I choose this right for reasons implied by the methods of symmetry and hermeneutics: comprehending seemingly strange and esoteric rights requires learning more about the general patterns of rights discourse than does comprehending rights whose sense is immediately accessible. Thus, I now turn to showing the oppositional aspect of Founding rights regarding military affairs, religions, trials, and, in what turns out to be a right of free trade, the rights of Annapolis. In each example, I illustrate how the Founders' substantive commitments to protect particular entitlements, liberties, powers, or immunities against the threats posed by British policies influenced Founding articulations of rights.

Military affairs
Central to the Founding period, from the American perspective, was an eight-year war on home soil and the continued presence, or threatened presence, of a hostile army. Accordingly, rights concerning soldiers and armies and their relationships to civil government and individual civilians comprised a large subset of the overall discussion of rights at the Founding. These rights included rights against quartering troops in private homes, rights to freedom from martial law and standing armies, rights to civilian control of the military, rights to serve in the defense of one's colony, country, or state, and rights of conscientious objection. Some of these rights may seem unlike others, but the set of connected conditions that prompted their articulation make them all "culturally adjacent."[44]

---

[44] See the discussion of cultural as opposed to logical adjacency in note 30.

Reactive opposition to a specific set of adversities that the colonists faced unites them all.

Quartering, standing armies, martial law, and the relationship between military and civil powers were themes of American anxiety. The quartering of soldiers in domestic homes was a popular target of state constitutions.[45] Several state constitutions prohibited standing armies except under specified conditions, and establishing the people's right to bear arms was usually presented as the alternative to establishing a professional force.[46] When drafting their new constitutions, some states included the right of civilians not to be subject to martial law.[47] The Founders also broadened the right against martial law to include a general concern that the civil government be at all times superior to the military; the Declaration of Independence listed "rendering the military independent of, and superior to, the civil power" among the king's crimes, and several states banned army officers and merchants who dealt in military supplies from sitting in their state legislatures.[48] The federal Constitution restricted congressional power to fund the military, permitting no outlays for periods longer than two years; no other subject of government activity bore a like restriction. In one of its few restrictions on state power, the Constitution also forbade individual states to keep armed forces in peacetime without congressional consent.[49] Reciprocally, individual states sought to limit the national government's capacity to maintain armies. The Virginia ratifying convention, for example, proposed to amend the federal Constitution so that raising or keeping regular troops would require a two-thirds vote of both houses of Congress.[50]

Some Founding rights regarding military affairs predate that period, if in slightly different forms. The American Founders were

---

[45] See Delaware Declaration of Rights, 1776, section 21; Pennsylvania Constitution of 1790, Declaration of Rights, section 23; Massachusetts Constitution of 1780, Declaration of Rights, Article XXVII.

[46] See Virginia Bill of Rights, 1776, section 13; Delaware Declaration of Rights, 1776, sections 18–19; Pennsylvania Constitution of 1790, Declaration of Rights, sections 21–22; North Carolina Constitution of 1776, Declaration of Rights, section 16; Massachusetts Constitution of 1780, Article XVII.

[47] Massachusetts, for example; Constitution of 1780, Article XXVIII.

[48] North Carolina Constitution of 1776, Article XXVII; South Carolina Constitution of 1790, Article I, section 22; Georgia Constitution of 1777, section 17.

[49] U.S. Constitution, I.8 and I.10.

[50] Edward Dumbauld, *The Bill of Rights and What it Means Today* (University of Oklahoma Press, 1957), p. 187.

not the first English-speakers to codify rights against the depreda-
tions of a hostile professional army. The most obvious examples are
certain rights in the English Bill of Rights of the previous century,
notably the prohibition on the king's keeping a standing army on
British soil in peacetime without parliamentary consent and the
entitlement of Protestant subjects to have arms for their own
defense. Those rights were forerunners of the Second Amendment.[51] The range of the Founders' claims, however, exceeded the
scope of earlier guarantees, creating a broader network of rights
regarding military affairs than had existed theretofore. Reaction to
contemporary conditions and attitudes inherited from previous
times both contributed to the shape of Founding ideas about rights,
and here as elsewhere the Founders operated under both influences.
Appropriating the aforementioned parts of the English Bill of
Rights and filtering them through contemporary experience to
produce the Second Amendment was an instance of past/present
rights synthesis.

Standing armies

The right to bear arms, the apparent centerpiece of the Second
Amendment, was a direct product of the Founders' fear of standing
armies. The link between opposition to standing armies and a right
of citizens to bear arms was not new at the time of the American
Revolution, of course: the two issues had been prominently con-
joined during the English political crises of the previous century. As
just mentioned, the English Bill of Rights of 1689 prohibited the king
from maintaining a standing army in the kingdom in peacetime
without parliamentary consent and guaranteed Protestant subjects
the right to keep arms for their own defense.[52] English Protestants
had worried that the Stuart monarchy would use a standing army as
a tool of repression. They therefore sought to prohibit standing

---

[51] Second Amendment rights were thus inherited rights as well as reactive rights in 1791, but it
is noteworthy that the 1689 origins of those rights were themselves reactive. Before the
English Bill of Rights listed its provisions, it set forth a list of the crimes by which James II
forfeited the crown. The list included his "raising and keeping a standing army within this
kingdom in time of peace, without consent of Parliament," and his "causing several good
subjects, being Protestants, to be disarmed, at the same time when Papists were both armed
and employed contrary to law." Thus, inherited rights are not wholly outside the pattern of
concrete negation; sometimes a right that is inherited in a later period may arise
oppositionally in the earlier period from which it is inherited.
[52] Bill of Rights of 1689, sections 6 and 7.

armies and to guarantee that ordinary citizens could bear arms, both so as to make standing armies unnecessary and so as to be able to resist repression if it came.[53] During the American Revolution and Founding, the link between civilians' bearing arms and opposition to standing armies was again prominent, partly as an inheritance from seventeenth-century England and partly because Americans actually experienced occupation by a hostile standing army during the years of war. Consider part thirteen of the Virginia Bill of Rights:

That a well regulated militia, composed of the body of the people, trained to arms, is the proper, natural, and safe defense of a free state; that standing armies, in time of peace, should be avoided, as dangerous to liberty; and that, in all cases, the military should be under strict subordination to, and governed by, the civil power.

The phrase "a well regulated militia," which opens the Second Amendment, here stands in opposition to a standing army. The argument of the Virginia Bill could be paraphrased as follows: The state needs a defense force, but standing armies are bad, and a good way to fulfill the need for defense without making recourse to standing armies is to have a popular militia. Between the adoption of the Virginia Bill of Rights in 1776 and the ratification of the federal Bill of Rights in 1791, the Articles of Confederation declared that no state should keep standing forces in peacetime, "... but every State shall always keep up *a well regulated and disciplined militia*, sufficiently armed and accoutred."[54] Other instances where militias are presented as the alternative to standing armies could be adduced almost without limit.[55] Once we recognize that the Founders understood providing for a militia to be a way of providing against standing armies and that the Second Amendment announced a

---

[53] For a discussion of the roots of the standing army issue, see Edmund S. Morgan, *Inventing the People: The Rise of Popular Sovereignty in England and America* (Norton, 1988), pp. 153–173. Morgan explicates Harringtonian and other republican theories about the superiority of amateur yeomen as soldiers, which was bound up (in the English-speaking world) with the idea that the English military was superior to the French. Morgan also casts some doubt upon that belief, as well as on the validity of the idea, prominent in early American rights discourse, that militias were less likely than standing armies to act as instruments of repression. See also John Miller, "The Militia and the Army in the Reign of James II," *Historical Journal* 16 (1973), 659–679.

[54] Articles of Confederation, Article VI, paragraph 4. Emphasis added.

[55] E.g., Pennsylvania Constitution of 1776, Declaration of Rights, Article 13: "That the people have a right to bear arms for the defense of themselves and the state; and as standing armies in the time of peace are dangerous to liberty, they ought not to be kept up."

popular right to bear arms for the sake of constituting a militia, it becomes clear that the Second Amendment's right of the people to bear arms arose as a right against standing armies.

As early as the 1760s, American colonists had begun to decry the evils of the British army in North America. At a time when his home town of Boston was under occupation, Sam Adams declared that "Introducing and quartering standing armies in a free country in times of peace without the consent of the people either by themselves or by their representatives, is, and always has been deemed a violation of their rights as freemen."[56] The Continental Congress, in its Declaration and Resolves of 1774, prefigured the Second and Third Amendments when, in successive clauses, it declared illegal "the keeping of a standing army in these colonies" and "the Act passed in the same session for the better providing suitable quarters for officers and soldiers in His Majesty's service in North America."[57] Hamilton foresaw a domino effect of lost liberties flowing from the standing army: once standing armies appeared, he wrote, "we might soon expect the martial law, universally prevalent to the abolition of trials by juries, the *Habeas Corpus* act, and every other bulwark of personal safety."[58] Oliver Noble delivered a creative tirade against standing armies in the form of a sermon on the biblical Book of Esther. Preaching one month before open war erupted, Noble described a good but lavish and not particularly intelligent king deceived by his advisors into authorizing the destruction of close to a million of the king's honest and industrious subjects. A large force was gathered to destroy them. The targeted people, however, stood in their own defense and, with the help of God, triumphed. Americans, Noble proclaimed, must heed the lesson and stand in their own defense:

To *repel* armed force, by force of the same kind, is LAWFUL by Heaven's decree. Therefore be of good courage, *nothing is lost that is not given over for lost.* – STANDING ARMIES MUST BE REMOVED, or they will reduce us to a state of SLAVERY worse than DEATH ... That God who delivered his people of old, when brought to the brink of ruin by a wicked *Minister* of *State*, can deliver

---

[56] Sam Adams, "Proceedings of the Town of Boston," in *Writings*, vol. II, pp. 359–369. Compare Jefferson's more abstract route to precisely the same conclusions: "Summary View," in Thomas Jefferson, *Basic Writings of Thomas Jefferson*, ed. Philip Foner (Wiley, 1944), pp. 17–18.

[57] First Continental Congress, Declaration and Resolves, October 1774.

[58] Hamilton, "The Farmer Refuted" (23 February 1775), in *Papers*, p. 94.

us. And is there not reason to hope, yea firmly to believe that he will remove the MONSTER of a standing ARMY from our land?[59]

After the war, during the process of codifying rights in the federal union, the desire never again to face standing armies pervaded discussion of the Constitution and the proposed amendments. At the Virginia ratification convention, Patrick Henry warned that the powers granted to Congress to raise armies were intolerably broad. Henry worried that Congress would, on the pretense of providing for the general welfare, keep armies in the field continuously. Henry rejected in advance a counterargument that he expected and, in so doing, underscored that the rights for which he argued were concrete negations of the British regime's practices. "We shall be told that, in England, the king, lords, and commons, have this power [of raising standing armies]," he said. "How does this apply here? Is this government to place us in the situation of the English? ... This [military oppression] was one of the principal reasons for dissolving the connection with Great Britain."[60]

During the legislative deliberation on the Second Amendment, the House of Representatives debated a version in which the text "... but no one religiously scrupulous of bearing arms, shall be compelled to render military service in person" followed the wording that would eventually be adopted. The measure was primarily intended to address the concerns of Quakers. Given that the topic of the amendment was understood to be the composition of the army, it seemed a logical venue for specifying exemptions. This text did not survive the Senate. We can only speculate as to the reasons for its defeat there, because the Senate did not leave records of those early debates, but we may infer certain likely arguments from the records kept in the House, where the conscientious objection clause passed with only one spare vote. In the House, Elbridge Gerry spoke against the proposal. "What, sir, is the use of a militia? It is to prevent the establishment of a standing army, the bane of liberty," he began. "Whenever Governments mean to invade the rights and liberties of the people, they always attempt to destroy the militia, in order to raise an army upon their ruins. This was actually done by Great Britain at the commencement of the late

---

[59] Oliver Noble, *Some Strictures upon the Sacred Story Recorded in the Book of Esther* ... (E. Luntt and H. W. Tinges, 1775), p. 28. Emphases in the original. Preached as a sermon, 8 March 1775.

[60] Jonathan Elliot, *Debates in the Several State Conventions on the Adoption of the Federal Constitution* (J. B. Lippincott & Co., 1901), vol. III, pp. 410–411. Proceedings of 14 June 1788.

revolution." Gerry went on to argue that if the conscientious objection clause remained, Congress might declare great numbers of people religiously scrupulous, thereby preventing them from serving in the militia. Enough such enforced exemptions could weaken the militia to the point of insignificance and create a seeming need for a standing army, with which Congress could then oppress the people.[61] Gerry's views were more paranoid than most, but his argument does reflect the hostility that most of the Founders felt toward standing armies.

Many states followed the pattern, mentioned earlier, of presenting rights against standing armies as immunities not from government in general but from the executive. Several of the states whose constitutions restricted standing armies merely prohibited the raising of troops in peacetime without the consent of the legislature. Charles Pinckney of South Carolina similarly submitted for inclusion in the federal Constitution the phrase "No troops shall be kept up in time of peace, but by consent of the Legislature."[62] This restriction might seem a clause with no teeth; a modern reader might not even consider the possibility of troops prowling around without legislative consent. To explain this and similar constitutional provisions, however, we must presume that many of the Founders seriously considered that possibility. Pinckney, we may infer, thought it plausible for an army to roam through South Carolina with no legislative authorization. Viewed in that context, the Founders' preoccupation with rights against standing armies is eminently understandable. And because the experience that made such a scenario plausible for Pinckney stemmed from executive rather than legislative abuses, it was against the executive that he sought to secure a right.

Domestic quartering

Domestic quartering, the other major military policy to call forth an American constitutional right, began in a relevant sense in 1765, when the first Quartering Act prescribed the quartering of British troops in barracks and vacant buildings, though not in private homes. Only in 1774 did the passage of the second Quartering Act extend mandatory quartering of troops to private homes. Thus,

---

[61] *Annals*, vol. I, pp. 749–750.
[62] Max Farrand, ed., *The Records of the Federal Convention of 1787* (Yale University Press, revised edn., 1966), vol. II, p. 341.

colonial complaints before 1774 about quartering in homes being "illegal" are admissible on positivist terms. The complaints, however, did not cease when Parliament changed the law and made domestic quartering legal. As with standing armies, writers throughout the colonies attacked the practice of quartering as despotic, dangerous, and violative of American rights.[63]

The right against quartering is a good illustration of the oppositional origins of rights because we can differentiate among areas where more and less quartering occurred during the war and then ask whether it is from the more affected areas that the right came. In fact, what became the Third Amendment is the only one of the first eight amendments that did not have a forerunner in the Virginia Bill of Rights. As an oppositional theory of rights discourse would predict, quartering was less common in Virginia than elsewhere. The state hardest hit by the Quartering Act was New York. The British army occupied New York City for most of the war, and at one point the state had its legislature suspended for refusing to comply with the Quartering Act. In 1788, New York proposed an amendment to the federal Constitution banning quartering as practiced by the British during the war. Furthermore, the first New York Constitution contained a long paragraph demanding that there must be a militia, in all circumstances of war and peace, consisting of every man in the state, "armed and disciplined, and in readiness for service," immediate and perpetual. Magazines and armories were to be "forever hereafter ... continued in every county in this State."[64] No other state had such emphatic constitutional provisions for its militia. New York, suffering under an occupation, had an immediate hatred of standing armies to vent. Its legislature therefore saw great importance in its militia, and it located that importance in the section of the state constitution dedicated to conferring rights. Similarly, New York enacted the following law in 1787:

That by the Laws and Customs of the State, the Citizens and Inhabitants thereof cannot be compelled, against their Wills, to receive Soldiers into their Houses, and to sojourn them there; and therefore no Officer, military or civil, nor any other Person whatsoever, shall, from henceforth, presume to place, quarter or billet any Soldier or Soldiers, upon any Citizen or Inhabitant of this State, of any Degree or Profession whatever, without his

[63] For two examples, see Bland, *Rights of the British Colonies*, and Sam Adams, in the *Boston Gazette* on 17 October 1768, reproduced in Adams, *Writings*, vol. I, pp. 251–253.

[64] New York Constitution of 1777, Article 40.

or her Consent; and that it shall and may be lawful for every such Citizen and Inhabitant, to refuse to sojourn or quarter any Soldier or Soldiers, notwithstanding any Command, Order, Warrant, or Billeting whatever.[65]

By comparison with measures against quartering in other states, this one is unusually strong. Most other states built in exceptions to the right with phrases like "... except when in cases of war or insurrection the public peace shall require it," or "except by consent of the legislature." New York, having borne the brunt of the British occupation, gave immunity from quartering a higher degree of importance. Possessed of a stronger sense of the need to keep soldiers out of private homes, New York codified an unqualified anti-quartering right.

Religion

The history of religious toleration in colonial America is intricate, varying widely from place to place. At one pole, the laws of Rhode Island had always guaranteed relatively broad freedom of worship.[66] At the other, several colonies approached outright theocracy.[67] Between the two extremes, colonies practiced different degrees of toleration, often criminalizing certain behavior on religious grounds and demanding some sort of approved church affiliation from all residents, though not necessarily with the established church.[68] In the seventeenth century, issues of religious establishment and toleration were of great importance in the British colonies, just as they were in Britain. After the Restoration, however, those concerns receded. In the first half of the eighteenth century, only one pamphlet on the subject of religious liberty was published in British North America.[69] The issue re-emerged as critical during and after

---

[65] An Act concerning the Rights of the Citizens of this State [i.e., New York], 1787, section 13.

[66] See Plantation Agreement at Providence, 1640, in Thorpe, *Constitutions*, vol. VI, p. 3205. Although Rhode Island was exceptionally tolerant of different religions by the standards of the seventeenth and eighteenth centuries, it did not always grant full religious liberty in the modern liberal sense. Catholics and Jews, though not actively persecuted in Rhode Island, were often denied the rights to vote and to hold office. See Thomas J. Curry, *The First Freedoms: Church and State in America to the Passage of the First Amendment* (Oxford University Press, 1986), pp. 90–91.

[67] See, e.g., Fundamental Orders of Connecticut, 1639, in Thorpe, *Constitutions*, vol. I, p. 519; Original Constitution of New Haven, 1639, ibid., p. 523.

[68] The Carolina Constitution, written by Locke himself, required that all adult residents be members of some church. Fundamental Constitutions of Carolina, 1669, in *Old South Leaflets* (Boston: Directors of the Old South Work, 1896–1909), vol. VII, #172.

[69] Curry, *First Freedoms*, p. 97. The sole pamphlet was Elisha Williams, *The Essential Rights and Liberties of Protestants* (S. Kneeland and T. Green, 1744). Williams was a Congregationalist

the French and Indian War, in which the overwhelmingly Protestant British colonies fought against Catholic Quebec. Religious liberty then remained a leading political concern through the Founding generation, during which every American state altered its church–state arrangements. Most states proclaimed a right to freedom of religion. Nevertheless, many states retained and even reinforced religious laws, established churches, and religious qualifications for holding government office. How the Founders could consider freedom of religion to be compatible with such strictures calls for explanation, and the explanation lies in the answer to the question of what precisely the Founders were trying to protect by proclaiming a right to freedom of religion. As I will show, the reasons why the Founders articulated and codified rights of free conscience in the ways they did had a great deal to do with perceived threats to their own religious liberty during the 1760s and 1770s. The rights of conscience they claimed were largely intended to protect themselves from hostile churches, especially the Catholic and the Episcopal; the religious laws they retained served the same purpose.

When Americans wished to argue for rights of freedom of religion, Enlightenment philosophy provided a ready framework. Jefferson and Sam Adams urged full toleration with arguments that could have come directly from Locke.[70] But religious liberty was sometimes recommended for more local reasons as well. Patrick Henry, for example, argued for toleration as an economic policy, noting that Virginia needed immigrants and should not be too restrictive about what kind of (Protestant) faith they practiced.[71] Isaac Backus, representative of the New England Antipaedobaptists, argued for religious freedom as a kind of tax reform: Massachusetts supported

minister and a former president of Yale College, and he wrote in opposition to a Connecticut law of 1742 that banned unlicensed preaching. The law had been written by "Old Light" opponents of the itinerant evangelizers of the "Great Awakening," a religious revival that swept the colonies at the time. (For more on the Great Awakening, see Alan Heimert, *Religion and the American Mind from the Great Awakening to the Revolution* [Harvard University Press, 1966].) The argument that Williams made exhibited an important characteristic of Founding attitudes toward religious liberty: it pointedly excluded Catholics from the tolerated spectrum. Throughout this section, I argue that anti-Catholicism, far from existing in tension with Founding notions of the right to freedom of religion, was actually a supporting element of enthusiasm for that right as the Founders understood it.

[70] Jefferson, "A Bill for Establishing Religious Freedom" (1779), in *Basic Writings*, pp. 48–49; Samuel Adams, *Writings*, vol. II, pp. 322–323, and "Rights of the Colonists" (1772), ibid., pp. 351–357.

[71] Patrick Henry, "Religious Tolerance" (1766), in Anson Phelps Stokes, *Church and State in the United States* (Harper & Brothers, 1950), vol. I, pp. 311–312.

churches with public revenue, and Backus claimed that members of his sect should not be "taxed on religious accounts where we were not represented."[72] Given the prevailing rhetoric about taxation and representation, this argument might have seemed a good way to advance the cause of minority believers. As it happened, however, Backus's arguments went unheeded.[73] In contrast, the Founding-era arguments that did succeed in establishing rights of religious freedom were expressed in oppositional terms by people who believed that British colonial policies threatened their own religious liberty. One of the chief worries involved Catholicism and Quebec, and another involved the possible establishment of an American Episcopate.

Episcopal establishment

For two generations before the Founding, Congregationalists and Anglicans in New England fought over the question of religious establishment. In Massachusetts and Connecticut, Congregationalists were locally dominant and in practice the established church. Anglicans, who were far less numerous, claimed that their church was established throughout the empire and therefore in New England as well. The two groups coexisted uneasily.[74] By the 1760s, American Anglicans had begun asking the church leadership in England to create an episcopate in America, thus establishing their church. Congregationalists and other dissenters were extremely upset at this possibility.[75] According to John Adams, Americans of dissenting sects worried that the same Parliament that taxed them despite their protests would "establish the Church of England here, with all creeds, articles, tests, ceremonies, and tythes, and prohibit

---

[72] Isaac Backus, in Stokes, *Church and State*, vol. 1, pp. 308–309. Backus's opposition to public financing of churches should not be taken to imply a general civil libertarianism on questions of church and state. For example, in line with the general anti-Catholicism that suffused the politics of religion at the Founding, he believed that Catholics should not be allowed to hold public office. See Curry, *First Freedoms*, pp. 212, 177.

[73] See William G. McLoughlin, ed., *Isaac Backus on Church, State, and Calvinism: Pamphlets, 1754–1789* (Harvard University Press, 1968), pp. 22–25.

[74] Curry, *First Freedoms*, pp. 108–114.

[75] Heimert says that among some dissenting sects, the passion for rights against the British administration generally had its roots in the crusade against this supposed British intention to establish an American Episcopate. See Heimert, *Religion and the American Mind*, pp. 351–352. See also, generally, Jonathan Clark, *The Language of Liberty, 1660–1832* (Cambridge University Press, 1994) on the role of conflict between Anglican and dissenting churches during the revolution.

all other churches, as conventicles and schism-shops."[76] New England preacher Jonathan Mayhew described the possible establishment of an episcopate and the work of Anglican missionaries as "carrying on the crusade, or spiritual siege of our churches, with the hope that they will one day submit to an episcopal sovereign."[77] The Anglican church, for its part, did little to allay such fears. The Society for the Propagation of the Gospel in Foreign Parts, an Anglican body ostensibly dedicated to organizing missionaries among the Native American population, aroused suspicion by erecting offices in places like Cambridge, Massachusetts, a Congregationalist town where no Native Americans had lived for decades. By the end of the 1760s, most members of nonconformist American sects suspected that the Church and the state of England were working together to bring all English subjects into the Anglican Church.[78]

In their quest to protect their own liberty of worship – or, in Hohfeldian terms, their immunity from the authority of the Anglican Church – many American dissenters applied the language of rights to issues of religion. "The various attempts ... to establish an American Episcopate," wrote Sam Adams, were

... a great grievance, and also an infringement of our rights, which is not barely to exercise, but also peaceably and securely to enjoy, that liberty wherewith Christ has made us free ... We think therefore that every design for establishing the jurisdiction of a bishop in this Province, is a design both against our civil and religeous [sic] rights.[79]

Protests that religious establishments violated the rights of citizens should not, however, be understood as arguments for disestablishment. Massachusetts, where Adams articulated the dominant opinion about the Episcopate, maintained its Congregational church establishment until 1833, more than fifty years after American independence. Opposition to an Episcopal establishment in the 1760s and 1770s should be understood less as opposition to the establishment of a church per se than as opposition to establishment of the wrong church. Indeed, the phrase "liberty wherewith Christ

[76] John Adams, *The Works of John Adams, Second President of the United States*, ed. Charles Francis Adams (Little, Brown, 1850–1856), vol. x, pp. 187–188.

[77] Jonathan Mayhew, *Observations on the Charter and Conduct of the Society for the Propagation of the Gospel in Foreign Parts* (Edes and Gill, 1763), p. 57.

[78] Bailyn, *Ideological Origins*, pp. 95–96.

[79] Samuel Adams, "Proceedings of the Town of Boston" (1772), in *Writings*, vol. II, pp. 359–369.

has made us free," which Adams used in the quotation above, was a New England Puritan formula meaning not the liberty to choose one's faith but the liberty to practice the *correct* faith.[80] Thus, the liberty at stake was not the liberty to be free of established religion but the liberty to maintain a Congregational establishment. In that light, Founding assertions of rights against the establishment of an American Episcopate emerge even more clearly as an example of rights arguments motivated less by a general principle of tolerance than by opposition to a specific practice that the colonists feared: the establishment of a disliked church.

The Quebec Act

The Founders articulated their greatest chorus of religious rights claims in opposition to the Quebec Act. In 1774, that Act of Parliament retained the existing French legal code for newly British Quebec, guaranteed French Quebecois Catholics who were now British subjects the "free Exercise of the Religion of the Church of Rome, subject to the King's Supremacy," and extended the boundaries of Quebec southward to the Ohio River. The Quebec Act horrified American Protestants. Fear and hatred of Catholicism were long-standing features of colonial American thought, and most Americans regarded Quebec as the nearest incarnation of the Catholic threat. For British colonists, the war of 1756–63 had been a war against Quebec, and the danger had been great enough for the normally quarrelsome Protestant sects to work together during what they considered the "dark day of popish invasion."[81] From the American point of view, the Quebec Act revived and in two ways even augmented the old threat. First, it awarded to Catholic Quebec the territories that the previous war had been fought to prevent Quebec from controlling. Second, it made the king head of the Roman Catholic church in a British colony. In a climate already worried about an American Episcopate, the Quebec Act exacerbated fears of religious coercion. Moreover, fear of the Episcopate and fear of Quebec easily worked in tandem, because many Americans regarded Episcopalianism as virtually identical with Catholicism: when the New England preacher Israel Holly gloomily

---

[80] Curry, *First Freedoms*, p. 6. This conception of liberty is of the same family of conceptions as what Isaiah Berlin called "positive liberty." Berlin, *Two Concepts of Liberty* (Clarendon Press, 1958).

[81] Heimert, *Religion and the American Mind*, p. 324.

prophesied the establishment of an American Episcopate, he warned that "we must have imposed upon us, the superstitions and damnable heresies" not of Anglicanism but "... of the church of Rome."[82] Fears like these prompted American colonists to defend their own Protestantism, and for that protective purpose they made arguments about rights of free religious exercise.[83]

Most American Protestants did not distinguish between toleration of Catholicism in Quebec and its establishment there, and those few who recognized the official distinction dismissed it. Philip Livingston rhetorically asked Americans to "Look thro' Europe. See if Popery is in any other manner established in any one country, than by payment of tythes, and protection of Priests. Is not this an establishment?" The prospects, he said, were dire. "Whenever a wicked monarch in vengeance shall arise; there shall we behold him, the civil and religious tyrant, of a province which extends over half the Continent of America."[84] Hamilton similarly prophesied that Britain would use Catholic Quebec to subdue the Protestant colonies. "We may see an inquisition erected in Canada," he wrote, "and priestly tyranny may hereafter find as propitious a soil, in America, as it ever has in Spain or Portugal."[85] According to the Continental Congress,

---

[82] Israel Holly, *God Brings About his Holy and Wise Purpose or Decree ...* (Eben. Watson, 1774).

[83] Any discussion of early American anti-Catholicism must account for the existence and role of American Catholics, but that wrinkle poses little trouble here. In no colony or state at the Founding were Catholics enough of a presence to exercise great influence over political affairs. Even Maryland, which was originally a Catholic colony, was half Protestant by 1650. The colony was reorganized with the Church of England as the established religion in 1688, and by 1715, the then Lord Baltimore was himself a Protestant. Maryland, the most Catholic of the colonies, was a Protestant colony throughout the Founding era. See Stokes, *Church and State*, pp. 11–37.

[84] Livingston, *The Other Side*, pp. 23–24.

[85] Hamilton, "Remarks on the Quebec Bill" (June 1775), in *Papers*, vol. 1, pp. 167–168. In the fiercely anti-Catholic environment of British North America, the Inquisition represented the horrors that the Catholic church could be expected to visit on any non-Catholics within its grasp. Accordingly, raising the specter of the Inquisition was one of the most common motifs of Founding political rhetoric. In addition to Hamilton, Paine and Jefferson argued for religious freedom by presenting the Inquisition as the logical alternative. Paine, *Rights of Man*, p. 109; Jefferson, "Notes on Virginia," in *Basic Writings*, p. 158. Use of the Inquisition bogeyman transcended religious issues. Josiah Quincy, Jr., compared the indemnity Parliament levied on Boston in retribution for the Tea Party to the practices "of a Spanish Inquisition" in *Observations on the Act of Parliament Commonly Called the Boston Port Bill* (Edes and Gill, 1774), pp. 21–22. At the Massachusetts convention called to ratify the federal Constitution in 1788, Abraham Holmes of Rochester worried that the new form of government would create a Congress "possessed of powers enabling them to institute judicatories little less inauspicious than a certain tribunal in Spain, which has long been the disgrace of Christendom: I mean that diabolical institution, the *Inquisition*" (Elliot, *Debates*,

the dominion of Canada is to be so extended, modelled, and governed, as that by being disunited from us, detached from our interests, by civil as well as religious prejudices, that by their numbers swelling daily with Catholic emigrants from Europe, [they might] be fit instruments in the hands of power, to reduce the ancient free Protestant Colonies to the same state of slavery with themselves.[86]

Contemporary observers recorded that American colonists generally shared this assessment that the danger from Catholic Quebec was serious and that Britain was entirely to blame. General Thomas Gage, the British military commander in Massachusetts, noted that Protestant farmers believed that the British intended to curtail their religious freedom. The Quebec Act, he believed, energized rural evangelical Protestants for the rebel cause.[87]

If a Catholic establishment in Quebec was cause for worry (even though the Quebec Act actually entailed no such establishment), a Catholic establishment created by the same Parliament that legislated for the other colonies was cataclysmic. "Does not your blood run cold, to think that an English parliament should pass an act for the establishment of arbitrary power and popery?" Hamilton asked the people of New York. Worse still, the looming pontiff was not some foreign potentate who might still be stopped at the gates but the colonists' own king, already reigning over them. Hamilton drew the obvious conclusion within the paranoiac view of Catholicism that then prevailed. Parliament, he warned, "may as well establish popery in New-York and the other colonies as they did in Canada. They had no more right to do it there than here."[88] Protestantism in America was in no danger, of course. In hindsight, it seems incredible that the colonists could have feared that a Protestant king and a Protestant Parliament would want to establish Catholicism throughout their American domain – but no more incredible, perhaps, than George III's becoming ecclesiastical head of the

---

vol. II, p. III, emphasis in the original). As Rakove notes, the Founders' notion of the "experience" from which they drew political lessons included certain narrated experiences from history as well as what they themselves lived through (Rakove, *Original Meanings*, p. 18). The merging of the inherited fear of the Inquisition with contemporary worries about Catholic Quebec thus presented another opportunity for past/present synthesis.

86 Continental Congress to the People of Great Britain, 21 October 1774, in Phillip Kurland and Ralph Lerner, eds., *The Founders' Constitution* (University of Chicago Press, 1987), vol. V, p. 61.

87 Heimert, *Religion and the American Mind*, p. 387.

88 Hamilton, *A Full Vindication of the Measures of the Congress, from the Calumnies of their Enemies* (James Rivington, 1774), pp. 68–69.

Catholic church in an enlarged province of Quebec seemed to the colonists. Feeling what they thought to be the threat of imposed Catholic power, Protestant colonists vehemently embraced a right to the free exercise of religion.

Against this background, the widespread practice in the original state constitutions of establishing one or multiple Protestant sects as the official or enfranchised religion of the state and simultaneously declaring a right of free religious exercise is less contradictory than it might appear. The freedom that that right was chiefly meant to confer was the freedom from Roman Catholicism. Both the Protestant establishments and the rights of free conscience served that end. Although the principle of toleration was frequently honored and even claimed as a right before the widespread fears of an American Episcopate and before the Quebec Act, toleration changed dramatically in the years immediately following the Quebec Act. In all the colonial laws written before the Quebec Act, only Pennsylvania and Carolina prohibited seditious behavior in the guise of religion; at the Founding, bans on seditious speech under the guise of religious preaching, or worse yet as actual religious preaching, became more common. The three states bordering pre-war Quebec took special care to prevent religious subversion. In New Hampshire, the only changes to the religious status quo contained in a proposed 1779 constitution would have forbidden laws that infringed the "rights of conscience," the laws of God, or "the Protestant religion."[89] Vermont's Constitution of 1777 required state legislators to take an oath of belief in the Protestant religion.[90] New York, with the longest border with Quebec of any state, forbade clergymen from ever holding civil or military offices.[91] New York also required all immigrants to renounce any allegiance to foreign ecclesiastical powers.[92] Officeholders were required to take a similar oath, and Catholics were thereby excluded from political office until well after the Founding era.[93]

The fear of conspiratorially imposed Catholicism survived the revolution and played a role in forming the national right of free

---

[89] Curry, *First Freedoms*, p. 186.

[90] Vermont Constitution of 1777, chapter 9, section 9, in Thorpe, *Constitutions*, vol. VI, p. 3737.

[91] New York Constitution of 1777, Article 39. Other states, including both Carolinas and Georgia, had similar provisions. Note the parallel with certain states' bans, discussed in the section on military affairs (page 100), on military officers holding government positions.

[92] New York Constitution of 1777, Article 42.

[93] Curry, *First Freedoms*, p. 162.

exercise as well. A common concern was that the national government would make laws limiting the diverse religious practices of people in the various states. Some delegates even worried that Congress would use its powers to force Catholicism on Americans. As one delegate at the North Carolina ratification convention put it, "It is feared, by some people, that, by the power of making treaties, [the central government] might make a treaty with foreign powers to adopt the Roman Catholic religion in the United States, which would prevent the people from worshipping God according to their own consciences."[94] Worries like these, expressed at the North Carolina convention and others, prompted the drafting and approval of the First Amendment right to freedom of religion.

Trials

The right to trial by jury had very old roots in English common law, but the precise content of those rights fluctuated. How they came to take the form of their eventual Founding codification had much to do with British policies of the time that made certain aspects of trials into critical issues. When specific British policies threatened or abolished aspects of the trial system that the colonists thought should be protected, the colonists responded with protests and polemics asserting rights to the relevant practices. The contours of Founding-era protest and pamphleteering guided those who later codified rights. As with other kinds of rights, what rights state and federal laws guaranteed was largely a function of what rights pro-independence protesters had asserted against the British, which was in turn largely a function of what practices important to that political class had been endangered by British policies. Of course, trial rights were already present in the Anglo-American legal world before the Founding, and some revolutionary protests against British violations correlate with Founding rights because Americans protested on the basis of rights already established. Nevertheless, that pattern can account for only a part of American ideas about trial rights, because those ideas were not coextensive with previously recognized rights. In some cases, Americans denounced British actions that had been valid law in England for centuries. Rather than simply reasserting an inherited system of rights, the Founders formed their ideas about

---

[94] Henry Abbot, speaking on 30 July 1788, in Elliot, *Debates*, vol. IV, pp. 191–192.

trial rights under the combined influences of historical rights and opposition to specific contemporary troubles.

Colonial charters and constitutions from the very early stages of settlement sought to extend English common-law criminal procedures to America. Sometimes, as in Virginia, importation of the common law was explicit and wholesale; sometimes, as in East New Jersey, provisions of the common-law tradition were incorporated piecemeal.[95] Some trial rights remained substantially the same through the Founding. Others changed. The right to challenge jurors, for example, which some colonies had recognized in their seventeenth-century constitutions, disappeared completely.[96] That right appears nowhere in the Founding discourse, not in the federal or the state constitutions nor in any of the declarations of rights nor in the polemics and pamphlets of the revolution. It was not an issue of the crisis, not threatened and therefore not defended. Today, more than two hundred years after the Founding, the right to challenge jurors is a hotly contested legal question, and its resolution is uncertain partly because there is no firm constitutional statement of whether such a right must be respected.[97] Had the practice of challenging jurors been threatened during the Founding era, the Founders would probably have articulated rights of challenge among the other jury-trial rights that they wrote into the Constitution. Because challenging jurors was not an issue of the Founders' crisis, they did not constitutionalize a right to challenge, and twentieth-century courts were more free to whittle away at the practice. By that pattern, historical contingencies of rights discourse can have long-term effects on the rights that people have.

The Stamp Act of 1765 set off the first major round of American protest over the rights of criminal trial. Suspected violators of the Stamp Act were to be tried not by juries in civil courts but by military officers in courts of admiralty, thus linking trial issues with military issues. In response, the colonial congress that gathered to protest the Stamp Act quickly asserted "That trial by jury is the inherent and invaluable right of every British subject in these

---

[95] Virginia Ordinance and Constitution of 1621, in Thorpe, *Constitutions*, vol. VI, p. 812; Fundamental Constitutions for the Province of East New Jersey, 1683, Article XIX, ibid., vol. V, pp. 2580–2581.

[96] See Frame of Government of Pennsylvania, 1682; The Charter or Fundamental Laws of West New Jersey, 1676, chapter 17.

[97] See, e.g., *Batson v. Kentucky*, 476 U.S. 79 (1986); *J. E. B. v. Alabama*, 511 U.S. 127 (1994).

colonies."[98] Richard Bland railed against the courts of admiralty, denouncing the "dragging" of colonists "before Prerogative Judges, exercising a despotick Sway in Inquisitorial Courts."[99] John Adams detailed the evils of admiralty courts as follows:

In these Courts, one Judge alone, presides – No Juries have any Concern there. – The Judges Commissions are only during Pleasure. – Nay, the most mischievous of all imaginable Customs has become established there, that of taking Commissions on all Condemnations – so that the Judge, single and dependent as he is, is under a pecuniary Temptation always against the subject ... What Justice and Impartiality are we ... to expect from a single Judge, without a Jury, dependent, perhaps ignorant, perhaps wicked ... What after all this can be wanting but the appointment of a weak or a wicked Man for a Judge ... to render Us the most sordid and forlorn of Slaves?[100]

This protest against Stamp Act judicial procedures contained the seeds for at least two different trial-related rights that would be codified in early American law: rights of individuals to jury trials and, as mentioned earlier, rights of the people collectively to independent judiciaries.

In 1772, acting pursuant to common-law precedent older than the oldest American colony, Parliament passed an Act under which Americans could be transported to England to be tried for crimes relating to the navy.[101] Undeterred by long-standing practice, the colonists charged that their rights were being violated. Without citing any source or rationale, Samuel Adams called the new Act "a violent infringement of our rights," and Moses Mather declared that all Englishmen had a right against far-away imprisonment.[102] Given that Parliament had common-law precedent on its side, it is clear that not every American invocation of common-law rights – as jury trials were generally considered – actually had common-law backing. Nevertheless, such a right would successfully oppose a specific adversity visited on Stamp Act violators, and Americans claimed the right so as to negate that imminent threat.

---

[98] Stamp Act Congress, Declaration of Rights, in Morrison, *Sources and Documents*, p. 33.

[99] Bland, *Rights of the British Colonies*, p. 29.

[100] John Adams, "Instructions of the Town of Braintree on the Stamp Act" (original draft, Braintree, September 1765), in John Adams, *Papers*, vol. I, pp. 134–135.

[101] An Act for the better preserving his Majesty's dock Yards, Magazines, Ships, Ammunition and Stores, 12 Geo.III, c.24. For an illustration of the legal precedents to this Act, see statute of 35 Henry VIII, in Morrison, *Sources and Documents*, p. 119.

[102] Samuel Adams, "Proceedings of the Town of Boston," p. 10; Moses Mather, *America's Appeal to the Impartial World* (Ebenezer Watson, 1775), pp. 13–14.

In Massachusetts, where local conflict between radicals and the colonial administration was especially sharp, methods of jury selection became an issue of concern. Daniel Leonard, a Tory, proposed in a local newspaper that the sheriff *ex officio* should select juries. John Adams responded, writing that allowing the sheriff *ex officio* to select juries was simply a way of stacking every jury in the colony against the rebels. The chosen sheriff, he wrote, would surely be a Tory, and he would pick Tory jurors. The solidly Tory juries would surely return verdicts against rebels, Adams wrote, no matter what the law or the evidence in a given case.[103] Thirteen years later, exactly one state convention called to ratify the federal Constitution discussed a people's right against having juries "appointed by the sheriff ex officio."[104] The state, of course, was Massachusetts, where the specific issue of whether sheriffs could appoint juries had recently been contested.

During the constitutional ratification process, debate over trial by jury did not focus on whether the right existed, or whether it was important, or even what its specific provisions were, but whether the proposed Constitution secured it adequately. As with other common-law rights, some people elevated jury trial to the plane of natural or self-evident rights. No one, however, saw fit to argue the question of its origins, perhaps because no one disputed the existence of such a right. Everyone, Federalist and anti-Federalist, seemed to agree on the importance of juries.[105] Furthermore, no one bothered to argue about whether juries must have twelve members, or whether convictions must be unanimous, despite the fact that different states had different answers to these basic questions. Like peremptory challenges, these practices remain live legal issues because of the contingent historical fact that they presented no specific adversities during the Founding and were therefore not codified, oppositionally, as constitutional rights.[106]

In contrast, the guarantee of jury trials in all cases had been

---

[103] Letter #5 of Novanglus [i.e., John Adams], printed in the *Boston Gazette* on 20 February 1775 and addressed "To the Inhabitants of the Colony of Massachusetts-Bay," in John Adams, *Papers*, vol. II, pp. 282–283.

[104] Elliot, *Debates*, vol. II, p. 110.

[105] See Hamilton, *Federalist* no. 83, for pro-ratification argument; Richard Henry Lee to Edmund Randolph, 16 October 1787, in Lee, *Letters*, vol. II, p. 45, for anti-ratification argument. On the unanimity of opinion, see also Washington to Lafayette, 28 April 1788, in Kurland and Lerner, *The Founders' Constitution*, vol. IV, p. 400.

[106] See, e.g., *Williams v. Florida*, 399 U.S. 78 (1970); *Johnson v. Louisiana*, 406 U.S. 256 (1972).

threatened, and the Founders accordingly used rights language to protect that guarantee, writing into the federal Constitution that "The Trial of all Crimes, except in Cases of Impeachment, shall be by Jury."[107] So great was the worry about endangerment of jury trials, however, that many people worried that even so clear a guarantee was insufficient. In the Virginia ratifying convention, an alarmed Patrick Henry actually charged that the right of jury trial had been taken away. Because the Constitution only specified a guarantee of jury trials in *criminal* cases, Henry worried, civil trials could be conducted entirely by judges, and undoubtedly corrupt ones at that. Trials would then be an instrument of oppression in the hands of the central government.[108] Henry and others who demanded explicit and detailed rights to trial by jury completely ignored questions about how juries would operate, such as how many members a jury must have and how many votes would be necessary for conviction. The aspects of jury trial that interested the Founders were exactly those that had been threatened or eliminated under the British: the use of juries as opposed to judges, the use of civil as opposed to military courts, and the trying of cases locally as opposed to far away. Accordingly, those were the aspects of jury trials that they used rights language to prioritize and protect.

Some who remembered the British practice of trying offenders far from home invented ingenious ways to discover the same threat lurking in the federal Constitution. One anti-Federalist author wrote, "I have it in my power to prove that under the proposed Federal Constitution, *the trial of facts in civil cases by a jury of the Vicinage* is entirely and effectually abolished." According to his argument, "the *appellate* jurisdiction as to law and *fact* which is vested in the superior court of the United States" was the undoing of local juries:

How is it possible that the supreme continental court, which we will suppose to consist at most of five or six different judges, can travel at least twice in every year, through the different counties of America, from New Hampshire to Kentucky [sic] and from Kentuckey to Georgia, to try facts by juries of the vicinage. Common sense will not admit of such a supposition. I am therefore right in my assertion, that *trial by jury in civil cases, is, by the proposed constitution entirely done away, and effectually abolished.*

Let us now attend to the consequences of this enormous innovation, and daring encroachment, on the liberties of the citizens ... Suppose therefore,

---

[107] U.S. Constitution, III.2.iii.
[108] Storing, *The Complete Anti-Federalist*, vol. v, bk. 16, p. 24.

that the military officers of congress, by a wanton abuse of power, imprison the free citizens of America, suppose the excise or revenue officers [or] a constable, having a warrant to search for stolen goods, pulled down the clothes of a bed in which there was a woman, and searched under her shift, – suppose, I say, that they commit similar, or greater indignities, in such cases a trial by jury would be our safest resource, heavy damages would at once punish the offender, and deter others from committing the same: but what satisfaction can we expect from a lordly court of justice, always ready to protect the officers of government against the weak and helpless citizen, and who will perhaps sit at the distance of many hundred miles from the place where the outrage was committed? – What refuge shall we then have to shelter us from the iron hand of arbitrary power?[109]

In this amazing suggestion, the author sets out from a rather benign-looking proviso of the Constitution, specifically that the Supreme Court would have standing as an appellate court of fact in civil cases, subject to exceptions as Congress might declare.[110] He vaults directly to tyranny and degradation, cataclysm in his tone, throwing in a healthy mixture of search warrants and standing armies. The letter reads like a summary sketch of the worst colonial nightmares under British rule. That theme was probably the guiding image behind his argument: all the terrors he lists must be avoided, and he would support no government that did not provide unquestionable rights against them.

Free trade and the rights of Annapolis

Many of the Founders were enterprise-oriented people in a mercantile age, and their documents reflected that general milieu. The federal Constitution guaranteed that Congress would not levy export taxes, give preferential treatment to ports in different states, or require duties on interstate shipping. The Constitution also provided against laws "impairing the obligation of contracts."[111] Nevertheless, the ways in which rights of free trade were and were not guaranteed stand in need of more detailed explanation. That the colonists were not free-trade absolutists is clear from their arguments against parliamentary taxation policies. In the early stages of the conflict, many prominent colonists distinguished between taxes whose purpose was to regulate trade and taxes whose purpose was to raise revenue, and it was the second category that drew more

---

[109] Letter of "A Democratic Federalist," printed in the *Pennsylvania Herald*, 17 October 1787, in Storing, *The Complete Anti-Federalist*, vol. III, bk. 5, pp. 6–9. Emphasis in the original.
[110] Article III, section 2.   [111] Article I, sections 9–10.

objections. Parliament's right to regulate trade was more freely conceded.[112] After independence, some kinds of trade were to be more free than others: the same Constitution that banned duties in interstate ports empowered Congress to regulate other forms of interstate commerce. For some reason, a right to free trade existed on the water to an extent that it did not exist on land.

Something, it seems, was special about ports, and political pamphlets of the Founding era demonstrate a connection between the special protection of ports and Parliament's Boston Port Act. Passed in 1774 as collective punishment for the Boston Tea Party, the Boston Port Act essentially closed the port of Boston and threatened the city with economic collapse. The Act attracted attention far beyond Boston. It was, for example, upon receiving news of the Boston Port Act that the government of Virginia called for a Continental Congress. In Founding discussions of the right to free trade, the Boston Port Act appears again and again. Just after passage of the Act, in what was ostensibly a review of English history under Charles II, Jefferson wrote about the tyrannical abridgment of "the exercise of a free trade with all parts of the world, possessed by the American colonists, as of natural right."[113] One year later, the Continental Congress listed Britain's interdicting the commerce of Massachusetts as one of its reasons for taking up arms.[114]

One fascinating line of development leads directly from the Boston Port Act to an obscure right in the Maryland Constitution of 1776, the guarantee that "the city of Annapolis ought to have all its rights."[115] Bailyn is fond of citing this right to show how haphazard and humorous rights discourse at the Founding was, because the right seems so completely inscrutable. In traditional common-law usage, references to rights of cities often refer to rights of businesspeople in those cities to trade freely, especially in their use of ports and waterways: an early model is Magna Carta's guarantee of the rights of the City of London, where "the City" is understood to have commercial connotations. Accordingly, as Bailyn points out, the "rights of the city of Annapolis" refers to a right of the people of

---

[112] Dickinson, "Letters From a Farmer, no. 5," in *Writings*, pp. 335–338. See also Robert Middlekauff, *The Glorious Cause* (Oxford University Press, 1982), pp. 68–69, 124–126, 156.
[113] Jefferson, *Summary View*, p. 8.
[114] Continental Congress, *A Declaration by the Representatives of the United Colonies of North America, Now Met in General Congress in Philadelphia, Setting forth the Causes and Necessity of their taking up Arms* (Newbury-Port, 1775), p. 4.
[115] Maryland Constitution of 1776, Declaration of Rights, section 37.

Annapolis to trade through the town's port. It is not clear, however, what the source of a right to use the port of Annapolis might be or why so specific and pedestrian a right should merit constitutional status. In the context of reaction to the Boston Port Act, however, a simple story emerges to explain the motive behind that clause.

Just after passage of the Boston Port Act, an anonymous pamphlet appeared in New York, noting that if the closure succeeded in subduing the rebellion in Boston, there was every reason to believe that Parliament would close other ports to drive other cities into submission. In short, the pamphleteer warned, the Boston Port Act portended ruin for residents of port cities throughout the American colonies.[116] In all, roughly forty pamphlets were published in reaction to the Boston Port Act. Not surprisingly, the majority were published in Boston. One pamphlet, which announced the Virginia House of Burgesses' condemnation of the Act, was published in Williamsburg, the seat of the Virginia government. With that single exception, every pamphlet protesting the Boston Port Act was published in a port city. Newport, not usually a site of pamphleteering, published a pamphlet. Hartford, an inland town which frequently did publish pamphlets, was silent. Eight pamphlets appeared in New York and six in Philadelphia. Of all the pamphlets published outside of Boston, New York, and Philadelphia, the three largest cities and largest ports in America, half were published in Maryland, where anger ran high in the port town of Annapolis.[117]

On 25 May 1774, a "meeting of the inhabitants of the city of Annapolis" passed a series of resolutions on the Boston Port Act. The meeting announced that all of the colonies must unite to obtain the repeal of the Act, that a boycott of Britain was in order, that Annapolis would stop exports to Britain immediately and stop imports when a larger cartel would be organized, that there would be no payments of debt to Britain until the Boston Port Act was repealed, and that Annapolis would boycott any colony that did not join in a colonial majority boycotting Britain. Some of these resolutions passed unanimously, and none met with significant dissent.[118] Perhaps no other city in America – Boston excepted –

[116] *A Serious Address to the Inhabitants of the Colony of New York, Containing a full and minute Survey of the Boston-Port Act* (New York: Holt, 1774).

[117] See Charles Evans, *American Bibliography: A Chronological Dictionary of all Books, Pamphlets, and Periodical Publications printed in the United States of America* (Peter Smith, 1941), vol. v, index on p. 443, indexed pamphlets throughout.

reacted as ferociously to the Boston Port Act as did Annapolis. Certainly, no city its size or smaller generated as much oppositional activity. Viewed in that context, a constitutional declaration shortly thereafter that "the city of Annapolis ought to have all its rights" is not at all strange. It is perfectly comprehensible. It establishes the rights of the city to trade and to use its port, and it became a constitutional right because of local reaction against the Boston Port Act.

CONCLUSION

In chapter 1, I explained that I would approach the nature of rights not through ontological inquiry nor by abstraction from a set of agreed rights but by analyzing how people in a given linguistic culture use the language of rights in normative political argument. Rights discourse, I argued, is a social practice in the sense described by Taylor and Searle, and identifying the features of that practice helps clarify what people are doing when they assert, deny, or codify particular rights. The political discourse of the American Founders illustrates many of the most important patterns in the practice of rights argument. Following the hermeneutic principle that I have called "nonviolence," I have interpreted instances of rights language as legitimate uses of the practice to the greatest extent possible, counting ostensible uses of the practice as intelligible as long as doing so would not make the practice incoherent.

In some ways, the practice of rights discourse at the Founding – a primarily political enterprise – differed from modern academic rights theory. Notably absent from Founding rights discourse was the pattern, typical of the philosophical mode, of formulating formal definitions on the basis of which to limit the substantive scope of rights. The Founders did not limit their use of rights language to moral imperatives deriving from a certain kind of source, or attaching to a certain kind of bearer, or embodying a will theory or a welfare theory. The alleged sources of the rights they claimed were

---

[118] Broadside, Annapolis, 25 May 1774, New York Historical Society collection, Evans, *Bibliography*, #13119. A meeting in Baltimore one week later passed substantially the same platform, and Maryland actually did boycott Newfoundland fish under these resolutions. Broadside, Baltimore, 31 May 1774, New York Public Library collection, Evans, *Bibliography*, #13130; broadside, Baltimore, 1 May 1775, Maryland Historical Society, Evans, *Bibliography*, #13820.

many and varied, sometimes internally contradictory, and frequently of little relevance to the content of the rights they were supposed to support. Rights were predicated sometimes of individuals, sometimes of government institutions, sometimes of "the people" as a collective, sometimes of abstractions like colonies or countries. In other respects, however, the political rights discourse of the Founding shares important traits with the rights discourse of modern academic theorists. Both conversations obey the two constitutive rules of rights practice, using the language of rights to prioritize and protect entitlements, liberties, powers, and immunities. Moreover, both conversations tend to value most highly, and therefore to classify as rights, propositions that oppose particular experienced adversities. The Founders spoke of rights when they wished to claim special protection for something that their contemporaneous circumstances endangered. To be sure, it was always possible to reason deductively about rights from abstract first principles, and some Founders kept nearer to that model than others when advancing claims of rights, just as some academics theorize about rights in ways that are more ontological and *a priori* than others. But the desire to oppose specific British abuses heavily informed Founding rights discourse, and most of the Founders' discussions of rights were sensitive to the desired oppositional outcomes. The content of rights codified at the Founding derived largely from the Founders' attitudes about what was important coupled with their experientially informed ideas about which important things needed protection, and their conclusions continue to influence American rights philosophy today, both in politics and in the academy.

Sometimes the Founders made explicit the connection between specific adverse conditions of the British colonial administration and Founding attitudes about which entitlements, liberties, powers, and immunities were important and endangered enough to merit the protection of rights language. Consider, for example, the South Carolina Constitution of 1776. In its opening statement, before it listed rights of the people, that constitution protested against non-consensual taxes, against admiralty courts in the place of jury trials, against trial in Britain for offenses committed in America, against the blockage of Boston harbor, against the establishment of Catholicism in Quebec, against restrictions on colonial trade, and against the fleets and armies stationed in America. Only then did it specify what the rights of South Carolinians were.[119] The protest list is an index to the specific adversities that the rights were intended to correct and prevent.

Events of the period also influenced how rights were grouped together. Sometimes, which rights were considered in groups with which other rights was a matter of analytic categorizing. For example, the rights of press, petition, and assembly could all be considered together under the heading of rights to control the legislature. Often, however, the groupings of rights were not analytic but determined by historical events: several analytically unconnected rights would be asserted and defended in the same place if they were all reactions against the same British activity. Thus, rights to free trade, against standing armies, and against courts of admiralty would all appear together in papers whose purpose or theme was condemnation of the Boston Port Bill. As another example, the Stamp Act Congress in 1765 composed a list of rights possessed by British colonists in America. The list included the right not to be taxed without consent, the right to representation, the right to trial by jury, and the right to petition the king and Parliament.[120] It did not include the rights to freedom of religion, freedom of speech, freedom of the press, or civil control of the military. The Stamp Act Congress declared the rights it did because of the specific abuses to which it was responding. Similarly, Moses Mather ten years later announced three categories of American rights: legislation, trial, and taxation.[121] He thought about those categories because of the Acts of Parliament then in force in his home colony. The Massachusetts Government Act suspended the state legislature, the Administration of Justice Act empowered admiralty judges to try and sentence civilians, and the Tea Act imposed duties on tea, to the much-celebrated ire of Bostonians.

Throughout the Revolution and the Founding, American conceptions of rights involved syntheses or at least opportunities for syntheses, both of inherited rights with present circumstances and of theory with experience. Past/present synthesis involved what Gadamer would call a fusing of historical horizons, as formulations of rights inherited from earlier eras influenced the way that Americans conceived of and argued about rights. When the federal

---

[119] South Carolina Constitution of 1776, in Thorpe, *Constitutions*, vol. VI, p. 3241.
[120] Resolutions of the Stamp Act Congress, New York, 19 October 1765, in Dickinson, *Writings*, pp. 183–187.
[121] Mather, *America's Appeal*, p. 7.

and state conventions codified American rights toward the end of the period, they were also familiar with and influenced by lists of rights from the revolutionary tracts of the preceding several years. In most of those texts, rights are grouped according to the events to which they responded, not by analytic categories into which they fall. The process of choosing, editing, and redacting rights into constitutions, amendments, and declarations preserved many of those oppositionally based groupings, as authors and committees lifted phrases and paragraphs from earlier documents for inclusion in later ones. Reading lists of rights of the Founding as if they were analytic surveys of topics in human or political rights, therefore, assumes a kind of structure that is often not there. It mistakes the genre of the text being read and misconstrues it accordingly.

In subsequent American history, lawyers, politicians and philosophers have tried to identify coherent analytic principles that underlie the Founding conception of rights so that such principles can then be deployed in legal, political, or philosophical debate. To imagine that such a set of principles exists on the formal level, however, specifying analytic criteria for what kind of thing can be a right, seems mistaken on all but the most general level. Within very broad parameters, Founding rights discourse was driven by substantive political commitments about things like armies, trials, religion, and trade, and those commitments were largely about opposition to experienced abuses. The discourse was not much limited by formal constraints on the nature of rights. And as I will illustrate in the coming chapters, those features of rights discourse were not unique to the Founding. In the nineteenth and twentieth centuries as well as in the eighteenth, substantive political commitments and especially the impulse to negate specific adversities continued to drive the discourse of rights.

CHAPTER 4

Rights and Reconstruction: syntheses and shell games

American rights discourse in the middle of the nineteenth century was both continuous and discontinuous with the rights discourse of the Founding. In some ways, the great transformations of American rights that emerged after the Civil War were fulfillments or extensions of Founding-era principles. Those who favored emancipation and equality found it easy to associate their visions with the Declaration of Independence and the ethos that went with it. At the same time, the changes in American conceptions of rights during the nineteenth century were not simply products of an inherited theory. Rights discourse in the nineteenth century was heavily conditioned by reactions against specific adversities that Americans faced during that time, just as Founding rights discourse had been influenced by reactions against adversities of that time. Much as their eighteenth-century predecessors had done, nineteenth-century Americans used rights language to prioritize and protect specific entitlements, liberties, powers, and immunities that they believed to be under threat. Part of the reconstruction of American conceptions of rights was the attempt to synthesize rights born of the concrete negations of different experiences at different times into a coherent whole.

There were many such attempts; the synthesis that emerged was not the only way in which Americans tried to fuse the legacies of Founding rights discourse with the crises of the nineteenth century. Before the Civil War, the relationships between the rights of the Founding and critical issues like slavery, free labor, property, and federalism were deeply contested. All sides used rights language to support their claims. Northerners and Southerners both claimed that fundamental rights named in the Declaration of Independence settled the sectional controversy, albeit in different directions. There is a plausible story to be told under which emancipation and equality proceeded from Founding principles, but Southerners told an alter-

native story and continued to tell it even after the war, though
without being able to command a national audience. To ensure that
their version prevailed, Northerners after the war found it necessary
to pass three constitutional amendments. The document as inherited
did not entirely reflect the Reconstruction Republicans' views, even
when those views were said to be rooted in principles inherited from
the Founding. Reconstructing American conceptions of rights required not just elaboration but synthesis, and successful synthesis
required acts of political will.

Moreover, the dominant rights theory was not static even during
the period of Republican dominance during Reconstruction, when
many leading competitors had been forced off the scene. Reconstruction rights discourse was partly a product of proximate political
circumstances, and changing political circumstances prompted
changes in the discourse of rights. The most interesting example of
substance-driven revision to formal theories of rights in Reconstruction concerned a typology by which political and legal actors
classified rights as "civil," "political," or "social." According to
prominent modern scholars in both history and law, understanding
the conceptual distinctions among those kinds of rights is essential
for understanding the constitutional legacy of Reconstruction. Akhil
Amar, for example, has constructed elaborate constitutional arguments based on this typology.[1] That scholarship, I suggest, has
overestimated the theoretic integrity of the classifications. The
categories were unstable, and a right called political in one place
might easily be called civil in another. The most consistent feature of
the scheme was that only "civil rights" were guaranteed to all
persons equally, and particular rights moved about among the
categories in a kind of constitutional shell game depending on
whether legislators or judges wanted to confer those rights on blacks.
By treating the categories as more stable and less functional than
they actually were, modern commentators like Amar attribute a
more elegant theory of rights to the Reconstruction Republicans
than they actually held. Of course, it should not be surprising that
an ostensibly formal theory of rights arose and operated primarily to
support a practical political agenda. If even the highly self-conscious
rights philosophy of academic theorists like Dworkin and Sunstein is
conditioned by substantive political commitments, how much more

[1] See, e.g., Amar, *Bill of Rights*, pp. 48, 258–259, 271–274.

crudely should we expect the less reflective rights discourse of judges and politicians to privilege desirable outcomes over philosophic consistency?

In its broadest sense, Reconstruction rights discourse included an immense range of conversational circles, ranging from the most to the least powerful members of society, from high federal office-holders to black freedmen and disfranchised Southern whites. As in the study of the Founding, I focus on elites.[2] The centerpiece of elite rights discourse during Reconstruction was the constitutional transformation enacted by the Thirteenth, Fourteenth, and Fifteenth Amendments, which I will call collectively the "Reconstruction Amendments." The paradigmatic rights of Reconstruction, as seen in these sources, are the right against slavery, the rights of access to, due process of, and equality before the law, rights of contract and property, the right to "the privileges and immunities of citizens of the United States," and the right to vote. The Reconstruction Amendments, other landmark legislation like the Civil Rights Act of 1866, and the judicial interpretations of those measures lie at the core of long-standing legal and historiographical debates about the meaning of Reconstruction rights, and they occupy a central place in this analysis.

This chapter has two main parts, the first of which examines the dynamic of synthesis in Reconstruction rights discourse. As I outlined in chapter 2, rights discourse develops through a pattern of adversity, reaction, and synthesis; to appreciate the synthesis, it is necessary to see that the history of American rights has not all been straightforward. Accordingly, the first section below contrasts a view of Reconstruction rights as flowing naturally from Founding rights with a view according to which much of American rights discourse in the mid-nineteenth century, even among Northern Republicans, was the product of reaction against contemporary adversities. The second set of influences should not be underestimated. The second section of this chapter, which concentrates on the years of Reconstruction proper, examines how Republicans and Northerners generally developed and adapted an ostensibly formal theory about the nature of rights in order to legitimate a set of substantive political

---

[2] In chapter 2, I identified a focus on elites as an important way in which the approach of this book differs from that which West prescribes in his criticism of Rorty's methods. What this analysis shares with West is the commitment to examine discourses other than that of university intellectuals, notably those of politics and law.

commitments. Those commitments, which included the a commitment to the preservation of their own political power, were themselves heavily informed by the impulse to negate the specific adversities of the previous generation's struggle.

The "underlying principle" approach

Looking backward from the beginning of the twenty-first century, it is easy to imagine a connected line of development that led naturally from the Founding rights discourse of the eighteenth century to emancipation and other egalitarian rights in the nineteenth. The more natural the progression, the less remarkable would be any efforts to bring the two sets of rights together: there is little difficulty in "synthesizing" two things that are already the same. I suggest, of course, that the two sets of rights were not the same. Some important themes were common to both, but the nineteenth-century Americans who codified Reconstruction rights acted against a background of experiences that their eighteenth-century predecessors did not share. Looking forward from the end of the eighteenth century, nobody could have predicted with certainty how American rights discourse would progress through the nineteenth.

Many commentators have nevertheless presented the Founding and Reconstruction as stages in a natural path of development, the rights of the Founding implying, if not directly entailing, the rights of Reconstruction. According to this view, Reconstruction brought the logical fulfillment of a vision of rights that the Founders articulated but did not fully implement. This view can be summarized as follows: the Founders espoused a good set of rights but, owing to specific adverse historical circumstances, applied them only to part of the population. It was left to later generations to extend the principles that underlay the rights of the Founding to their proper, broader limits. The Civil War and Reconstruction redeemed the promise of the Founding in areas like race and slave labor, areas where the Founders had not applied their principles properly. Thus, the role of Reconstruction was to fulfill what the Founding had moved toward but not managed to achieve in its own time. Sunstein takes such a view in *The Partial Constitution*. As noted earlier, Sunstein tries to tell a story about American constitutional development in

which a few organizing principles underlie constitutional law generally, and he acknowledges that his account aims at adducing a
"usable past." In other words, his account is an attempt at synthesis.
When he turns to Reconstruction, he naturally argues that Reconstruction "fortified" the "original commitment" to the principles
that he earlier identified as central to the Founding, extending those
principles to people previously excluded from their scope.[3] It is true,
of course, that certain features of political debate, including ongoing
arguments about the nature of equality and about the rights and
duties of citizens, are common to the Founding, Reconstruction, and
contemporary America. It is also true that some figures of the earlier
two eras advanced arguments that, if accepted, would have implications for current disputes. As a historical claim, however, this
"underlying principle" view is overly simple. Nineteenth-century
understandings of Founding rights were not limited to the egalitarian
version that the "underlying principle" approach favors, nor was the
Founding the sole influence on the normative discourse of Reconstruction politics.

In his book *Conscience and the Constitution: History, Theory, and Law of
the Reconstruction Amendments*,[4] David A. J. Richards presents a more
extensive version of an "underlying principle" approach to Reconstruction-era conceptions of rights. His treatment is sensitive to
certain ways in which the rights discourse of one time differs from
that of another. He recognizes, for example, that Reconstruction
required an interpretation and not just an application of Founding
rights. Going forward in time from Reconstruction, however, Richards's presentation of an underlying principle approach becomes less
subtle, obscuring differences between Reconstruction rights discourse and that of modern America. Reconstruction conceptions of
rights, he argues, were rights-based principles still applicable today,
and he maintains that those principles are the principles of universal,
egalitarian, human rights. The theory of rights that Richards
attributes to abolitionists and Reconstruction Republicans is essentially John Rawls's theory of justice, stressing individualism, "public
reason," and what Rawls would call the "equal basic liberties
principle"; through an exposition of the thought of Francis Lieber, a
not insignificant figure of nineteenth-century Republican thought,

---

[3] Sunstein, *The Partial Constitution*, p. 136.
[4] David A. J. Richards, *Conscience and the Constitution: History, Theory, and Law of the Reconstruction Amendments* (Princeton University Press, 1993).

Richards is also at pains to urge a Kantian strain in American abolitionist philosophy, another way to bring Reconstruction together with Rawls.[5] Before the Civil War, Richards contends, slavery posed a problem for Founding ideas of equality, contractarianism, and inalienable rights. After the war, the major congressional backers of the Reconstruction Amendments aimed at "bringing the Constitution of 1787 unambiguously in line with rights-based political theory" such that black Americans would be "included in the American political community on terms of principles guaranteeing them equal protection of their basic human rights."[6] Accordingly, the Reconstruction Amendments were constitutional exercises in "a general political theory of human rights ... that leading abolitionist and related thinkers powerfully developed."[7] The preceding quotation contains at least three separate commitments, all of which Richards insists upon: one, that Reconstruction proceeded along a general theory rather than piecemeal or haphazardly; two, that the theory was one of human rights; and three, that abolitionist arguments dominated the framing of those rights.[8] Each of these commitments is questionable. For present purposes, where the dominant concern is conceptions of rights, the most problematic is the second.

Although Richards constantly discusses Reconstruction in terms of human rights, the vocabulary of "human rights" was all but unused during Reconstruction. Natural rights, civil rights, political rights, social rights, and certain other kinds of rights were frequently discussed, but "human rights" played little role. As the next chapter will show in greater depth, the vocabulary of "human rights" is largely an innovation of the mid-twentieth century. In presenting Reconstruction in terms of "human rights," Richards reads twentieth-century commitments about rights – notably the idea of universalism – back onto a nineteenth-century context.[9] Richards here

---

[5] Richards, *Conscience and the Constitution*, e.g., pp. 70, 149, 223, 256. In his most recent book, Rawls himself also endorses this synthetic "underlying principle" view. The Reconstruction Amendments, Rawls maintains, "brought the Constitution more in line with its original promise," rectifying the "blatant contradiction" between the rights of the Founding and slavery and racial subjugation. Rawls extends this analysis forward from Reconstruction as well, arguing that the same principles of the Founding that condemned slavery are applicable to contemporary problems like sexual inequality. John Rawls, *Political Liberalism* (Columbia University Press, 1993), pp. xxix, 238–239.

[6] Richards, *Conscience and the Constitution*, pp. 73–80, 123, 153–154.   [7] Ibid., p. 19.

[8] Ibid., pp. 3, 114, 153–154.

[9] In chapter 5, I provide a more thorough discussion of the distinctively twentieth-century

transgresses the basic principle that past political debate should be interpreted within the conceptual limits imposed by the linguistic and conceptual apparatuses of the agents involved. If Richards's use of the term "human rights" has any distinctive force, it must refer to some concept in play at the time considered. Following Skinner's principle that, though words and concepts are not the same, use of a concept is standardly signaled by the use of some corresponding term, the virtual absence of the term "human rights" from Reconstruction discourse suggests that no such concept played a major role at that time.[10] Overcoming that presumption would require a demonstration that Reconstruction Americans used some other vocabulary to denote what moderns would understand as "human rights," but Richards does not undertake such a demonstration. Instead, he identifies various nineteenth-century rights as "human rights," regardless of whether the rights discussed had the properties (e.g., universality) standardly associated with human rights, and he proceeds to infer attitudes of universal rights among Reconstruction Republicans. Just as some forms of the underlying principle approach to American rights discourse collapse Reconstruction too easily into the Founding, Richards here collapses twentieth-century ideas too easily into Reconstruction. In so doing, he obscures the degree to which Reconstruction and twentieth-century innovations required active syntheses of different ideas about rights, and he simultaneously strengthens the very synthesis he obscures by bringing those different sets of rights together.

Richards's account is far from the only scholarly work to view Reconstruction as having been primarily concerned with underlying principles of individual rights and racial equality and to lend support to intertemporal syntheses of systems of rights accordingly. Consider William Brock's *An American Crisis*, an analysis of the Reconstruction Congress published in 1963.[11] According to Brock, Reconstruction was above all else an ideological struggle about black equality. Republicans saw their party as the embodiment of a moral crusade,

---

concept of "human rights," including a consideration of the similarities and differences between human rights and natural rights.

[10] Skinner, in "Language and Political Change," p. 8.

[11] William R. Brock, *An American Crisis: Congress and Reconstruction, 1865–1867* (Macmillan, 1963). Brock's British nationality might be thought to compromise his status as representative of a relevantly American view of Reconstruction, but the importance that his book assumed in the United States suggests that he articulated the views of a substantial body of Americans.

not as just another political organization, and they believed that the strength of their party lay in "its adherence to principle, and that embodiment of its principles, equality of rights among men." Although not every Republican of the day was a thoroughgoing egalitarian, he says, the most important rights legislation of the period was carried out "in the cause of disinterested justice."[12] Eleven years after the publication of *An American Crisis*, Michael Les Benedict credited Brock and a school of like-minded contemporary historians with having reversed the scholarly view of Reconstruction. A generation earlier, the radical Republicans had been villains; now they were heroes.[13] Peter Novick similarly notes that the historiographical view of abolitionists became dramatically more favorable during the 1950s and 1960s. Between the world wars, historians tended to write about the American Civil War in the same way that they thought about World War I, that is, as the pointless tragedy of a blundering generation. Then, when World War II replaced the first as the dominant historical prism, people began to write about the American Civil War as a great moral crusade.[14] This reversal occurred simultaneously with the rise of the civil rights movement; it is not an accident that histories of the Reconstruction era emphasizing principles of legal equality appeared during a time of intense preoccupation with extending legal rights to disfranchised Americans. When Richards seeks to substantiate the march-of-principle view of Reconstruction rights, he draws upon the generation of historians who reversed understandings of the Civil War in the 1950s and 1960s.[15]

The "underlying principle" approach was not a twentieth-century invention. Prominent figures of Reconstruction engaged in synthetic argument at the time, maintaining that their project was the fulfillment of Founding-era principles of rights. Immediately upon his election as Speaker of the House of Representatives for the first

---

[12] Ibid., passim, esp. pp. 2–14; direct quotes from pp. 62–67, 10, Brock quoting radical senator Ben Wade from *Congressional Globe*, 38th Congress, 2nd session, p. 165; ibid., pp. 113–115.

[13] Michael Les Benedict, *A Compromise of Principle: Congressional Republicans and Reconstruction, 1863–1869* (Norton, 1974), p. 13.

[14] Peter Novick, *That Noble Dream: The "Objectivity Question" and the American Historical Profession* (Cambridge University Press, 1988), pp. 224–238, 350–351.

[15] Richards, *Conscience and the Constitution*, p. 114n. See also Jacobus tenBroek, *Equal Under Law* (Collier, 1965); Kenneth Stampp, *The Era of Reconstruction, 1865–1877* (Knopf, 1965). For further discussion of the rights climate of the 1950s and 1960s of which these books were a part, see chapter 5.

post-war Congress, Schuyler Colfax invoked the spirit of the Founding as the guide to the mission of the Congress. Colfax told the Congressmen that their task was to reestablish the state governments that had been overthrown during the Civil War so as to "afford what our Magna Charta, the Declaration of Independence, proclaims is the chief object of government – protection to all men in their inalienable rights."[16] The "underlying principle" view of Reconstruction tends to understand remarks like these as if Colfax and the Congress were, to use Dewey's image again, spectators, striving to see some fixed meaning of the Declaration and the rights it entailed.[17] But Colfax was not merely reporting static facts about the Declaration and its relationship to the Reconstruction Congress. He was engaging in what Gadamer calls a fusing of horizons, helping to synthesize Reconstruction rights with those inherited from the Founding by interpreting the Declaration so as to attribute a specific meaning to the activities of his own Congress. After all, documents and events of the Founding admitted of more than one meaning with regard to the rights issues of slavery, secession, and Reconstruction. When people like Colfax used Founding texts for Reconstruction purposes, they tried, sometimes successfully, to persuade their audiences to adopt some of those possible meanings rather than others.

Given the central place of emancipation and the rights of blacks in Reconstruction, synthesizing Reconstruction with the Founding required a suitable account of the relationship between the Founding and slavery. Thus, the "underlying principle" view of the relationship between the Founding and Reconstruction presents emancipation as the necessary consequence of Founding ideas about universal rights to human freedom. That argument, however, rests on the problematic presumption that slavery was incompatible with the rights that the Founders had asserted. As David Davis has shown, many leading Americans at the Founding saw no contradiction between their revolution and their slaveholding.[18] On some readings, slavery was a supporting pillar of American liberty. Harrington had argued that liberty relied upon the independence of people from

[16] *Congressional Globe*, 39th Congress, 1st session, 4 December, 1865, p. 5.
[17] John Dewey, "The Need for a Recovery of Philosophy," in *John Dewey: The Middle Works, 1899–1924* (Southern Illinois University Press, 1980), vol. 10, esp. pp. 22–23.
[18] David Brion Davis, *The Problem of Slavery in the Age of Revolution, 1770–1823* (Cornell University Press, 1975), pp. 245–284.

government and that such independence relied upon freehold
property, and freehold property in America commonly meant
slaves.[19] Edmund Burke had suggested that black slavery may have
in fact made Americans fiercer advocates of their own liberties, as
the specter of an entirely unfree life raised their regard for their own
freedom.[20] Chief Justice William Cushing of Massachusetts ruled in
1783 that slavery was incompatible with his state's constitution, but
not all jurists, or even all Northern jurists, resolved the tension in the
same way: in 1794, the highest court in Pennsylvania ruled that
slavery was consistent with that state's declaration of rights.[21] The
difference between these rulings did not stem from differences in the
codifications of rights in the two states, which were alike on the
relevant points, but from sincere disagreements as to whether blacks
had a right not to be slaves and whether free Americans had a right
to human slaves as a form of property. In the end, the Founders as a
class were profoundly multifold in their attitudes toward slavery.
That reality made synthesizing Founding rights discourse with that
of Reconstruction a project of political will, not merely a foregone
conclusion.

Concrete negation

Before the war: threats to Northern liberty
The rights of Reconstruction had roots in nineteenth-century crises
as well as in the ideas and experiences inherited from the Founding.
Accordingly, ambiguity among the Founders is only one of two
major reasons why the rights of Reconstruction cannot be understood as the proper, race-blind application of Founding principles to
areas where the Founders failed to apply them. The other is that

[19] On the Harringtonian influence in America, see J. G. A. Pocock, "Machiavelli, Harrington,
and English Political Ideologies in the Eighteenth Century," *William and Mary Quarterly*, 3rd
series, 22 (October 1965), 565 and passim. See also Pocock, *The Machiavellian Moment:
Florentine Political Thought and the Atlantic Republican Tradition* (Princeton University Press,
1975), pp. 385–387.
[20] See Burke's "Speech on Conciliation with America," in Edmund Burke, *The Works of
Edmund Burke* (Little, Brown, 1881), vol. II, pp. 123–124. As Judith Shklar noted, these ideas
about the compatibility of slavery and American liberty operate at the level of psychology
rather than morality. Burke may have described an attitude that slaveholding Americans
held, and that attitude is psychologically comprehensible but, Shklar maintained, morally
incoherent. See Judith N. Shklar, *American Citizenship: The Quest for Inclusion* (Harvard
University Press, 1991), p. 40.
[21] See Davis, *Problem of Slavery*, pp. 164–184, 319.

much of the rights discourse that set the stage for Reconstruction grew not from timeless principles but from reactions against adversities that did not commence until the Founding was long over. If anything, framing rights as matters of philosophy and abstract principle was much less common during Reconstruction than during either the Founding era or the post-World War II era, and the relative role of ad hoc reaction to specific adversities was correspondingly greater.

Northern whites began erecting a system of rights against what they perceived as Southern "Slave Power"[22] encroachments on their own liberties, powers, immunities, and entitlements well before the Civil War. Abolitionists and others who articulated rights against the Slave Power as matters of disinterested or universal justice had substantial impacts upon the rights discourse of the time, and their contributions to shaping American rights discourse through Reconstruction give great comfort to synthetic accounts that connect principles of Reconstruction both backward to certain elements of the Founding and forward to progressive twentieth-century movements. Nevertheless, the concrete regard of many Northerners for their own rights was also an important condition shaping the political discourse that eventually dismantled the Slave Power. As I will illustrate below, many Northerners became energized in the sectional conflict because of perceived threats to their own rights, including their rights of petition, free press, and free speech.

It is relatively easy to understand attitudes toward slavery among those who believed, for religious or philosophical reasons, that slavery was evil and that morality demanded certain basic rights of freedom for everyone. That attitude is familiar, and it is therefore not difficult for us to imagine people coming to hold that position merely by virtue of its internal strength. After all, the moral or rational power of an idea is one reason, often a strong reason, for the adoption or longevity of that idea. For many anti-slavery Americans, however, the causal reasons for which anti-slavery ideas gained hold were not identical with, or limited to, the direct philosophical justifications of those ideas. Elster's approach to the reasons for

---

[22] The "Slave Power" was the name that Northerners gave to an ill-defined but unquestionably pernicious cabal of Southerners and their agents supposedly dedicated to controlling government and society entirely in the interest of a few rich Southern planters. I will discuss the "Slave Power" and the impact of its image in more detail later in the chapter.

beliefs provides a good way to understand the pattern whereby Northern whites frequently established rights for blacks, Northern and Southern, as means to something else rather than as ends in themselves. As discussed previously, the causes of beliefs often differ from their justifications. Elster counsels that it therefore makes sense to seek causal and historical explanations even for beliefs that appear rational, because the rationality of a belief is not necessarily the reason for which it is adopted.[23] The causal reasons for many Northerners' having endorsed anti-slavery rights before and during the Civil War, as well as for their endorsing certain equality rights during Reconstruction, lay at least in part in historical circumstances external to ideas about the rights themselves.

Passage of the Reconstruction Amendments involved a coalition among people who embraced abolition and some kind of egalitarianism for many different reasons. Those reasons included *a priori* philosophizing about inalienable rights at one extreme and cynical political calculations at the other, and Elster's analysis is less applicable as one approaches either extreme. If a belief is really based on *a priori* philosophizing, then it is hard to differentiate its contents from the reasons for its being held; if someone adopts a normative political stance for purely cynical reasons, there is a sense in which there is no belief at all to be explained. But those two extremes did not exhaust the range of Republican opinion. There was also a large middle ground in which political and other factors contributed over time, in Elster's fashion, to the formation of beliefs in what would become the rights of Reconstruction. It would not be accurate to say that people occupying that middle ground did not sincerely believe in the rights that they promoted, nor would we fully understand their relation to those beliefs if we neglected the historical circumstances that conditioned them.

Rights of speech and petition: the Gag Rule

An early instance of threats to a right enjoyed by Northern whites prompting anti-slavery sentiment in the North concerned the so-called Gag Rule, a provision in the House of Representatives that prohibited discussions of slavery. In December 1835, Representative James Hammond of South Carolina proposed that Congress should

---

[23] Elster, "Bias, Belief, and Ideology," pp. 147–148; see also Bohman, *New Philosophy of Social Science*, pp. 198–199.

not receive anti-slavery petitions. John Calhoun, also of South Carolina, introduced a parallel motion in the Senate three weeks later. Many Southerners in Congress knew that the proposal might fall foul of the First Amendment right of petition, thus allowing abolitionists to win friends by aligning anti-slavery with the Bill of Rights. Some tried to finesse the issue legalistically, proposing that petitions should be received and immediately rejected or else referred to a committee which would have instructions to report against them.[24] In May 1836, the House finally moved to consider a resolution to receive but take no action whatsoever on any petitions regarding slavery or abolition. During the next week, Southern representatives repeatedly blocked Northern efforts, notably those of John Quincy Adams, to force open debate on the issue. Adams and other Northern representatives saw the Gag Rule not only as a protection of slavery but also as an abridgment of First Amendment rights, including legislators' rights to free speech and the public's right of petition: Adams called the Gag Rule "a direct violation of the Constitution of the United States, the rules of this House, and the rights of my constituents."[25]

When Congress adopted the Gag Rule despite these objections, public reaction was fierce. Determined to protect their right of petition against what they considered a dangerous encroachment, vast numbers of Americans sent slavery-related petitions to Congress in the year following the Gag Rule's passage. The number of anti-slavery petitions that Congress received rose from 23,000 in the year before the Gag Rule to 300,000 in the year after. Total membership in abolition societies in America at the time was only 100,000, suggesting that many people not firmly in the abolitionist camp moved toward anti-slavery because of their disgust at the Gag Rule. John Botts, a Representative from Virginia, believed that the Gag Rule "made more abolitionists in one year, by identifying the right of petition with the question of slavery, than the abolitionists would have made for themselves in twenty-five years."[26]

The rights of petition, free speech, jury trial, and habeas corpus became strong anti-slavery issues in the succeeding years, as Northerners saw those liberties restricted at the hands of the South. While

---

[24] William Freehling, *The Road to Disunion* (Oxford University Press, 1990), vol. I, pp. 311–330.
[25] *Congressional Globe*, 24th Congress, 1st session, 1837, pp. 383, 406.
[26] Russel B. Nye, *Fettered Freedom: Civil Liberties and the Slavery Controversy, 1830–1860* (Michigan State College Press, 1949), pp. 37, 53.

the Gag Rule hinted that the institution of slavery could ignore First Amendment rights, enforcement of the Fugitive Slave Laws repeatedly showed Northerners that slavery could override and eliminate traditional safeguards to individual liberty like jury trial and habeas corpus, both of which were denied to people captured as suspected runaway slaves. One fascinating instance in which Northerners opposed their rights to the institution of slavery occurred in 1842 when Adams presented a constituent petition asking for dissolution of the United States on the grounds that the federal government was abridging the rights of the people. Adams did not actually move for dissolution, saying instead that he merely presented to Congress a petition that his constituents had asked him to present as their representative. He did, however, argue that his constituents had a strong claim, and he invoked the Declaration of Independence's advocacy of changing or removing governments that abridged the people's rights. When asked to withdraw the petition, Adams refused, saying that to do so would be to sacrifice "the right of petition ... the right of habeas corpus ... the right of trial by jury ... [the rights of free press, free speech, and] every principle of liberty ... that might not be pleasing to members of the 'Peculiar Institution'" of slavery.[27]

Adams's use of the Declaration of Independence points to the question of the sources of the rights that Americans claimed at the time. Generally, rights discourse from the mid-nineteenth century through Reconstruction relied less upon abstract sources like nature and reason than did Founding rights discourse, placing more emphasis on positive law and the writings of the Founders themselves. Just as during the Founding, however, people on both sides of the major political rifts used the same sources to argue for the rights they favored. The Declaration is a prime example. Southern Congressmen excoriated Adams for invoking the Declaration on behalf of the rights of his petitioning constituents, but their successors a generation later routinely read the Declaration as conferring their right to secede. Jefferson Davis ended his monumental apologia for the Confederacy by invoking "the eternal principles of the Declaration of Independence ... the Bills of Rights ... [and] the natural rights of man" in favor of secession and the Southern cause generally.[28] Northerners

---

[27] Freehling, *Road to Disunion*, pp. 350–351.
[28] Jefferson Davis, *The Rise and Fall of the Confederate Government* (Thomas Yoseloff, 1958), vol. II, p. 763.

who felt that the inalienable rights of man expounded in the Declaration were directly opposed to the institution of slavery might have found this Confederate invocation of that document hypocritical, or at least astigmatic. Southerners, after all, were generally skeptical that the rights claims of the Declaration had political or legal force – except for the rights of revolution and secession, which they claimed more and more frequently as 1860 approached. Such selective readings would be hard to justify by any rules of textual interpretation.

The pattern of outcome-driven rights reasoning whereby one identifies some desirable entitlement, liberty, power, or immunity and only later associates it with some normatively binding source, whether or not such association is logically defensible, was neither unique to the South nor new to the nineteenth century. It was present throughout the Founding, and it recurred in the years leading up to the Civil War. Northerners found the anti-slavery right to liberty in the Declaration; Southerners found the right to secede. Northerners emphasized constitutional rights like free speech and petition, while Southerners emphasized constitutional rights to property and to freedom from a coercive central government.[29] In short, each side used rights language to defend its substantive political commitments, and each side "proved" the rights it claimed with the same sources. As during the Founding, the substantive commitments often drove the use and reading of sources rather than the other way around.

The right of free press

The right to petition was one right whose endangerment encouraged Northerners to regard slavery as inimical to their system of rights. Freedom of the press was another. During the late 1830s, abolitionist presses and mailings came under attack in some parts of the South. After a mob broke into a post office and burned mailings in Charleston, South Carolina, local officials began to censor abolitionist periodicals.[30] In Tuscaloosa, Alabama, a grand jury actually indicted a New York publisher for printing a monthly anti-slavery pamphlet, and the governor of Alabama asked New York to extradite the publisher.[31] These attempts at censorship on behalf of the

---

[29] James MacPherson, *Battle Cry of Freedom* (Oxford University Press, 1988), p. 241.
[30] Nye, *Fettered Freedom*, pp. 56–58. See also Freehling, *Road to Disunion*, pp. 291–292.
[31] New York declined. Nye, *Fettered Freedom*, p. 59.

institution of slavery helped to associate abolitionism with the right of free press, and many targets of censorship made political capital accordingly. For example, James G. Birney, who had published the anti-slavery *Philanthropist* in Kentucky and then been forced out of that slaveholding state, moved to free-soil Ohio and began printing the newspaper again. Once in Ohio, he described his cause more in terms of the right of free press than in terms of abolition.[32]

The most celebrated pro-slavery attack on freedom of the press involved Elijah Lovejoy, who was killed defending his printing press against an anti-abolition mob at Alton, Illinois. Lovejoy, who opposed slavery but did not regard himself as an abolitionist, had published an anti-slavery paper called the *Observer* in St. Louis, in the slave state of Missouri. Local opponents warned him that "Freedom of speech and press does not imply a moral right . . . to freely discuss the subject of slavery." Lovejoy was unimpressed. "Today a public meeting declares that you shall not discuss slavery, tomorrow another meeting decides it is against the peace of society that the principle of popery be discussed," he said.[33] "The next day a decree is issued against speaking against distilleries, dram shops, and drunkenness. And so on to the end of the chapter." Forced to leave St. Louis, Lovejoy reestablished his press across the river at Alton. On 23 August 1837, a mob destroyed his press. Lovejoy appealed to the public for contributions to rebuild in the name of free press, received sufficient contributions, and published anew. Although in a free state, Alton was still within the cultural ambit of the slave territory just across the river, and in November a town meeting there prohibited any discussion of slavery in local newspapers. Lovejoy announced that he would disregard the prohibition, and he gathered armed supporters to protect his press. On 7 November, a mob attacked the warehouse where the press was kept, killed Lovejoy, burned the building, destroyed the press, and dumped its remains into the Mississippi River.[34]

The attacks on Lovejoy and other publishers did a great deal to associate the anti-slavery movement with "rights" – that is, the

---

[32] Ibid., pp. 100–101.

[33] It is a bit ironic to a modern observer that the right to condemn slavery should have been justified in terms of the right to express anti-Catholic prejudices. For Lovejoy, however, the legitimacy of condemning Catholicism was probably safe ground for consensus with his audience, even if the legitimacy of condemning slavery was in dispute.

[34] Nye, *Fettered Freedom*, pp. 115–119.

rights of whites – in the minds of moderate Northerners. Rights language is usually used to protect something endangered, and Northerners increasingly articulated rights against the Slave Power as slavery-related threats to particular liberties and sometimes lives became manifest. That Southerners would censor Northern mail and drive publishers out of their cities was bad enough. The idea, made vivid with Lovejoy's death, that the attack on free press could extend beyond the slave states and into the free North was particularly frightening.[35] Viewing these incidents together with the Gag Rule in Congress, many Northerners saw a dangerous undermining of their own rights. The possibility that Southern slavery might subvert the liberties of the free states seemed to become more and more real. E. P. Barrows wrote that "The tendency of [slavery] to suppress the freedom of speech and press is most alarming. Let this freedom, guaranteed to every citizen of the United States by the constitution, be once destroyed on this point, and it will be an easy work to destroy it on every other point."[36] Salmon P. Chase, who during Reconstruction would be Chief Justice of the United States, entered the anti-slavery movement out of disgust at violence against abolitionist printers.[37] William Ellery Channing, a prominent New England preacher, had opposed the abolitionists as dangerous and closed-minded fanatics until attacks on abolitionist presses changed his mind. He then decried a "systematic effort to strip the citizen of freedom of speech." In the attacks on abolitionists, he wrote, "the most sacred rights of the white man and the free man have been assailed. They [i.e., the abolitionists] are sufferers for liberty of thought, speech, and the press; and, in maintaining this liberty

---

[35] The reach of the Slave Power into Northern territory for purposes the North found odious was not new, of course. It had earlier manifested itself in connection with the fugitive slave laws, under which runaway slaves who reached free territory had to be returned to the South if captured by Southern slavehunters. In keeping with the general argument about rights and reactivity, I will note that several Northern states passed "personal liberty laws" in response to the fugitive slave laws. These Northern statutes gave fugitive slaves the rights of testimony, habeas corpus, and trial by jury when apprehended by slavehunters. Massachusetts, in response to a particularly well-publicized case of fugitive slavecatching, passed a law that refused to admit as evidence any statements that an alleged fugitive might make tending to indicate that he or she was, in fact, a runaway slave. For more on this topic, see Thomas Morris, *Free Men All: The Personal Liberty Laws of the North, 1780–1861* (Johns Hopkins University Press, 1974).

[36] Nye, *Fettered Freedom*, pp. 98–99.

[37] Eric Foner, *Free Soil, Free Labor, Free Men: The Ideology of the Republican Party Before the Civil War* (Oxford University Press, 1970), pp. 100–101.

amidst insult and violence, they deserve a place among its most honored defenders."[38]

The Slave Power conspiracy

By the 1850s, Northern concern that all civil liberties would fall victim to a Southern assault had spread beyond abolitionists. In large numbers and with increasing confidence, Northerners believed in a deliberate conspiracy to subjugate all of America to slaveholder interests. The conspiracy, organized by a demonic force called "the Slave Power," was thought to be operating throughout the country and at the highest levels of government.[39] Charles Francis Adams charged in 1855 that the Slave Power consisted of "three hundred and fifty thousand men, spreading over a large territorial surface, commanding the political resources of fifteen states" and all of "the official strongholds in the general government."[40] Abraham Lincoln echoed the conspiracy theme in his famous "House Divided" speech of 1858 when he described an alleged program of encroaching slavery, carried out over several years by high-level conspirators in the federal government.[41]

As David Davis describes in *The Slave Power Conspiracy and the Paranoid Style*, Northern fear of a Southern conspiracy to wreck the rights of ordinary Northern citizens could and did exaggerate wildly.[42] Nevertheless, Northerners had some reason to be concerned by the time of Lincoln's speech. One year earlier, the Supreme Court had ruled in *Dred Scott v. Sandford* that slaveholders could take their slave property with them into free territory without the slaves becoming free. In 1858, members of the Buchanan administration took the next logical step. If slaveholders could keep their slaves while traveling through "free" states, they reasoned, slavery could not really be prohibited anywhere in the United States. Some Southern congressmen predicted triumphantly that slavery would soon extend to the Canadian border.[43] In 1860, a case testing

---

[38] Nye, *Fettered Freedom*, p. 108.   [39] See Foner, *Free Soil*, pp. 97–102.

[40] Charles Francis Adams, *What Makes Slavery a Question of National Concern?* ... (Little, Brown, 1855), p. 27.

[41] Don E. Fehrenbacher, ed., *Abraham Lincoln: A Documentary Portrait Through His Speeches and Writings* (Stanford University Press, 1964), pp. 94–102.

[42] David Brion Davis, *The Slave Power Conspiracy and the Paranoid Style* (Louisiana State University Press, 1969).

[43] William Wiecek, *Liberty Under Law: The Supreme Court in American Life* (Johns Hopkins University Press, 1988), p. 81.

the constitutionality of the state slavery ban in New York went to the Supreme Court. The outbreak of the Civil War prevented the Court from ever ruling in the case, but, had it done so, it would probably have ruled against New York's law, and slavery would have come to the North.[44] Given what Northerners already knew about the effects of slavery on individual liberties – "the right of petition ravished and trampled ... the right of peaceable assembling violently wrested ... free speech struck dumb ... free presses cast into the streets and their fragments strewed with shoutings" – they had good reason, as they saw it, to believe that their own rights were in peril.[45]

In 1864, when the wartime Congress took up the question of a constitutional amendment to abolish slavery, its discussions reflected concern for the rights of Northern whites as well as for the rights of blacks. Important liberties, powers, and immunities of Northern whites had been threatened, and many in Congress were quick to use rights language in their defense. Charles Sumner, speaking in favor of the proposed Thirteenth Amendment abolishing slavery, charged that slavery violated rights of free speech, free press, and free transit.[46] Sumner also talked about "rights of sovereignty" and "rights of war" as they related to the propriety of emancipation. "The defiant pretensions of the master, claiming control of his slave, are in direct conflict with the paramount rights of the national Government," Sumner said, opposing the master's rights not only to the rights of the slave but also to the rights of the *government*. Among Sumner's less radical peers, uses of rights language to privilege Northern white liberties comprised a still greater proportion of anti-slavery arguments. Prominent Republicans like Senator Lyman Trumbull of Illinois and Representative James Ashley of Ohio routinely charged that slavery threatened basic rights such as free speech and free press, and they proposed to abolish slavery in order to secure those rights to the free people of the North.[47] In these anti-slavery arguments, political actors used rights language to prioritize what they considered to be important and in need of protection, which often meant their own liberties or the liberties of people like themselves.

---

[44] *Lemmon v. People*, 20 N.Y. 562 (1860). See also Foner, *Free Soil*, pp. 97–98.
[45] Theodore Dwight Weld, in tenBroek, *Equal Under Law*, pp. 125–126.
[46] *Congressional Globe*, 38th Congress, 1st session, 1863–64, p. 523.
[47] *Congressional Globe*, 38th Congress, 1st session, 1863–64, p. 1313; tenBroek, *Equal Under Law*, p. 166.

Some defenders of slavery understood this pattern. Senator Willard Saulsbury of Delaware, an opponent of emancipation, offered an alternative amendment just before the Senate adopted the Thirteenth Amendment, hoping to persuade the Senate to stop short of abolition. Saulsbury's proposed amendment would have protected the rights of free religion, free press, free speech, assembly, access to voting, and habeas corpus. The amendment would also have banned slavery or slave transit north of the Missouri compromise line and secured jury trials to persons accused of being fugitives.[48] This proposal was a last-ditch effort to derail abolition, and its chosen tactic was to appease all the related complaints. Northerners accused slavery of poisoning their rights to free press, so this amendment would protect free press, and so on for each of the other provisions. Saulsbury's amendment failed, but his assessment of the motivation of the legislative majority was perceptive. He recognized that the North was about to abolish slavery for a combination of first- and second-order reasons: not just because slavery infringed rights of people held as slaves but also because it endangered other rights of non-slaves. Fearing for their own rights, Northerners moved to destroy the endangering force, the Slave Power, and then, to prevent its return, created a new set of rights: the rights against being held as a slave.

After the war: commitments to the rights of labor and the rights of blacks
The interplay between inherited principles and concrete negation of recent adversities in the formation of rights discourse continued through the Civil War and into the years of Reconstruction proper. Many codifications of rights during Reconstruction used very broad language that evoked principles of the Founding. The Fourteenth Amendment's language of equal protection, due process, and life, liberty and property provides obvious examples. To the authors and authoritative interpreters of the Reconstruction Amendments, however, the landmark rights codifications of the time actually protected only narrow subsets of the rights that their language would guarantee if read as broad statements of principle. Courts often held the rights announced in the Reconstruction Amendments to be applicable only where there was some link to the central institution against which Reconstruction had reacted: black slave labor. That

---

[48] *Congressional Globe*, 38th Congress, 1st session, 1863–64, pp. 1489–1490.

pattern had two variants. First, courts frequently showed greater zeal in protecting Reconstruction rights pertaining to labor issues than those pertaining to other matters. Second, instead of applying rights to all Americans regardless of race, Reconstruction rights were frequently interpreted as conferring rights particularly on blacks. These limited applications of rights that were codified in much broader terms reflected a contemporary understanding of what was most important and in need of protection – the basic criteria for the formation of conceptions of rights. Even where the influence of broad principles of political morality fostered sweeping declarations of rights, Reconstruction often realized only those rights that also drew upon the concrete negation of specifically disfavored experiences.

Special regard for free labor rights

The courts guarded vigilantly against slavery-like subversions of market freedoms. In Maryland in 1867, a former slave named Elizabeth Turner signed a contract with her former master, ostensibly apprenticing her to learn to be a domestic servant. The contract substantially limited Turner's personal liberty. She subsequently sought to be released from the contract, and Chief Justice Salmon Chase, riding circuit, found in her favor. According to Chase, the terms of the contract were "subterfuges for slavery" and thus violated the Thirteenth Amendment.[49] On strictly formal grounds, Chase could have found that Turner's rights were not being abridged, because the limitations imposed upon her were contractual. Chase, on the lookout for slavery, chose to see a deeper reality and concluded that Turner's rights had been violated.

Where other kinds of rights were concerned, however, the courts read much more narrowly. One particularly egregious example occurred in *Blyew v. United States*, a Kentucky case in which the only witnesses to the murder of a black woman were black. Kentucky courts did not admit black testimony, and a federal court declined to overrule that restriction under the Civil Rights Act. The Civil Rights Act, the court said, granted rights of judicial access to black citizens only in cases "the decisions of which might injuriously affect them either in their personal, relative, or property rights." None of these

---

[49] *In re Turner*, 24 F. Cas. 337 (1867); Harold Hyman and William Wiecek, *Equal Justice Under Law: Constitutional Development 1835–1875* (Harper & Row, 1982), p. 434.

applied in the case at hand, because the woman affected was dead and therefore, the court held, without rights.[50] Similarly, the Supreme Court in *US v. Cruikshank* held that Louisiana whites who had murdered blacks could not be indicted in federal jurisdiction under any of the Reconstruction laws or amendments, because murder did not violate a federal right.[51] If, as the Court would later claim, the right to contract and to free labor generally could be found in the Fourteenth Amendment guarantee of "life, liberty, and property," then the reasoning of *Cruikshank* appears thoroughly precarious. If deprivations of property contravened a federal right, then so must deprivations of life. A defender of the Court could point out that, in a formal sense, the Amendment only protected rights against state actions and that the murders in *Cruikshank* were private acts. In light of Chase's willingness in the Turner case to find slavery where a contract formally existed, however, it is clear that the judiciary was sometimes willing to consider realities deeper than the surface if the rights being violated were sufficiently important. Why the *Cruikshank* Court could not have found that the state of Louisiana violated black citizens' rights to life or access to law by failing to pursue and punish murderers of blacks on equal terms with murderers of whites thus requires explanation. Prosecution, after all, is state action, as is a decision not to prosecute, and it was only Louisiana's failure to prosecute the white murderers of black victims that made federal action necessary. Without the specific historical background of the struggle against the Slave Power, it would be difficult to understand why any court would place a higher priority on finding a way to break a domestic service contract than on finding a way to punish murderers. The historical background, however, is essential, and it points to the reason for the difference in judicial approach between these cases. One dealt with labor, property, contract: the issues of the Slave Power struggle. The corresponding rights enjoyed high priority. The other case, in contrast, did not resonate with concrete negation of Slave Power adversity as Reconstruction Republicans understood it. There was therefore less motivation to find a way to vindicate the rights at issue.

In 1883, in a connected set of cases called the *Civil Rights Cases*, the Supreme Court ruled explicitly on whether the Constitution

---

[50] *Blylew v. United States*, 80 U.S. 581 (1873).
[51] *United States v. Cruikshank*, 92 U.S. 542 (1875).

after Reconstruction allowed Congress to guarantee equal rights to black citizens broadly or whether blacks held only rights against involuntary servitude, narrowly construed. The Court upheld the narrow interpretation.[52] In a solitary dissent, Justice John Marshall Harlan wrote that the purpose of the Thirteenth Amendment was to abolish slavery in America. Because that slavery "rested wholly upon the inferiority, as a race, of those held in bondage," he wrote, "their freedom necessarily involved immunity from, and protection against, all discrimination against them, because of their race, in respect of such civil rights as belong to freemen of other races."[53] Harlan's dissent captured the insight that whatever rights blacks could obtain during Reconstruction would have to be rooted in reactions against slavery. It was as necessary conditions of their freedom – that is, their non-slavery – that Harlan argued for broader rights for blacks. Racial subordination was not, however, the aspect of slavery that repulsed most of the Court. Harlan's argument was as reactive as that of the Court's majority; where they differed was in their conceptions of the thing being reacted against. Harlan thought that the evil of slavery lay in the subordination of one race to another. The majority, however, located the problem elsewhere, in the endangerment of established rights and the denial of free labor, and the Court's reaction against slavery construed as something other than racial subordination yielded rights other than rights of racial equality. In light of later history, Harlan's dissent seems to imply that blacks could only come to possess broader rights of equality when Americans reacted against the concept of "inferiority as a race." In other words, Harlan saw racial equality as important and in need of protection, and he therefore took a broader view of black rights than did his contemporaries, whose view of what was important and in need of protection was focused elsewhere. For Harlan's position on black rights to be adopted, the dominant conception of what it was that was important and to be protected would have to change. That would happen only sixty years later.

---

[52] Among the issues on which the cases turned was the technical distinction, popular in Reconstruction-era constitutional law, between "civil rights" and "social rights" mentioned in this chapter's introduction. I discuss that distinction in greater detail, including its application to the Civil Rights Cases, in the second part of this chapter.

[53] *Civil Rights Cases*, 109 U.S. 3, at 36 (1883).

Special regard for the rights of blacks

That Reconstruction rights discourse did not aim at general black equality does not mean that blacks were always disadvantaged in the application of Reconstruction rights. Sometimes, the opposite was the case. Even when the Reconstruction Amendments or other legislation used racially nonspecific language to confer rights, those rights were often interpreted as applying only to blacks. Rights as various and as important as free labor, suffrage, and standing at law were interpreted to belong to black Americans under the post-war Amendments and civil rights acts but not to belong to certain classes of non-black Americans, even though the relevant legislation did not name blacks as a privileged class. For example, Representative Robert Hale of New York said that the Fourteenth Amendment was intended to protect only "American citizens of African descent."[54] The language of the Fourteenth Amendment, of course, does not single out Americans of any particular "descent." An amendment whose racially nonspecific language is held to apply only to a specific racial group is, of course, a text in which meaning and expression are importantly distinct and therefore a prime candidate for hermeneutic analysis. In this case, the underlying coherence in the problematic text lies in the then-dominant Republican conception of what Reconstruction rights were supposed to protect. The more directly a phenomenon was connected to black slave labor, the more likely Reconstruction Republicans were to articulate and enforce rights against it. Just as the rights of labor had special force, so sometimes did the rights of blacks, and for substantially the same reason.

In the so-called *Slaughterhouse Cases* of 1873, the Supreme Court held that a group of white Louisiana butchers could not claim the protection of the Thirteenth and Fourteenth Amendments.[55]

---

[54] *Congressional Globe*, 39th Congress, 1st session, 27 February 1866, p. 1065.

[55] Once Reconstruction rights were codified in law, their authoritative interpretation passed from legislators to judges, and members of Congress, as at other times in history, were not always happy with judicial interpretations. One cannot rely upon court rulings to indicate legislative intent – indeed, one cannot even be sure that legislative records indicate legislative intent. It is not even clear what "legislative intent" might meaningfully be, given that allies within a legislature can and usually do have different reasons for supporting a certain measure. When I discuss judicial opinions on questions of Reconstruction rights, I aim to establish not authorial intent but authoritative interpretation. The courts determined how Reconstruction rights would be made part of the larger American rights system and how those rights would be applied for the several decades following. Throughout this book, I present the legal sphere as an interpretive rationalizer of successive strata of rights, and it is with that intent that I present court rulings on Reconstruction rights.

Louisiana had required all butchers in a certain area to use a single designated facility for their work, effectively creating a state-regulated monopoly. The butchers argued that the state of Louisiana, by dictating where and under what conditions they could work, violated their rights under the Thirteenth Amendment by imposing a form of involuntary servitude and under the Fourteenth Amendment by depriving them of liberty and property. The Supreme Court disagreed. True to the understanding of men like Hale, the Court held that the Reconstruction Amendments had been written and adopted for the purpose of ending black slavery and that the rights they conferred should be interpreted accordingly. For white citizens to claim the protection of those Amendments, the Court ruled, would distort their true meaning. The Court was also untroubled by the possibility that the Fourteenth Amendment's equal protection clause required that any rights accorded to blacks be accorded to whites as well. "We doubt very much," the Court wrote, "whether any action of a State, not directed by way of discrimination against the negroes, as a class, will ever be held to come within the purview of that provision."[56] Reconstruction rights discourse, like rights discourse in general, tended to confer rights-status on particular propositions if those propositions were important and in need of protection, and importance and endangerment tend to be functions of specific historical conditions. Accordingly, the Court interpreted Reconstruction rights in the *Slaughterhouse Cases* as applying specifically to blacks because the specific historical conditions that then obtained made black free labor a more critical issue than white free labor, as well as more in need of protection.

The right of suffrage, discussed in greater detail below, was another right whose expansion was limited to blacks. In the heavily Republican state of California, for example, the majority favored black suffrage but opposed suffrage for Chinese immigrants and their American-born descendants.[57] It is similarly noteworthy that the Fifteenth Amendment's text, prohibiting discrimination in voting based upon "race, color, or previous condition of servitude," was adopted only after Congress rejected a broader proposal under which discrimination would have been banned with reference to officeholding as well as to voting and with respect to "nativity,

---

[56] *Slaughterhouse Cases*, 83 U.S. 36, 81 (1873).
[57] William Gillete, *The Right to Vote* (Johns Hopkins University Press, 1969), pp. 153–158.

property, education, or religious beliefs" as well as the categories that the eventual amendment named. (Female suffrage did not even get that far.) The Republican Congress's refusal to prohibit discrimination in those categories is partly comprehensible in electoral terms: in the North, immigrants, the poor, and the uneducated tended to support the Democrats. But the willingness to recognize a right to vote for blacks and not for other disfranchised people is also partly comprehensible in terms of specific concerns made important by recent political crises. The country had just fought a war over the status of blacks, not the status of the poor or the illiterate, and it was accordingly upon blacks that new rights would be conferred.

Another example of broad expressions of rights carrying narrow and racially specific meanings involved the right of access to law. As a "civil" rather than a political or a social right, access to law was supposedly made race-blind by civil rights legislation. The relevant principle of equality, however, was that *blacks* should enjoy the right equally with whites, not that all people should enjoy the right regardless of race. In 1869, a California court highlighted this narrow understanding of equality when it dismissed a criminal case involving a black defendant and a Chinese witness for the prosecution. According to the court, blacks had the same rights as whites. One of those rights, in California, was the right not to be testified against by Asians. The black defendant could not be convicted without this witness's testimony and was therefore released in accordance with his "equal" rights.[58]

If Asian-Americans were to benefit from the rights of Reconstruction, it would have to be in connection with prevailing commitments other than those which benefited blacks as such. The other major commitment of Reconstruction rights discourse, to free labor, sometimes served the purpose. In *Yick Wo v. Hopkins*, the Supreme Court ruled that city officials in San Francisco were violating the rights of Chinese laundry workers by arbitrarily denying them operating licenses. "The very idea that one man may be compelled to hold his life, or the means of living, or any material right essential to the enjoyment of life, at the mere will of another, seems to be intolerable in any country where freedom prevails, as being the essence of slavery itself," the Court held, granting the laundry workers relief under the Thirteenth and Fourteenth Amendments.[59] Thus, Recon-

---

[58] *People v. Washington*, 36 Cal. 658 (1869).   [59] *Yick Wo v. Hopkins*, 118 U.S. 356 (1886).

struction rights were not interpreted in a way that systematically excluded Asians.[60] *Yick Wo* was not, however, decided as a matter of racial equality; that its petitioner was an Asian-American was more or less incidental. It was decided with reference to a non-racial issue, free labor, that resonated as specifically with the Slave Power struggle as did blackness.[61]

CIVIL, POLITICAL, AND SOCIAL RIGHTS: A CONSTITUTIONAL SHELL GAME

During the debate over the Thirteenth Amendment, some Republicans had assumed that, with the abolition of slavery, the rights enjoyed by whites would be extended to blacks on equal terms.[62] That is the position that scholars like Richards and Brock consider the essence of Reconstruction. But the Republicans who held that view were a minority; most wanted to grant some rights to blacks while refusing them the equal enjoyment of other rights, and that was how Reconstruction in fact proceeded. In keeping with the pattern by which concrete negations of adversity shape rights discourse, which rights were extended to blacks was largely influenced by the content of the evils that Republicans had recently faced. The political commitments that most heavily informed Reconstruction's dominant theory of rights were shaped in reaction to the struggle against the Slave Power. As many Northern Republicans saw it, the fight against slavery had been chiefly a fight against slave

---

[60] The same rights deemed available to Asian-Americans were, however, systematically denied to women. In *Bradwell v. Illinois*, 83 U.S. 130 (1873), the Supreme Court ruled against a white woman who argued that her right to choose a profession was unconstitutionally violated by a state law requiring that lawyers be male. Even if this right extended beyond blacks, it was not held to apply to all people.

[61] The Court's holding in *Yick Wo* might be thought at odds with its doctrine in *Slaughterhouse* that Fourteenth Amendment rights applied only to blacks, but it is possible to make sense of the difference in approaches between the two cases. *Slaughterhouse* involved only regulation of professional conduct whereas *Yick Wo* involved complete exclusion from a profession, and the right to choose one's occupation is not the same as the right to practice an occupation in whatever way one likes. Some regulation of professional conduct is bound to fall within a state's police powers. Moreover, thirteen years and a major shift in political conditions separated *Yick Wo* from *Slaughterhouse*. In 1873, the year of *Slaughterhouse*, the national government was still actively involved in trying to guarantee the rights of Southern blacks. By 1886, when *Yick Wo* was decided, Reconstruction was officially dead and white state governments controlled Southern affairs with little federal interference. The substantive commitment to the rights of blacks had faded, but the commitment to rights of labor and contract persisted for another two generations.

[62] Foner, *Reconstruction*, p. 67; Hyman and Wiecek, *Equal Justice Under Law*, pp. 276–278.

labor rather than against the personal or racial subordination of blacks. Most Republicans during and after Reconstruction were accordingly concerned with guaranteeing blacks the rights necessary to a free labor system, such as rights of contract, property, movement, and access to courts of law, but most Republicans saw no need to grant blacks rights to vote and hold office.[63] In the course of justifying this selective extension of rights to blacks, Reconstruction Republicans developed a theory about the nature of rights, a theory that acted as a vehicle for their reactively formed preferences.

The main feature of that theory was a division of rights into three categories: civil, political, and social.[64] No authoritative document ever defined those terms, and Reconstruction produced no definitive list of rights in which different rights were classified as one or the other. The many political and legal actors who spoke and wrote about rights using these terms did not always employ the categories in the same way. Most of the scholarship on Reconstruction rights, however, has sidestepped these inconsistencies, preferring to construct accounts of the tripartite typology as a coherent system. Historians like Brock, Hyman, Wiecek, and Foner have all produced similar though non-identical versions of the distinctions between civil, political, and social rights. Drawing on their work, Akhil Amar has developed what is probably the most robust version of such a theory in the field of constitutional law.[65]

All these accounts agree on certain aspects of the system. Perhaps most importantly, all agree that the dominant opinion among Republicans early in Reconstruction was that only civil rights attached to all persons equally. Where political and social rights were concerned, blacks were not necessarily entitled to the same rights as whites.[66] Existing scholarly accounts also largely agree on

---

[63] Foner, *Free Soil*, pp. 290–292, shows that Republicans held this position as early as 1858.

[64] "Natural rights" such as life, liberty, and the pursuit of happiness sometimes comprised a fourth class. The meanings of those terms were never settled, but at the very least respect for natural rights required the abolition of chattel slavery and minimal personal freedoms like locomotion. That natural rights attached to all persons equally was no longer controversial during Reconstruction, and the real work of the theory concerned the other three categories.

[65] See, e.g., Amar, *The Bill of Rights*, pp. 258–259, 271–274; Amar, "The Fifteenth Amendment and 'Political Rights'," *Cardozo Law Review* 17, 2225 (1996); Amar, "The Bill of Rights and the Fourteenth Amendment," *Yale Law Journal* 101, 1193, at 1198–1260 (1992); Amar, "The Bill of Rights as a Constitution," *Yale Law Journal* 100, 1131, at 1164, 1176, 1202–1203, and text accompanying n. 152 (1991).

[66] Brock, *American Crisis*, pp. 19–20; Foner, *Reconstruction*, pp. 67, 231; Wiecek, *Liberty Under Law,*

the substance of the three categories. "Civil rights" were conceived as the rights that people must hold in order to act as private individuals in civil society, capable of personal independence and self-sufficiency. The advisedly named Civil Rights Act of 1866 guaranteed black freedmen the rights "to make and enforce contracts, to sue, be parties, and give evidence, to inherit, purchase, lease, sell, hold, and convey real and personal property, and to full and equal benefit of all laws and proceedings for the security of person and property."[67] These rights were the minimum basic requirements for distinguishing free persons from slave laborers. Not coincidentally, they were the rights most readily extended to blacks. "Political rights," paradigmatically suffrage and the right to hold office, were not as quickly conferred. According to Amar's thick theory of Reconstruction rights, the category of political rights encompassed all the rights associated with the Republican tradition of participatory citizenship, including not just suffrage and officeholding but also the right to sit on juries and the right to serve in the military.[68] "Social rights" dealt on some accounts with personal and private matters, such as access to privately organized schools; slightly different accounts, including Sunstein's, maintain that social rights encompassed access to education generally, as well as access to public transportation and public accommodations.[69]

At the same time, Reconstruction scholarship often contains

---

p. 94; Hyman and Wiecek, *Equal Justice Under Law*, pp. 276–278. See also *Civil Rights Cases*, *Ex Parte Virginia*, 100 U.S. 339 (1880), especially dissent of Justice Field.

[67] Harold Hyman, ed., *The Radical Republicans and Reconstruction, 1861–1870* (Bobbs-Merrill, 1967), pp. 308–318.

[68] Amar, "The Bill of Rights and the Fourteenth Amendment," pp. 1261–1262; Amar, "The Bill of Rights as a Constitution," pp. 1164, 1176, 1202.

[69] Sunstein, *The Partial Constitution*, p. 42. The scheme was similar to that which T. H. Marshall presented in *Citizenship and Social Class* (Cambridge University Press, 1950), in which he famously distinguished civil, political, and social components of citizenship. The civil component, Marshall wrote, incorporates "the rights necessary for individual freedom," in which he included freedoms of speech, faith, and movement, rights of contract and property, and access to equal justice. Courts of law are the relevant institutions for the regulation and enforcement of civil rights. The political component, Marshall continued, incorporates the rights to elect and be elected, and the corresponding institutions are legislative government bodies. Finally, the social component included the right to minimum economic welfare and "the right to share to the full in the social heritage." The most relevant institutions for this social component are schools and social services (Marshall, pp. 10–11). Marshall's typology, designed with Britain rather than America in mind, does not completely map the Reconstruction system of classification. Nevertheless, it bears substantial resemblance to the classifications of rights popular in early Reconstruction.

conflicting claims about which rights fell into which categories. For example, Wiecek and Sunstein describe education as a social right, but Brock identifies it as a political right.[70] Scholarly accounts also sometimes conflict with important primary sources along the same lines: for example, Amar classifies the right to serve on juries as political, but the Supreme Court in the *Civil Rights Cases* classified it as civil.[71] Most such differences reflect not errors in scholarly reporting but the fundamental instability of the categories. During Reconstruction, whether a given right was civil, political, or social was often a matter of controversy, and the primary sources themselves are often in conflict about how rights are to be classified. Indeed, the very definitions of the categories were contested. For example, many people during Reconstruction defined "political rights" as those connected with participation in the political activities of citizenship, as Amar's account suggests, but others held that "political rights" were simply those which it was in the discretion of the political process to confer or withhold.[72] Under the second definition, the right to education and the right to use public transportation were sometimes considered "political rights," which they could not have been under the first. Brock is thus partially correct to say that education was a political right, and Wiecek and Sunstein are partially correct to say that it was social: depending on which documents one examines, one can find Reconstruction sources identifying it as one or the other. Similarly, Amar is partially correct to say that jury service was a political right. Some people at some times during Reconstruction held that view, but other people at various times did not.

The shortcoming in most modern scholarly accounts of the Reconstruction rights typology begins with the failure to recognize that many rights were not clearly fixed in one category or another. Existing scholarship on the typology sees it as static, with the categories "civil," "political," and "social" relatively determinate and given rights falling into their given places. But the typology was in fact dynamic: rights migrated from one category to another. Like coins in a shell game, rights seen at any given time under one category might quickly be gone from that category and appear

---

[70] Brock, *American Crisis*, pp. 19–20; Sunstein, *The Partial Constitution*, p. 42; Wiecek, *Liberty Under Law*, p. 94.
[71] Amar, *The Bill of Rights*, pp. 48, 271–274; *Civil Rights Cases*, at 17.
[72] See, e.g., *Ex Parte Virginia*, at 386 (Field, J., dissenting).

instead under another heading.[73] Moreover, the migration of rights among categories was not random. The major pattern of change was the transformation of social and political rights into civil rights, and that pattern holds the key to understanding the substantive political function that the typology performed. Partly because scholars who have tried to describe the civil/political/social scheme have seen the system as formal and static, they have treated the framework as descriptive of differences among rights rather than as constitutive of those differences. It has thus largely neglected the question of what substantive values or ends that system served or what work it was used to accomplish. But the typology arose in the specific political context of Reconstruction, and its ostensibly formal categories were a temporally specific articulation of a shifting set of political commitments.

Prior to the Civil War, American law did not know the scheme of civil, political, and social rights as it operated during Reconstruction. There were some broad conceptual links among jury service, military service, and suffrage, but those activities were not components of a known category called "political rights." Conversely, the terms "civil rights" and "political rights" were sometimes used, but not in a way that aligns with the Reconstruction typology. No less an antebellum authority than Joseph Story discussed civil and political rights in a way that directly contradicts what Amar, the

---

[73] In his most recent work on the subject, Amar recognizes a longer-term mutability of the categories, noting that the right to bear arms was decidedly political at the Founding but in some ways reimagined as civil during Reconstruction. Amar, *Bill of Rights*, pp. 258–259. For Amar, this change was bound up with a substantive change in the right. The Founding political right to bear arms was public and collective, he says, and its subject was communities organizing themselves into militias in the spirit of republican participation. The Reconstruction civil right was private and individualistic and largely about personal self-protection. Analyzing how particular rights assumed different meanings at different times is a central aim of my current argument, and Amar's chronicling of some such changes in conceptions of rights is, from my perspective, one of the great strengths of his book. I would, however, take his account of changes in the tripartite theory of rights farther than he does. More rights moved than Amar seems to notice. Moreover, Amar's account of a right migrating from one category to another, as above, may actually be a story about how one right – republican arms-bearing – is political and an analytically distinct right traveling under the same name – gun ownership – is civil. In that kind of "movement," what changes is the meaning people attribute to "the right to bear arms" rather than whether a right with some particular substance is civil or political. It is therefore compatible with there having been an analytically stable classification of rights as civil, political, and social. I suggest, in contrast, that key rights including jury service and suffrage actually moved from the political to the civil category without undergoing any analytic alteration, and that the tripartite theory was never as analytically stable as later scholarship has imagined.

most sophisticated modern explicator of the Reconstruction scheme, takes to be the fundamental relationship between them. According to Amar, civil rights are held by a broader class of persons than are political rights. That was certainly the case during Reconstruction. Amar takes the status of single white women in the nineteenth century to exemplify the condition of holding civil rights but not political ones, and if "civil rights" and "political rights" mean what Amar claims, which is roughly what they meant at the very beginning of Reconstruction, his example is well-chosen.[74] Unmarried women could own property, make contracts, and be parties to lawsuits, but they could not vote or serve on juries. But before the Civil War, Justice Story wrote that women enjoyed *political* rights even when marriage, which imposed certain legal incapacities on women at common law, extinguished some of their *civil* rights.[75] Clearly, Story cannot have meant by "political rights" what Amar means: women did not vote or serve on juries in Story's lifetime. He had a different conception of political rights entirely, according to which "political rights" meant rights derived from treaties and the law of nations. His statement that married women enjoyed political rights even when they did not enjoy full civil rights runs contrary to the idea that political rights are systematically more exclusive than civil rights. That hierarchical idea was new in Reconstruction, and it is sensible to ask what purpose that innovation in rights theory served. Reconstruction Republicans, I suggest, wanted to dismantle the Slave Power and grant certain rights to blacks, but most were not committed to full black equality in spheres not implicated by their generation's crisis. The tripartite theory of rights was a convenient vehicle for implementing the limited enfranchisement of blacks that their politics supported: rights that were to be extended to blacks could be called "civil," a kind of right that attached to everyone, and rights that might still be withheld could be called "political" or "social."

Inconsistencies in Reconstruction-era sources over whether a certain right fell in one category or another were often disputes not just about the analytic nature of the right in question but about the normative desirability of conferring that right on blacks. Over time, as blacks gained more and more of the rights previously denied to

---

[74] Amar, *Bill of Rights*, pp. 48, 260.
[75] *Shanks v. DuPont*, 28 U.S. 242, at 248 (1830). The "political right" in question in this case was a married woman's right to elect her country of citizenship.

them, more and more rights came to be described as "civil," that is, rights of the kind that attach to everyone. Trying to establish in which of the three Reconstruction categories particular rights "actually" belonged, I suggest, misses the real essence of the typology, as does asserting that a given right was "really" a political rather than a civil right. The best understanding of the tripartite scheme sees it as a way in which many Reconstruction politicians and judges used an ostensibly formal theory about the nature of rights to give force to their specific and changing political commitments, commitments largely formed reactively in the fight against the Slave Power.

The rights that most obviously had to be extended to blacks if the Slave Power were to be dismantled were the rights of contract, property, personal mobility, and access to law, and those rights were from the very beginning of Reconstruction classified as "civil." As time went on, more and more Republicans saw the need or the wisdom of extending other rights to blacks as well. Among the rights that blacks later came to enjoy were two rights that had originally been at the core of the category of "political rights": the right to vote and the right to serve on juries. According to Amar, the Fifteenth Amendment did for political rights what the Fourteenth had done for civil rights, that is, extended the rights in that category to all people regardless of race.[76] That claim offers a consistent analytic view of Reconstruction rights, but it does not map the actual usage of Reconstruction-era courts and legislatures. After the Fifteenth Amendment was passed, most legislative and judicial sources continued to maintain that blacks were guaranteed equality only of civil rights and began to speak of suffrage as a civil right, rather than saying that suffrage was a political right and that both civil and political rights applied equally to blacks and whites. Later, when racial discrimination was banned in jury service, people began to speak of jury service as a civil right as well.

The extension of these rights to blacks was piecemeal rather than systemic: one right and then another was extended, and each right was redescribed as "civil" by those who made it available to blacks. Nor was it only "political" rights that became civil in the mouths of those who advanced the rights of blacks: for example, the *Civil Rights Act* of 1875 granted blacks rights that most modern scholar-

---

[76] Amar, *Bill of Rights*, p. 274n; Amar, "The Fifteenth Amendment and 'Political Rights'," pp. 2225, 2227, 2228.

ship (and the Act's contemporary opponents) has classified as not civil but social, like the right to use public transportation and accommodations. Congress did not say, however, that it was making social rights available to blacks. It merely moved the rights that it made available under a different shell, calling them civil rights rather than social ones. By the end of Reconstruction, "civil rights" were clearly coterminous with the rights of blacks. In later generations when it was no longer possible to assert that blacks had some but not all the rights of whites, the distinctions among civil, political, and social rights were all but forgotten. "Civil rights" became synonymous with legal or constitutional rights in general, especially as connected with the rights of blacks.

The right to vote

At the start of Reconstruction, some Republicans pointedly denied that suffrage was a "right" at all, claiming that it was a "privilege" to which blacks were not necessarily entitled.[77] Distinguishing between rights and privileges echoes Hohfeld, but the echo is false – and nevertheless illuminating. Hohfeld maintained that rights and privileges were analytically dissimilar, and the Republicans who classified suffrage as a privilege and not a right implicitly agreed. The nature of the dissimilarity, however, is not the same in both theories. Hohfeld used the rights/privileges distinction to show the difference between situations involving duties and situations involving the absence of duties: A's right, according to Hohfeld, is correlated with B's duty toward A, and A's privilege is correlated with A's lack of a duty toward B. This view of the difference between rights and privileges is analytic only. According to Hohfeld, whether something is a right or a privilege has no normative import and no necessary political consequences. In contrast, the Republican contention that suffrage was a privilege but not a right relied upon the different political force of those two terms. The point of making that distinction was to justify continued disfranchisement of blacks. To deny black Americans a *right* would be unjust, this Republican might argue, but *privileges* are legitimately vested in some people and not others. Whether suffrage is a right or a privilege is in that context a political question and not, as it would be under Hohfeld's scheme, a

---

[77] Foner, *Reconstruction*, p. 231.

purely analytic one.[78] That the question of whether suffrage was a right as opposed to a privilege was thoroughly political suggests a key shortcoming in Hohfeld's typology, as I argued in chapter 1: in American political discourse, rights enjoy a priority and a claim to special protection that privileges do not, and no theory of rights that ignores that aspect is adequate for understanding the place of rights in American political or moral debate.

There were, however, other Republicans who did regard suffrage as a right, albeit not a right enjoyed by all people. For them, the question was what kind of a right it was. At the beginning of Reconstruction, many hoped to answer that question in some way that would not obligate them to enfranchise blacks. After all, most Republicans then opposed black suffrage. At the time of the Civil War, no state outside New England permitted blacks to vote. The Northern rump Congress in 1864 organized the Montana territory with white-only voting, and even after the war the solidly Republican states of the Upper Northwest were reluctant to grant voting rights to blacks. In 1865, referenda on black suffrage were narrowly defeated in both Minnesota and Wisconsin.[79] Given this opposition to black suffrage, mainstream Republicans who did conceive of voting as a right needed some way to explain why a black citizen who resembled a white citizen in all respects relevant to voting qualifications in a given state – sex, age, perhaps literacy and property – should be disqualified on the grounds of race. The prevailing division of rights into civil, political, and social categories served the purpose. As discussed earlier, only civil rights were held to apply to blacks and whites equally. Voting, classified as a political right, was withheld from blacks.[80]

And then, very quickly, the prevailing Republican position on black suffrage changed. Five years after the war ended, the final Reconstruction Amendment declared suffrage a right that could not be abridged on the grounds of race, color, or previous condition of servitude. The reasons for that change had a great deal to do with the Republican Party's interest in maintaining its political predominance. Under the constitutional system before the Civil War, representation in the House of Representatives had been apportioned in accordance with the number of free citizens plus three-

---

[78] Of course, Hohfeld would regard voting as neither a right nor a privilege but a power.
[79] Benedict, *Compromise of Principle*, pp. 78–79; Foner, *Reconstruction*, p. 223.
[80] Brock, *American Crisis*, pp. 19–20; Wiecek, *Liberty Under Law*, p. 94.

fifths the number of slaves in each state. This "three-fifths compromise" was an artifact of sectional bargaining at the original constitutional convention, at which Northern representatives wanted slaves to count for nothing in allocating congressional seats and Southern representatives wanted slaves to count fully, both sides seeking to maximize the power of their own sections. An irony of the emancipation, therefore, was that it threatened to increase the congressional power of the defeated Southern states. Southern blacks, who had previously counted in apportionment at three-fifths strength, would now count at full strength. It was by no means clear that the increased Southern representation would be elected by black freedmen as well as by white rebels; if blacks could not vote in most of the North, there was little reason to expect that they would vote in the South. Representation was apportioned with reference to people, not voters, so Southern representation would increase whether or not blacks could vote. Northerners suddenly faced the prospect of having their Southern enemies confront them in Congress again, this time with greater political strength for having lost the war.[81]

If the South was to have more power, Northerners wanted at least to keep that power out of rebel hands. "One thing I know," said Senator John Sherman of Ohio in a typical comment, "that never by my consent shall these rebels gain by this war increased political power and come back here to wield that power in some other form against the safety and integrity of the country."[82] Therefore, one of two conditions had to be met: either Southern representation must not increase, or else blacks must vote. For a time, Congress experimented with the first approach. One suggestion for changing the basis for representation in Congress would have allocated representatives "among the several States of the Union according to their respective numbers, excluding negroes, Indians, Chinese, and all persons, not white, who are not allowed the elective franchise."[83] Instead of gaining additional representation for the "missing" two-fifths of the black population, Southern representation under such a system would have fallen by the three-fifths of the black population

---

[81] Brock, *American Crisis*, pp. 21–22.

[82] *Congressional Globe*, 39th Congress, 1st session, 1865–66, p. 745. See also comments in Northern press quoted in Foner, *Reconstruction*, pp. 225–227, on Northerners coming to favor black suffrage as a response to the prospect of "rebel" political power.

[83] *Journal of the Joint Committee of Fifteen on Reconstruction*, ed. Benjamin B. Kedrick (Columbia, 1914), pp. 43–44.

that had previously been counted. Ultimately, Congress settled on a system whereby one or the other of the two conditions would be fulfilled, leaving each state to choose its poison: the Fourteenth Amendment changed the basis of representation from the total number of free inhabitants plus three-fifths of the slaves to the total number of residents (untaxed Indians excepted) *less* the percentage that any adult male citizens denied the vote bore to the total adult male citizen population. Thus, Southern states could not increase their representation without enfranchising blacks. If blacks were enfranchised, the Republicans reasoned, all would be well, because blacks would vote for Republicans. On December 18, 1865, Thaddeus Stevens of Pennsylvania laid out the practical implications of the proposed new suffrage formula.

If the Amendment prevails, and those [Southern] States withhold the right of suffrage from persons of color, it will deduct about thirty-seven, leaving them but forty-six. With the basis unchanged, the eighty-three southern members, with the Democrats that will in the best time be elected from the North, will always give them a majority in Congress and in the Electoral College. They will at the very first election take possession of the White House and the halls of Congress. I need not depict the ruin that would follow ... If they should grant the right of suffrage to persons of color, I think there would always be Union white men enough in the South, aided by the blacks, to divide the representation, and thus continue the Republican ascendancy. If they should refuse to thus alter their election laws it would reduce the representatives of the late slave States to about forty-five and render them powerless for evil.[84]

Stevens called the measure necessary "to render our republican Government firm and stable forever," but he seems to have aimed at preserving not just the republican government but the *Republican* one.[85] That aim was widely understood to be the policy behind the complex suffrage formula of the Fourteenth Amendment.

[84] *Congressional Globe*, 39th Congress, 1st session, 1865–66, p. 74.
[85] Stevens was a leading radical Republican, one of those most committed to abolition and equal rights for blacks. He favored a constitutional amendment that would have declared all state and federal laws applicable to persons of all races equally, and, at the same time as he presented the congressional calculus, he had urged that "Equal right to all the privileges of the Government is innate in every mortal being, no matter what the shape or color of the tabernacle it inhabits" (Brock, *American Crisis*, pp. 100–101, 126, 131; *Congressional Globe*, 39th Congress, 1st session, 1865–66, p. 74). He and Sumner had advocated black suffrage clearly and prominently for many years before the Civil War (Foner, *Reconstruction*, p. 230). It is therefore hard to say that the electoral calculus he voiced was his exclusive motivation for black suffrage: he may have favored black suffrage for other reasons which he simply muted in favor of what he thought would better persuade the House, or he may have been

The constitutional right to vote without regard to race, color, or previous condition of servitude is, however, located not in the Fourteenth Amendment but in the Fifteenth. Passage of the Fifteenth Amendment represented full reversal from the earlier position that suffrage was not a right of blacks on equal terms with whites; the Fourteenth Amendment left states the option of white-only voting, but the Fifteenth positively announced race-blind suffrage as a right. To understand the motives behind guaranteeing that right, let us begin by noting that, by the time the Fifteenth Amendment was passed, blacks in the South could already vote. Disgusted that former rebels were exercising power in the Southern states, Congress passed a Reconstruction Act in 1867 that imposed military rule, disfranchised certain classes of ex-Confederates, and, with the pragmatic approval of Southern Unionists, granted blacks the right to vote throughout the South.[86] Most Southern Unionists had originally opposed black suffrage but realized in 1865 and 1866 that they needed allies in order to stand against the more numerous former rebels. Reluctantly, many white Unionists came to accept that enfranchising blacks was the most plausible way to meet that need. By 1867, blacks could vote throughout the South. Thus, except to further entrench what the Reconstruction Act had already established, the Fifteenth Amendment did not change the voting status of Southern blacks. That further entrenchment was not insignificant, because Northern Republicans knew that elements of their program not placed beyond the popular will by constitutional amendment were likely to be overturned once Southern whites were reenfranchised.[87] Nevertheless, the passage of the Fifteenth Amendment did not immediately change the voting status of Southern blacks. It changed the voting status of blacks outside the South – in the border states and the Lower North.

Republicans could already see a future when whites would again

motivated simultaneously by egalitarian principles and political arithmetic. In whichever case, if so radical a spokesman as Stevens argued the question in terms of power politics, the more moderate mainstream is unlikely to have harbored enthusiasm about black suffrage as a matter of principle. Indeed, as Benedict shows throughout his analysis of Congressional Reconstruction, men like Stevens and Sumner were politically (if not rhetorically) marginal even among the radicals: the more they voiced their "authentic" egalitarianism, the less support they commanded on the floor. Stevens, for all his fame, lost more votes in the 39th Congress than any other Representative (Benedict, *Compromise of Principle*, e.g., pp. 23, 142–143).

[86] Foner, *Reconstruction*, pp. 186–190, 270–280.
[87] See Brock, *American Crisis*, pp. 11, 22–23.

control the South and dominate its politics, sending Democrats to
Congress. The Republicans could only maintain their majority,
therefore, if they held the loyal states solidly. In a few Lower North
and border states, notably New Jersey, Maryland, and Kentucky, the
Democratic Party was strong enough to challenge Republican
control. These states did not permit blacks to vote. If blacks could
vote in those states, Republicans reasoned, they would provide the
margin of Republican majority. The Republicans therefore used
their temporary coalition of the solid Republican Upper North and
Southern states controlled by blacks and Unionists under military
reconstruction to pass the Fifteenth Amendment. Not surprisingly,
the Amendment met its fiercest opposition in the Lower North,
precisely where it was supposed to bully states into enfranchising
blacks. New Jersey, for example, rejected the Amendment.[88]

In the end, the political forces that passed the Fifteenth Amendment were motivated by multiple reasons. Neither the Republicans'
partisan interest in gaining electoral control of a few border states
nor an abstractly motivated commitment to egalitarianism nor
principles of individual liberty inherited from the Founding was an
exclusive cause.[89] For all the practical political interests at stake,
there were also people who believed black suffrage to be a matter of
inalienable right and who promoted the Fifteenth Amendment as a

---

[88] Gillete, *The Right to Vote*, p. 150.
[89] Gillete may tend toward reductionism in his account of the passage of the Fifteenth
Amendment. In so doing, he fails to acknowledge that the Amendment was, at least in part,
an attempt to further strengthen and protect Southern blacks for their own sake (see
Benedict, *Compromise of Principle*, pp. 325–327). LaWanda and John H. Cox have also argued
that Gillete's largely inferential contention that only the electoral advantage motivated
passage fails to consider that the Fifteenth Amendment held electoral costs as well as
benefits for the Republicans. Enfranchising border-state blacks might alienate white voters
in those states from the Republican Party, thus defeating the tactical purpose of
enfranchisement (see Cox and Cox, "Negro Suffrage and Republican Politics: The Problem
of Motivation in Reconstruction Historiography," *Journal of Southern History* 23 [1967],
303–330). This was no idle worry: prominent Republicans believed that Republican
support for black suffrage cost the party white votes in every region of the country (see, e.g.,
speech of Senator Henry Wilson of Massachusetts, *Congressional Globe*, 40th Congress, 3rd
session, p. 672). Of course, this argument is not the last word, either. Other more radical
Republicans believed that the party would self-destruct if it compromised its fight for
universal manhood suffrage (Foner, *Reconstruction*, p. 238). Perhaps the most realistic
appraisal of the motives behind the Fifteenth Amendment must admit the inextricability of
pragmatic political and abstract ideological forces. Benedict argues that "Most Republicans
never had to choose between political expediency and political morality, for to a large
extent the political fortunes of the Republican Party were best served by fulfilling its liberal
ideological commitments" (Benedict, *Compromise of Principle*, p. 327). It may not be possible
to know whether either set of motivations could have carried the Amendment without the
support of the other.

way to enshrine the principle of race-blind suffrage in the Constitution and ensure its continuance after the military rule of Reconstruction ended.[90] Moreover, particular individuals did not necessarily support the Amendment for only one kind of reason. Different motivations coexist within political actors, making it difficult to say "He voted this way because of X and not because of Y." Not knowing precisely how much causal force to attribute to each of several motivations, however, does not entail an inability to identify certain motivations as among the important causes of a political decision, and we may safely conclude that specific electoral needs played a powerful role in establishing the Fifteenth Amendment right to suffrage. In 1866, when the issue was debated chiefly as a matter of abstract justice, most Congressional radicals believed that they could never muster the necessary numbers to pass an equal suffrage amendment. Benjamin Wade, who lost his Senate seat in 1866 after campaigning on a black suffrage platform, spoke of the generally poor radical performance in the elections of that year, saying, "We went in on principle, and we got whipped."[91] Over the next four years, however, the radicals focused their arguments on the lack of other viable ways to protect Unionists and Northerners from renewed rebel power and on the concrete interests of the Republican Party. These arguments were indispensable to passing the Fifteenth Amendment.[92] It was mostly in those terms that its supporters promoted it, and it was largely in those terms that commentators of the day understood it. Shortly after ratification, the *New York World* wrote that the "sole purpose" of the Fifteenth Amendment "was to strengthen the Republican party in the Northern States."[93] The *New York Times* went farther, promoting the Fifteenth Amendment on the eve of its adoption while explicitly disavowing principled discussion of extending the rights of suffrage, or indeed any package of "political" rights, across racial or other lines:

---

[90] Whether or not the Fifteenth Amendment served the purpose of protecting Southern black suffrage after Reconstruction depends upon the time frame under consideration. For most of a century, it would have been considered a miserable failure; later, when a new rights transformation emphasized rights against racial discrimination, the Fifteenth Amendment again became an important constitutional guarantee.

[91] Benedict, *Compromise of Principle*, p. 273.

[92] Benedict devotes several chapters of *A Compromise of Principle* to making this argument (see chapters 7–11, the summary on p. 222, and pp. 257–274). See also Brock, *American Crisis*, pp. 294–295.

[93] *New York World*, 1 April 1870.

The adoption of this [Fifteenth] amendment will put an end to further agitation of the subject [of suffrage], for a long time at least ... We do not concur with those who predict that the question of Suffrage for women will speedily demand public action or engross public attention, or that the right of men to hold office without distinction of color or race, will absorb any great degree of public time or public thought for a long while to come ... With the adoption of the Fifteenth Amendment, we may fairly look upon the Suffrage agitation as at an end, for the present political generation at all events ...

The changes already made in the provisions of the old Constitution in regard to suffrage, and which will be completed with the ratification of this amendment, have sprung not from any conviction of injustice or unfairness in their operation, but from the new emergencies created in the progress and by the results of the civil war – and until some new catastrophe shall occur, equally potent in changing the current of the nation's thoughts, there is not likely to arise any fresh demand for essential changes in the fundamental law in regard to suffrage.[94]

This *New York Times* editorial highlights the piecemeal nature of the extension of rights to blacks in Reconstruction and undermines the view of the Fifteenth Amendment as having been about a general package of political rights, rights that would have included "the right of men to hold office." The editorial explicitly separates that right from suffrage and predicts its obscurity for the foreseeable future.

Extending the right of suffrage to blacks, however, did constitute a major departure from the theory of distinct civil, political, and social rights as it had existed only a few years earlier. Voting had been the paradigmatic political right, and part of the strength of the theory of separate categories, from the early-Reconstruction point of view, was precisely it rationalized the continuing disfranchisement of blacks. Once blacks had secured the right to vote, those who espoused the idea of separate categories of rights had several options of how to reconcile the new reality with their theory. One option would have been to argue that political rights as well as civil rights now belonged to all people equally. Another would have been to argue that some political rights were to be enjoyed equally by all people but that others were not. Yet a third would have been to abandon the three-tiered theory altogether. For the most part, however, participants in the rights discourse of the day chose a fourth alternative: reclassifying voting as "civil" rather than "political."

After the adoption of the Fifteenth Amendment, the Supreme Court still argued that the Reconstruction Amendments had mandated equality only of civil rights, not of political ones.[95] But in case after case, the post-Fifteenth Amendment Court described voting as a civil right, not a political one.[96] By 1880, even Justice Stephen Field, who denounced his colleagues for fast-and-loose reshufflings of rights among the three categories, quietly omitted voting from his list of political rights.[97] The landmark *Civil Rights Cases* classified voting rights as civil even while curtailing the rights of blacks by taking a narrower view of civil rights than the one Congress had proposed in the last years of Reconstruction.[98]

Voting is quintessentially political, and it is hard to see how a theory could classify it as non-political and remain coherent. If, however, we understand the theory of civil, political, and social rights as a way of describing what classes of people get what rights rather than as an analytic approach to the nature of rights themselves, the rearranging of rights among categories is perfectly comprehensible. The Republican commitment to extend suffrage to blacks pushed the right of suffrage, against the formal logic of the classificatory scheme, into the category of civil rights. The legacy of this readjustment persisted through the twentieth century, during which voting rights were consistently considered matters of "civil rights": the "Civil Rights" Act of 1957 was mostly about voting rights, and the landmark "Civil Rights" Act of 1964 dealt with voting rights before any other issues.

Juries

The right to vote was not the only political right to become a civil right in the generation after the Civil War. The right to serve on juries moved as well. Before 1880, a West Virginia statute declared that "All white male persons who are twenty-one years of age and

---

[95] See *United States v. Reese*, 92 U.S. 214 (1876); *Civil Rights Cases*, 109 U.S. 3 (1883) at 30, 39–40, 48–49, 55–57, majority opinion and Harlan in dissent; *Ex Parte Virginia*, 100 U.S. 339, 363, 367–368 (1880) (Field, J., dissenting). That Field's remarks occurred in a dissenting opinion is here of little relevance, because the majority did not contest his characterization of the Reconstruction amendments nor of voting as a civil right.

[96] *Hornbuckle v. Toombs*, 85 U.S. 648, at 656 (1873); *United States v. Joseph*, 94 U.S. 614, at 616 (1876); *Neal v. Delaware*, 103 U.S. 370 (1880); *Dubulcet v. Louisiana*, 103 U.S. 550 (1880).

[97] *Ex Parte Virginia*, 100 U.S. at 368 (Field, J., dissenting).

[98] *Civil Rights Cases*, 109 U.S. 3, 17 (1883).

who are citizens of this State shall be liable to serve as jurors."[99] Just as the term "privilege" echoed Hohfeld in the context of voting, the word "liable" echoes Hohfeld in the context of jury service. The statute's use of the term was analytically consistent with Hohfeld's use: white male West Virginia citizens over twenty-one had a liability, Hohfeld would say, because they were subject to a legal power of another agent (the State) to compel them to do something. In Hohfeldian terms, that relationship defines a liability and not a right. But again, Hohfeld's rules miss the performative aspect of calling something a right, namely that calling something a right identifies it as important and deserving of special protection. The ability to serve on juries has long been recognized as a mark of enfranchisement, an instrument of power, and a trust bestowed only on those who hold the confidence of the community. When the Supreme Court in *Strauder v. West Virginia* considered the constitutionality of the West Virginia statute, it described jury service as a "right," despite the language of the statute.

As Amar and others note, jury service began Reconstruction as a political right.[100] The Supreme Court, however, did not remain convinced of that categorization. The *Strauder* court declared that a state could not exclude blacks from jury service, but it did not argue that blacks enjoyed the same political rights as whites. Instead, the Court noted that the Constitution guaranteed blacks "all the civil rights that the superior race enjoy" and struck down the statute as a violation of the Fourteenth Amendment.[101] There was some ambiguity in *Strauder* as to whether the right being litigated was the right to serve on a jury or the right of defendants to be tried by juries from which people of their own race had not been excluded: Amar has recently offered a reading on which the former right is political and the latter right civil. If the holding in *Strauder* is only about one or the other, the latter option is probably the stronger one, and the best assessment is probably that the Court did not clearly limit its analysis to one right or the other.[102] This murkiness makes it difficult to cite *Strauder* as conclusive proof that the Supreme Court in 1880 saw jury service as a civil rather

---

[99] West Virginia Acts of 1872–73, p. 102, quoted in *Strauder v. West Virginia*, 100 U.S. 303 (1880), at 305.

[100] Amar, *Bill of Rights*, p. 271.   [101] *Strauder v. West Virginia*, 100 U.S. at 306.

[102] Compare *Strauder*, at 305, 309, 310, discussing the right of the defendant, with page 308 of the same case, which discusses the right to serve as a juror.

than a political right, inasmuch as *Strauder* might merely hold that
the defendant's right was a civil right. Two companion cases to
Strauder, however, removed much of the ambiguity. *Virginia v. Rives*
explicitly analyzed exclusion from jury service as a denial of the
potential juror's civil rights.[103] In *Ex Parte Virginia*, the Court
upheld the detention of a state judge who had prevented blacks
from serving as jurors, and it identified the issue as an issue of civil
rights under the Fourteenth Amendment.[104] Three years later, the
Court reaffirmed in the *Civil Rights Cases* that jury service was a
civil right.[105] The Court used broadly egalitarian rhetoric in
Strauder and its companion cases, arguing that a racially discriminatory procedure for choosing juries would obviously be invalid if it
excluded white men or naturalized Irishmen and that it was no
more valid because the excluded group was black men. This
reasoning, however, was confined to civil rights and did not
impinge upon the manifestly unequal statuses of blacks and whites
with respect to political and social rights. In dissent, Justice Field
did not contest the unconstitutionality of inequalities in civil rights.
He contended, rather, that the right to serve on a jury was political,
not civil, and therefore not guaranteed to blacks.[106]

To the extent that the right in question was the right to serve as a
juror rather than a defendant's right to a racially nondiscriminatory
jury, Amar maintains that *Strauder* and its companion cases were
actually not Fourteenth Amendment cases or cases about civil rights
at all. Instead, Amar classifies *Strauder* as a Fifteenth Amendment
case about political rights. In brief, his argument holds that Justice
Field was correct to insist that jury service was a political right
rather than a civil one but wrong to believe that blacks did not enjoy
the same political rights as whites. The Fifteenth Amendment, which
extended suffrage to blacks, should actually be interpreted to extend
all political rights, including jury service, to blacks. Those were the
true constitutional grounds, Amar contends, vindicating the *Strauder*
decision.[107] Amar's theory is analytically cogent, and it may offer a

---

[103] *Virginia v. Rives*, 100 U.S. 313, at 315, 320 (1880).   [104] *Ex Parte Virginia*, at 345.
[105] *Civil Rights Cases*, at 17.
[106] *Strauder; Ex Parte Virginia*, at 685–687 (Field, J., dissenting).
[107] Amar, *The Constitutional and Criminal Procedure: First Principles* (Yale University Press, 1998),
    p. 164. Amar has written different pieces of this argument in different places and at
    different times, and, given the intricacy of the material and a certain amount of refinement
    in his thinking over time, there are small variations in the positions he articulates in
    different books and articles. Thus, on one reading of Amar, *Strauder* is a Fifteenth

more consistent theoretical grounding for the result in *Strauder* than the *Strauder* court itself offered. At the same time, because Amar's theory is not consistent with the *Strauder* court's own understanding of the issue, it does not illuminate conceptions held by the actors in the case it purports to explain. To say that *Strauder* should have been decided as a Fifteenth Amendment case does not establish that *Strauder* was a Fifteenth Amendment case, especially in light of the fact that neither the *Strauder* majority nor the majority in either of the companion cases ever mentioned the Fifteenth Amendment. To say that *Strauder* should have been understood as a case about equality of political rights does not establish that *Strauder* was such a case, especially in the face of the fact that the *Strauder* court never asserted equality of political rights for blacks. Both at the time of *Strauder* and thereafter, as in the *Civil Rights Cases*, the Court described the right to serve on a jury as a civil right, and the legal rationale for blacks' enjoying that right was simply that blacks enjoyed the same civil rights as whites.

To be sure, the scheme of civil, political, and social rights might make more sense as an analytic theory about the nature of rights if jury service were a political right. Such a scheme would certainly make more sense if rights would hold still as one kind of right or another rather than shifting among different categories. Amar's account has those analytic virtues, and measured by those criteria it is superior to the tripartite scheme that was actually operative during Reconstruction. That does not mean, however, that Amar's account establishes the nature of civil, political, and social rights after the Civil War. It may establish the shortcomings of a political and legal class as abstract theoreticians, but it is still that class whose thoughts and words determine the nature of rights during Reconstruction. The Reconstruction differentiation among civil, political, and social rights was a political and judicial construction, not a detached philosophical theory. It worked and changed with the political commitments that it carried.

Amendment case and Field's error is his failure to understand that the Fifteenth Amendment guarantees political rights to blacks, while on another reading of Amar, *Strauder* is not a Fifteenth Amendment case because it actually turns on the civil rights of the defendant to a racially nondiscriminatory jury rather than on the political rights of potential black jurors. On the latter reading, the companion cases and especially *Ex Parte Virginia* must, I assume, be about political rights.

John Harlan and the limits of reactively formed civil rights in Reconstruction

In 1883, in the *Civil Rights Cases,* Congress declared the Civil Rights Act of 1875 unconstitutional. In that Act, Congress banned racial discrimination in transportation and accommodations, securing for blacks equal access to public conveyances, inns, and so forth. In trying to extend these rights to blacks, Congress clothed them in the language of civil rights: after all, a right that fell in the civil category was a right that blacks should enjoy equally with whites. When the Supreme Court struck down the statute, it did not disturb the settled understanding that civil rights were to be enjoyed without respect to race. It merely said that the rights named in the statute were not actually civil. They were social, and Congress could not enforce rights of social equality.[108] In attempting to extend these rights to blacks, Congress had pushed the flexible category of civil rights farther than it could go.

That the category was not infinitely flexible shows that "civil rights" was not a talismanic formula that could secure majority approval for the racially neutral allocation of rights for any propositions whatsoever. The relationship between the labeling and the acceptance of a right was more complex: as people became more willing to extend a certain right to blacks, it became more and more plausible to speak of that right as civil, and the two changes occurred together, one reinforcing the other. Without some substantive reason for whites to favor extending a particular right to blacks, the invocation of the "civil rights" label alone was not necessarily sufficient to work the change. As is generally the case, a powerful part of the formation of people's attitudes about whether a given right should or should not be recognized stemmed from the desire to negate specific adversities, which in Reconstruction usually meant the issues of the Slave Power struggle. Concrete negation of the Slave Power could help support voting for blacks, because the alternative to black voting was a resurgence of white Southern political power. No similarly powerful concerns supported a race-neutral right of access to public transportation and accommodations.

Only Justice Harlan's dissent found adequate connection between the 1875 Civil Rights Act and the slavery crisis to warrant upholding

---

[108] *Civil Rights Cases,* at 3.

the law. Harlan, it will be recalled, saw the essence of slavery as racial subjugation, and anything that preserved that subjugation was for him part of what had to be negated by systems of rights after the Civil War. Because Harlan was the only justice to take such an expansive view of race and slavery, rights as far removed from the narrow issues of the previous era as access to transportation and accommodation could not be extended to blacks. The technique of describing rights to be conferred on blacks as civil rights, however, would persist, and when the substantive commitments of American rights discourse shifted sufficiently to permit recognition of rights of equal access to transportation and accommodation, the Act that announced the change did not purport to enforce "social" rights. It was again called a Civil Rights Act: the Civil Rights Act of 1964.

Harlan was to clash with the rest of the Court over the limits of civil rights again in the landmark case of *Plessy v. Ferguson*. Reconstruction was over by the time of *Plessy*, and American rights discourse no longer contained strong commitments to expanding the rights of blacks. *Plessy* concerned a Louisiana statute segregating railroad cars, and the Court upheld the segregation over Harlan's lone dissent. As in the *Civil Rights Cases*, the majority presented the issue as one of social equality and maintained that the Reconstruction amendments had not gone that far.[109] Harlan, arguing for black equality, again spoke of civil rights, and his dissent denouncing racial segregation has come to be regarded as among the greatest judicial dissents in the history of American law. Understanding the nineteenth-century typology of civil, political, and social rights, however, suggests a deep irony in the fame of that opinion. Harlan is remembered for having asserted that the Constitution is color-blind, neither knowing nor tolerating classes among citizens. But in the paragraph containing those famous words, Harlan three times asserts that he is discussing an issue of *civil* rights. It is in respect of civil rights, he says, that government can make no racial distinctions. If Harlan merely meant to argue that the Constitution is color-blind where civil rights, as opposed to social rights, are concerned, then what modern readers see as an egalitarian manifesto was actually a legal truism. Nobody in the *Plessy* case contested that the Constitution was color-blind in matters of civil rights. What they contested was whether the right that Homer Plessy sought was civil as opposed

---

[109] *Plessy v. Ferguson*, 163 U.S. 544 (1896).

to social. Harlan was indeed far more egalitarian than his colleagues, but his *Plessy* dissent reflected that difference in a different place than that usually remembered today, that is, in his willingness to characterize a right as "civil" rather than "social." Only at a later time when people had largely forgotten the narrow meaning that "civil rights" carried in a pre-egalitarian age could Harlan's dissent come to seem a ringing declaration of equality. It may not be a coincidence that that dissent, for all its fame today, was never cited in a subsequent case until 1961, at which time the Supreme Court was committed to full black equality and "civil rights" seemed coextensive with rights in general.

CONCLUSION

During the Civil War and Reconstruction, as during the Founding, Americans used the language of rights to claim special protection for liberties, powers, immunities and entitlements made critical or endangered by contemporary political conditions. Before the Civil War, pro-slavery Southerners spoke of slaveholding in terms of property rights, both positive and natural. Northerners used the language of rights for directly opposite purposes, charging sometimes that American slavery was creating a climate destructive of the rights of non-slaves, such as the rights of free speech and free press, and sometimes that slavery was itself a violation of natural or inalienable rights. As the secession crisis grew, Southerners located their right to secede in the same sources where abolitionists located inalienable rights of human freedom. In short, all parties to the conflicts presented their own preferred propositions as rights. Not only was clothing some proposition in rights language a way to protect and prioritize it, but denying the label of "right" was a standard way to strip something of protection and priority: recall the argument sometimes made early in Reconstruction that suffrage was a privilege rather than a right.

After the war, Congress and the courts adopted a formalistic theory about the structure of rights and ostensibly used that theory to frame the extension of rights to black Americans. That theory, however, was not simply an analytically founded reason for extending certain rights and withholding others. It was also an attempted rationalization of why some rights and not others were extended. Shaped by the struggle against the Slave Power, intent on dismantling the slave-labor system but not enthusiastic about thoroughgoing egalitarianism, Reconstruction Republicans endorsed a theory whereby blacks would enjoy "civil" but not other rights. The political and legal actors of Reconstruction were less concerned with reflective philosophic consistency than modern academic rights theorists are, and even modern theorists are often influenced by the substantive results their theories yield: certainly a large part of what appealed to Reconstruction Republicans about their tripartite theory was the conclusions that it permitted them to reach. Moreover, the theory admitted of substantial modifications when its driving political aims so required, and content triumphed over form in the reclassification of "political" rights like suffrage as "civil." The Reconstruction classificatory scheme of rights as civil, political, or social, often read as a theory about the form of rights, helped to advance a specific set of substantive political commitments, commitments largely formed in opposition to the Southern Slave Power as Northern whites understood it.

The manipulations of the scheme of civil, political, and social rights that legislatures and courts worked during Reconstruction were more crudely outcome-driven than are most modern academic theories of rights, but there are also important similarities between the rights discourse of some Reconstruction politicians and that of some modern academics. One concerns the attempted practice of rights synthesis. When Sunstein and Richards present the rights of Reconstruction as following necessarily from the rights of the Founding and, for that matter, as leading directly to still-contested rights, there is a sense in which their activity resembles that of men like Colfax and Sumner. In both cases, there is an attempt to integrate a new set of rights, or proposed rights, with an earlier, honored set. Successful synthesizers generally persuade their audiences to accept some interpretation of the older set that makes it align with, and support, the desired additions. Constitutional lawyers and political activists frequently attempt that kind of synthesis. A successful synthesis might be understood in Kuhnian terms as a change in paradigms or vocabularies, and a successful synthesizer might be what Harold Bloom calls a "strong poet."[110] In Bloom's usage, a strong poet often makes his audience understand

---

110 Kuhn, *Scientific Revolutions*, pp. 92–110; Harold Bloom, *The Anxiety of Influence* (Oxford University Press, 1973).

predecessor poets only through the lens that the later poet offers. In
Rorty's adaptation of the term, strong poets are people who
reinterpret a body of thought and change the rules, frameworks, and
vocabularies of ongoing debates: in other words, those who effect
Kuhnian revolutions.[111] Such a person is a poet (rather than a
lawyer, philosopher, or historian) because he or she departs from
verifiable modes of scholarship and language in pursuit of expressing
something that cannot be expressed within existing vocabulary.

But the lines separating poets – in this case, synthesizing politicians – from lawyers, philosophers, and historians are not so clear.
Colfax, Sumner and others interpreted the history and structure of
American rights so as to foster particular tendencies in the rights
discourse of their own day, and the measure of their success lies not
in whether later historians believe their accounts of the Founding to
have been objectively accurate but in the degree to which they
succeeded in transforming American conceptions of rights. A parallel analysis can apply to Sunstein and Richards. If we judge the
"underlying principle" view of Reconstruction rights as a historical
account of American rights discourse, we will find it deeply flawed.
There is, however, another aspect to the views that Sunstein and
Richards represent, specifically the attempt to affect current rights
discourse by persuading modern Americans to interpret the history
of rights in a particular way. That project is synthesis. Just as the
ostensibly formal rights theories of Dworkin, Feinberg, and others
are inescapably political, so are the attempts at rights synthesis in the
work of scholars like Sunstein and Richards. In different ways, they
are all supporting political commitments by reinterpreting the
language of rights.

---

[111] Rorty, *Contingency, Irony, and Solidarity*, pp. 20–43.

CHAPTER 5

Rights after World War II

Throughout the twentieth century, American conceptions of rights bore marks of Reconstruction, the Founding, and even earlier periods of history. Around the time of World War II, however, a new set of substantive political commitments reshaped both the form and the content of American rights. Once again, the transformation of rights discourse followed the pattern of adversity, reaction, and synthesis. The chief adversities this time stemmed from Nazi Germany and the Soviet Union. For a generation of mid-century Americans, the conflict with those two powers shaped politics and ideology. Sometimes, Americans collapsed the Nazi and Soviet threats into a single concept under the name of "totalitarianism." According to many American intellectuals from Hannah Arendt to Arthur Schlesinger, the obvious differences between the Nazi and Soviet orders were in fact less significant than their essential similarities, and it therefore made sense to see opposition to Germany and the Soviet Union as one struggle rather than two.[1] Whether American reactions against Nazi and Soviet adversity should be counted as one phenomenon or two is a question without an overarching answer: anti-Nazism and anti-Sovietism merged in some respects but not in others. No matter whether conceived as one project or two, however, the cumulative American reaction against European totalitarianism became so powerful a force in the world of legal and political ideas that it sometimes surpassed, though without ever completely eclipsing, the influences of the ideas and experiences of older eras. Just as Reconstruction changed the prism through which Americans viewed rights that had been inherited from the Founding, the confrontation with totalitarianism again reconfigured

---

[1] Hannah Arendt, *The Origins of Totalitarianism* (Harcourt Brace Jovanovich, 2nd edn., 1968); Arthur M. Schlesinger, Jr., *The Vital Center* (Houghton Mifflin, 1949). See also Novick, *That Noble Dream*, pp. 135–138.

the discourse of rights. Anti-totalitarian ideas did not completely displace older notions of rights any more than Reconstruction ideas had completely displaced the Founding. Instead, another synthesis took place, with anti-totalitarian agendas placing new interpretations on inherited notions of rights at the same time that pre-existing notions of rights helped shape what it was about totalitarianism that Americans so fiercely opposed. The mid-century transformation of American rights discourse thus stood at the juncture of two syntheses, one synchronic and one diachronic. In the former, American conceptions of rights simultaneously incorporated reactions against Nazism and against the Soviet Union, reactions which sometimes pushed conceptions of rights in the same direction but which often were at odds with each other. In the latter, the reaction against twentieth-century totalitarianism revised, and was itself shaped by, the legacy of earlier conceptions of rights.

In an attempt to ground their opposition to Nazi Germany and the Soviet Union, many Americans felt a need to articulate some set of normative precepts outside of and prior to positive law. As political-moral commitments of the highest importance, those ideas were expressed in terms of rights. Reaction against Sovietism and Nazism helped bring about major shifts in the rights of free expression, racial equality, and individual privacy. A new vocabulary of "human rights" arose to carry the content of those political commitments and to link them with a broader idea rarely seen in the generation before the war but ascendant thereafter: that certain rights exist and must be respected regardless of the positive law. Several legal and political theorists have noticed that American conceptions of rights underwent major shifts in the middle of the twentieth century, but they have generally not explained, or even explored, the roots of that transformation. Sandel, for example, notes that privacy rights have a much shorter history than other constitutional rights like free speech and freedom of religion. For Sandel, that observation is part of a larger argument about how the political ideology of the modern "procedural republic" that he opposes differs from that of earlier periods in American history. Sandel neglects, however, the question of why privacy rights and similar aspects of the "procedural republic" arose when they did.[2] The reaction against Nazi Germany and the Soviet Union supplies much of the solution.

---

[2] Sandel, *Democracy's Discontent*, p. 91.

Anti-totalitarianism helped shape twentieth-century academic rights discourse as well as the rights discourse of law and politics. Legal and political philosophers from Llewellyn, Hart, and Fuller to Dworkin, Sunstein, and Ackerman have been powerfully affected by the problems that Nazism and Soviet communism posed for their disciplines, and much of their work implicitly responds to those problems. Indeed, the relationship between those problems and the substance of their work is often more than implicit. The major transformations in American conceptions of rights that I suggest are traceable to reaction against totalitarianism – the resurgence of normative foundationalism in the form of "human rights" and other universal, non-positivist ideas, the thickening of rights against racial discrimination, against invasions of personal privacy, in favor of free expression – are as typical of academic rights discourse as they are of rights discourse in politics or law. To be sure, there are significant differences in the ways that academics and non-academics discuss questions of rights. The kind of interpretive theorizing associated with reflective equilibrium, as discussed earlier, is more typical of academic than of political debate. Nevertheless, some discursive patterns are common to both forums of the conversation. In both arenas, people use the language of rights to prioritize and protect the entitlements, liberties, powers, and immunities that they believe to be most important and most in need of protection. Moreover, the sets of propositions that people seek to prioritize and protect in the two arenas are largely coextensive. To the extent that academics and non-academics share the normative assumptions of a particular time, both having been shaped by the same adversities, this overlap makes a great deal of sense.[3]

The project of negating Nazi and Soviet totalitarianism has been the greatest new substantive influence shaping American conceptions of rights since World War II, but that influence never dictated a uniform set of outcomes. Indeed, the fact that the mid-century

---

[3] Someone could reasonably ask whether this attention to academics makes this analysis of rights discourse after World War II methodologically different from the analyses of the Founding and Reconstruction eras, in which little or no attention was given to professional academics. The answer, however, would be that it does not. As a distinct class, professional academics did not exist in significant numbers in the United States until late in the nineteenth century. The preceding chapters have not studied the discourse of professional academics because, at the relevant times, there was not much academic discourse to study. The twentieth century, however, had a large and thriving academic rights discourse, and that discourse should be included in a study of rights discourse as a social practice.

transformation of rights discourse reacted to two threats rather than one permitted a significant amount of indeterminacy in the direction that conceptions of rights would take. There is no exclusive way to negate even a single adversity; an era of simultaneous reaction against two similar but nevertheless distinct adversities carried many different possibilities for the form that concrete negation of adversity would assume. In a transformation with so much room for variation, other forces – like the rise of the welfare state, the political aspirations of minority groups and especially of black Americans, the pragmatic imperatives of the Cold War, and the women's movement – could significantly influence which of many possible oppositional attitudes Americans would adopt to guide their changing conceptions of rights. Furthermore, as I discussed earlier with reference to Gadamer's idea of multiple historical horizons, the rights discourse of a given time is influenced by events of several past eras simultaneously. Just as the rights discourse of the Founding retained elements of the rights discourse of the English Revolution and other earlier eras, and just as the rights discourse of late nineteenth-century America retained elements from the Founding, post-war rights discourse retained elements from each of those previous periods. Those legacies also contributed powerfully to shaping how twentieth-century Americans navigated the indeterminacies of attempting to negate two faces of totalitarianism.

A CHANGED FORM OF RIGHTS

It is well established that a major change in American conceptions of rights occurred sometime between the 1920s and the 1960s, but many scholars fail to give sufficient emphasis to anti-totalitarianism and especially anti-Nazism when trying to account for that transformation. Some contend that the important post-war innovations in judicially recognized rights stem from the battle over the constitutionality of the New Deal. During the Roosevelt administration, the Supreme Court at first disallowed sweeping new federal regulation of the economy as violative of individual rights of property and contract. Later, the Court shifted its position and allowed the New Deal to stand.[4] According to Ackerman, that shift was the key to the

---

[4] See *Schechter Poultry Corp. v. United States*, 295 U.S. 495 (1935); *Carter v. Carter Coal Co.*, 298 U.S. 238 (1936); *West Coast Hotel Co. v. Parrish*, 300 U.S. 379 (1937).

new view of constitutional rights that prevailed during the
generation after World War II. This view has merit. Important
elements of American rights certainly were rethought during the
1930s, and much of the structure of American law and politics
remained powerfully under the influence of the New Deal transformation for most of the twentieth century. Moreover, as Ackerman
has noted, we are now living at a time when it is easy to underestimate the importance of the New Deal and to overestimate the
importance of World War II and the Cold War in its place, because
people with personal experience of World War II and the Cold War
are still active on the political stage and in the academy, but there
are few and increasingly fewer active shapers of political discourse
with personal memories of the Great Depression.[5] It is thus important to give the New Deal its due as a transformative period in
American political thought.

Nevertheless, the notion that the New Deal was the most powerful
force shaping post-war rights discourse needs to be questioned. The
rights at issue during the 1930s were mostly economic, and economic
rights then seemed to be the centerpiece of rights generally, as the
New Deal and the depression that inspired it made economic issues
the dominant concerns of that decade. As late as 1944, President
Franklin Roosevelt spoke of establishing a second bill of rights to
secure economic needs of Americans as the first had secured political
needs. He included in this envisioned bill the right to employment,
the right to sufficient earnings for food, clothing, and recreation, the
right to trade without monopoly competition, the right to a decent
home, the right to medical care, the right to protection against the
economic problems of old age, accident, or illness, and the right to a
good education.[6] Such sweeping rights rhetoric from a president
who had substantially transformed American politics does warrant
attention.

Identifying the economic rights questions of the 1930s as the
origins of the great rights shifts of the 1950s and 1960s, however, fails
to recognize that a different kind of rights were at stake in those later
times. The signature rights of the post-war period were not primarily
economic. Their leading themes included personal privacy, police
procedures, free expression, and protection against discrimination,

---

[5] Ackerman, *We the People: Foundations*, p. 38.
[6] Speech given 11 January 1944, in B. D. Zevin, ed., *Nothing to Fear: The Selected Addresses of Franklin Delano Roosevelt, 1932–1945* (Hodder & Stoughton, 1947), pp. 387–397, at p. 396.

especially racial discrimination. The reaction against the depression that produced Roosevelt's call for an economic bill of rights had little connection to rights of privacy, racial equality, free expression and so on that were central to post-war rights discourse. In fact, the New Deal and post-war patterns in rights thinking are not only distinct but in some ways in conflict with each other. The New Deal required the judiciary to decline rigorous enforcement of individual liberties once thought fundamental, notably the "absolute property right." In contrast, judicial activism in the name of fundamental rights was a central feature of post-war rights discourse.[7] The tension between these two approaches to rights implies that the rights discourse of the post-war period operates under important influences different from those shaping the New Deal. As will be argued below, the agendas shaping post-war conceptions of rights have key roots not only in the 1930s but in the 1940s and beyond.

The return of foundationalism

In 1950, in the preface to *The Origins of Totalitarianism*, Hannah Arendt wrote that antisemitism, imperialism, and totalitarianism,

> ... one after the other, one more brutally than the other, have demonstrated that human dignity needs a new guarantee which can be found only in a new political principle, in a new law on earth, whose validity this time must comprehend the whole of humanity.[8]

Arendt here endorsed several overlapping themes of post-war American moral theory. The language of "human dignity" was one. Universality was another. A third was the need for a principle, a theoretical ground for opposition to the evils that totalitarianism had made manifest.[9] All of these themes were part of a general renewal

---

[7] For examples of the earlier period's concern with property rights and the Supreme Court's shift toward judicial restraint during the New Deal, see *Lochner*; *Nebbia v. New York*, 291 U.S. 502 (1934); *West Coast Hotel*. For renewed judicial activism regarding fundamental and even unenumerated rights after World War II, see *Brown v. Board of Education of Topeka*, 347 U.S. 483 (1954); *Griswold v. Connecticut*, 381 U.S. 479 (1965); *Roe v. Wade*, 410 U.S. 113 (1973). Whether these two courses of action are compatible was perhaps the central preoccupation of American constitutional scholarship in the last third of the twentieth century.

[8] Arendt, *The Origins of Totalitarianism*, p. ix.

[9] The version of classical liberal philosophy that makes the most use of the concept of "human dignity" – Kantianism – was rediscovered by American political philosophers in the post-war period and put to work to supply a new comprehensive theory of universal justice. The Kantian renaissance in America cannot, of course, be wholly ascribed to a social need to ground universal morality. Other incidental factors contributed to this pattern as well,

of political philosophy in the United States, a renewal substantially prompted by the confrontation with totalitarianism. The normative and foundationalist topics that political philosophers considered staple subjects in the second half of the twentieth century commanded little respect before the war. Legal realism, logical positivism and related ideas dominant early in the century had argued against the possibility of deriving ethics from logical foundations. As Edward Purcell has shown in his chronicle of scientific naturalism, most American intellectuals had by the early 1930s rejected the idea that a normative theory could be logically authoritative. Moreover, few worried about the practical implications of a theory according to which no particular system of ethics was necessarily correct.[10] During the years of the Nazi regime, however, the intellectual agenda changed. After the war, many Americans took normative foundationalism more seriously, responding, as Arendt put it, to the totalitarian demonstration of the need for a new political principle.

Consider, as an illustration of the shift in attitudes, the fate of legal realism during and after World War II. Central elements of realism included a skeptical critique of the claim that law could be neutral and apolitical and an equally skeptical view of the claim that formal legal reasoning could discover justice or humanitarian values. Prewar giants of American jurisprudence such as Oliver Wendell Holmes, Jr., and Roscoe Pound were confirmed realists. With the rise of Nazism, however, many prominent realists changed their views. In the 1920s, Yale Law School Dean Robert Hutchins had been a prominent realist, but by the late 1930s he urged a return to foundationalism and universal morality. In denouncing ideas he had formerly shared, Hutchins made explicit reference to the rise of Nazism. On the eve of the war, he bemoaned the skepticisms and empiricisms that completed "the journey from the man of goodwill to Hitler," and in 1940 he attacked legal realism by declaring that "There is little to choose between the doctrine that I learned in an

including the migration of German-trained academics such as Arendt to the United States as refugees before, during, and after the war. The influence of émigré intellectuals from Central Europe and the desire to find theoretical grounds for principled opposition to totalitarianism were mutually reinforcing, and both contributed to the increased importance of Kant to post-war American liberalism. Rawls's *A Theory of Justice*, the centerpiece of American political philosophy in the half-century after the war, is the most obvious product of this trend.

[10] Edward A. Purcell, Jr., *The Crisis of Democratic Theory: Scientific Naturalism and the Problem of Value* (The University Press of Kentucky, 1973), pp. 5–72.

American law school and that which Hitler proclaims."[11] At roughly the same time, the great realist Karl Llewellyn abandoned several of his earlier positions, announcing that any legal thinker must "need correction at once and, if need be, with a club" if he denied that "the heart and core of Jurisprudence" is justice.[12]

In the late 1940s and on into the 1950s, a flood of articles in major American law journals engaged and embraced natural law or other forms of foundational rights theory.[13] Frequently, these articles contained prominent reference to the wartime encounter with Nazism. The status of Nazism in those discussions was more than that of an excellent example used to make a broader conceptual point that would have been supported with other examples had the Nazi example not been available. Instead, the confrontation with Nazism was substantially constitutive of the discussion. Without the problem of Nazism, these discussions would probably not have taken place at all. Indeed, before the rise of Nazism, there was no such discussion. In the entire decade of the 1930s, neither the *Harvard Law Review* nor the *Yale Law Journal* published a single article on natural law or universal rights. Both of those publications reviewed dozens of books every year, but the *Harvard Law Review* reviewed only two books on natural law or universal rights topics during that decade and the *Yale Law Journal* not a single one.[14] The *Notre Dame Lawyer*, the law review of the most prominent Catholic law school in America and accordingly the journal in which natural law thinking should have been most apparent, published only two articles about natural law or related topics from its founding in 1925 until the

---

[11] Ibid., pp. 74–94, 147–158.

[12] Karl Llewellyn, "On Reading and Using the Newer Jurisprudence," 40 *Columbia Law Review* 581 (1940).

[13] See, e.g., Brendan F. Brown, "Racialism and the Rights of Nations," *Notre Dame Lawyer* 21, 1 (1945); Sheldon Glueck, "The Nuernberg Trial and Aggressive War," *Harvard Law Review* 59, 396 (1946); Edmond N. Cahn, "Justice, Power, and Law," *Yale Law Journal* 55, 336 (1946); Harold MacKinnon, "Natural Law and Positive Law," *Notre Dame Lawyer* 23, 125 (1948); Miriam Theresa Rooney, "Law Without Justice," *Notre Dame Lawyer* 23, 140 (1948); Ben Palmer, "The Natural Law and Pragmatism," *Notre Dame Lawyer* 23, 313 (1948); Myers S. McDougal and Gertrude C. K. Leighton, "The Rights of Man in the World Community," *Yale Law Journal* 59, 60 (1949); Max Radin, "Natural Law and Natural Rights," *Yale Law Journal* 59, 214 (1950). The Hart–Fuller debate, discussed later in this chapter, is also part of this trend.

[14] The two books reviewed were *American Interpretations of Natural Law*, by Benjamin F. Wright, reviewed by Roscoe Pound, *Harvard Law Review* 46, 864 (1933), and *Natural Law and the Theory of Society, 1500–1800*, by Carl Joachim Friedrich, *Harvard Law Review* 49, 677 (1936).

outbreak of war fourteen years later.[15] Thus, the flood of articles published on natural law and related rights topics in the years following the war was a real change in the academic discussion of rights, a change whose timing with respect to the war was not coincidental.

The universalist and anti-positivist dimensions of rights discourse during and after World War II were tied to the relationship between certain substantive commitments and the totalitarian regimes in which those commitments were most obviously contravened. During and after World War II, people used the language of rights to support commitments they felt to be important and in need of protection in the age of totalitarianism. One such commitment was to protection of the individual against the arbitrary power of a police state. Another was to free expression. Perhaps the most important commitment was that against unjust discrimination, especially discrimination by the state against individuals on the basis of race or religion. Armed with a theory of universal or *a priori* rights, an American could assert that European regimes that contradicted those commitments were in moral error, regardless of the content of their positive law.[16]

---

[15] Thomas F. Konop, "The Fundamental Rights of Man," *Notre Dame Lawyer* 10, 341 (1935); William P. Sternberg, "Natural Law in American Jurisprudence," *Notre Dame Lawyer* 13, 89 (1938). The Konop piece is not even a bona fide article; it is a transcript of a radio question-and-answer session with a faculty member. It should also be noted that the "natural law" in which Catholic institutions like Notre Dame maintained some slight interest was often Thomist rather than Lockean-liberal natural law; the latter was even more scarce.

[16] Half a century after World War II and a decade after the collapse of the Soviet Union, some of the most pressing issues in contemporary rights discourse can no longer be accounted for strictly within that anti-totalitarian scheme. The most prominent limiting case is the issue of sexual discrimination. For nearly a generation after the war, issues of racial discrimination commanded much more attention than did issues of sexual discrimination. When issues of sexual discrimination became more prominent, one powerful paradigm – the liberal-feminist or egalitarian approach – sought to apply to issues of sex basically the same principles of equality that had earlier been applied to issues of race and religion. Accordingly, it could use many of the same general arguments used for other kinds of post-war egalitarianism. The case is otherwise with respect to other approaches, such as difference feminism and various radical feminisms that reject the liberal-egalitarian framework. Some of these feminisms use the language of rights, and some do not; one interesting question to ask is whether the use of rights language serves a mainstreaming function for the feminisms that do use it. It is not yet clear how those approaches will play out, and part of the challenge that they pose for contemporary political theory lies precisely in the fact that they are breaking out of – or at least stretching – a paradigm that has been dominant for more than fifty years.

The discourse of anti-Nazism

Images of and allusions to Nazism pervaded many of the most important discussions of rights issues in the generation following World War II. In the first Japanese-American internment case, Justice Frank Murphy expressed his reservations about detaining Americans of Japanese descent by noting that "it bears a melancholy resemblance to the treatment accorded to members of the Jewish race in Germany."[17] After the war, the theme of the country's recent "death struggle against the apostles of racism" appeared in successful Supreme Court briefs filed by lawyers for the National Association for the Advancement of Colored People (NAACP).[18] In the heyday of the civil rights movement, President Kennedy asked Americans whether they would be comfortable saying that America had "no ghettos, no master race, except with respect to Negroes."[19]

The pervasiveness of references to Nazism in moral debate is unlikely to mean that the evil of Nazi Germany provides the best examples for all possible questions of political morality. Nazism, for all of its horrors, was a historically specific occurrence with particular parameters, and it would strain credulity to maintain that *every* evil imaginable was presented there in its strongest form. A more plausible way to explain the discursive pattern is to say that invoking Nazism was, and is, a powerful rhetorical device. Many uses of the Nazi trope were, and are, instrumental, reflecting someone's tactical belief that associating some rival position with Nazism will be a strong attack against it. To be successful, however, a rhetorical device must capture some aspect of an audience's worldview. Rhetorical uses of Nazism have had instrumental value only because anti-Nazism has been a prominent feature of post-war conceptions of injustice. Accordingly, Nazi examples occur frequently in post-war normative argument not only because they fit well into a larger theory and not only because they are instrumentally or rhetorically valuable but also because anti-Nazism has played a large constitutive role in shaping the conversation.

American reaction against Nazism prompted changed attitudes in domestic affairs along the lines of the substantive commitments

---

[17] *Hirabayashi v. United States*, 320 U.S. 81, at 110–111 (1943).
[18] Petitioner's brief in *Morgan v. Virginia*, 328 U.S. 373 (1946).
[19] John F. Kennedy, speech of 11 June 1963, in Leon Friedman, ed., *The Civil Rights Reader: Basic Documents of the Civil Rights Movement* (Walker and Company, 1968), pp. 196, 66.

listed above. During the war, American intellectuals paid increasing attention to issues of racism and tolerance. Publishing of both fiction and nonfiction books on racial themes steadily increased, newspaper coverage of minority issues rose sharply, and hundreds of new interracial groups dedicated to improving minority rights were formed.[20] A broad civil rights coalition began to take shape, composed largely of blacks fighting for an end to discrimination and Jews propelled into increased activism against prejudice by wartime events: in 1945, the American Jewish Committee announced a comprehensive plan to combat prejudice in the United States on the theory that eliminating anti-Jewish prejudice required eliminating prejudice in every form.[21] Many members of racial minority groups were optimistic that the American caste system would have to give ground to the logical implications of one of America's leading explicit reasons for fighting the war.[22] Reciprocally, the domestic issues of racial equality colored the way that Americans came to understand what the core evils of Nazism were. It was partly because the problem of racial discrimination was already present in American minds that racism is what Americans saw when they looked at Nazi Germany. This is not to say that Americans imputed racism to the Nazis fallaciously or superfluously: theories of racial superiority were indeed central to Nazi ideology and practice. But the idea that the central evil of Nazism was one of racism was not always obvious to all concerned, or even to all Americans concerned. During the war, for example, many senior officials in the Roosevelt administration regarded the chief Nazi crime as the instigation of aggressive war rather than any racial atrocities that the Nazis were committing. Others who were more concerned with issues of race, however, saw the racial component of Nazism as its chief evil. Perhaps because concern with racial equality was already present in American rights discourse from Reconstruction, the synthesis of anti-Nazism with the extant discourse of American rights could naturally seize upon and emphasize issues of race.

The effect of reaction against Nazism on what would become the

---

[20] Donald R. McCoy and Richard T. Ruetten, *Quest and Response: Minority Rights and the Truman Administration* (The University Press of Kansas, 1973), pp. 10–18.

[21] American Jewish Committee, *On Three Fronts: Thirty-ninth Annual Report, 1945* (American Jewish Committee, 1946), esp. pp. 27–30.

[22] McCoy and Ruetten, *Quest and Response*, p. 16.

civil rights movement was explicitly recognized already in the 1950s. C. Vann Woodward wrote in 1955 that

The foremost of the Axis powers against which the United States fought in World War II was the most forceful exponent of racism the modern world has known. The Nazi crime against the minority race, more than anything else, was the offense that branded the Reich as an outlaw power. Adolph Hitler's doctrine of the "master race" had as its chief victim the Jew, but the association of that doctrine with the creed of white supremacy was inevitably made in the American mind. That association is not likely to be broken very easily. American war propaganda stressed above all else the abhorrence of the West for Hitler's brand of racism and its utter incompatibility with the democratic faith for which we fought. The relevance of this deep stirring of the American conscience for the position of the Negro was not lost upon him and his champions. Awareness of the inconsistency between practice at home and propaganda abroad placed a powerful lever in their hands.[23]

Robert Penn Warren echoes Woodward's point about American war propaganda, noting that wartime propaganda and newsreels used the figure of Lincoln to personify the United States and thus to present America as essentially opposed to doctrines of racial supremacy.[24] This synthesis between Reconstruction and the twentieth-century transformation also helped remake the meaning of Reconstruction. After all, Reconstruction had not been a pure anti-racist crusade. Many Reconstruction Republicans were white supremacists willing to limit black "equality" severely, as with the scheme of civil, political, and social rights. Opposition to the Slave Power was not coextensive with racial egalitarianism. Linking opposition to Hitler to the image of Lincoln, however, naturally directed attention to what the two projects had in common, thus highlighting the egalitarian strains within Reconstruction. In this way, reactions against different adversities in different centuries helped shape each other's dominant face, and the resulting synthesis placed heavy emphasis on racial nondiscrimination within American rights discourse.

Predictably, those who opposed increased minority rights as well as those who favored them invoked totalitarian imagery in support of their positions. In 1964, civil rights workers in the South and politicians pushing civil rights legislation in Washington self-

---

[23] C. Vann Woodward, *The Strange Career of Jim Crow* (Oxford University Press, 1955), p. 119.
[24] Robert Penn Warren, *The Legacy of the Civil War* (Random House, 1961), p. 79.

consciously tried to draw lessons from the experience of Nazism by applying anti-racist principles to the situation of American blacks.[25] But those on the political right in civil rights disputes also structured arguments in terms of anti-Nazism and, more frequently, anti-Sovietism. One Southern newspaper called the 1964 Civil Rights Act "an outrage belonging in Russia" on the grounds that it would violate rights of property and free association.[26] A Southern senator opposed the bill in the name of the "continuous struggle [against] totalitarianism," saying that the Act would destroy the checks and balances that protect individual rights.[27] Anti-Nazism figured in such arguments as well: when President Eisenhower sent federal troops to integrate Central High School in Little Rock, Arkansas in 1957, Senator Richard Russell of Georgia angrily compared the soldiers to Hitlerian storm troopers.[28]

Attacking a position or policy by linking it somehow to Nazism is among the most familiar facets of post-war political rhetoric. It is also one of the most familiar tropes of post-war political philosophy. For example, the debate over morality and legal positivism between Lon Fuller and H. L. A. Hart, conducted in the *Harvard Law Review* in 1958 and still canonical today, is a barely concealed dispute over whether the road to Nazism was paved with a positivist theory of law. As I will discuss below in more detail, Fuller attacks positivism as having led to the Nazi regime in Germany, and Hart concedes that positivism must disentangle itself from Nazi associations if it is to be a viable theory.[29] It seems commonly accepted, in that debate and throughout normative political theory, that to associate a political theory with Nazism is to present a dispositive case against it. Leo Strauss noted this pattern in academic discourse shortly after the war, describing – and denouncing – an increasingly common argumentative technique that he labeled *reductio ad Hitlerum*.[30]

---

[25] Elizabeth Sutherland, ed., *Letters from Mississippi* (McGraw-Hill, 1965), p. 10; *Congressional Record*, 1964, p. 6091.

[26] *Little Rock Democrat*, 10 March 1964, quoted in *Congressional Record*, 12 March 1964, p. 5074.

[27] Senator Hill of Alabama, in *Congressional Record*, 9 March 1964, p. 4759.

[28] Robert L. Branyan and Lawrence H. Larsen, eds., *The Eisenhower Administration, 1953–1961: A Documentary History* (Random House, 1971), vol. II, pp. 1135–1156.

[29] H. L. A. Hart, "Positivism and the Separation of Law and Morals," *Harvard Law Review* 71, 593 (1958); Lon Fuller, "Positivism and Fidelity to Law – A Reply to Professor Hart," *Harvard Law Review* 71, 630 (1958).

[30] Leo Strauss, *Natural Right and History* (University of Chicago Press, 1950), pp. 42–43. To see the pervasiveness of anti-totalitarianism at the time, consider that the book in which Strauss derided *reductio ad Hitlerum* was itself partly a product of anti-totalitarianism and presented

The prevalence of anti-Nazism in normative political philosophy after the war is notable for what it shows about the substantive commitments present in that philosophical discourse. Indeed, the very form that that discourse took was substantially conditioned by the content of those commitments. As noted earlier, foundationalist political philosophy had been out of fashion before the war, but theories of universal rights suddenly gained credit in the 1940s. That renaissance, I submit, was largely due to a set of substantive political commitments that required the support of universalist theories. In those theories, the substantive commitments of the time found expression in a rights discourse more abstract than that which followed the Civil War three generations earlier. Two reasons for this contrast have roots in a fundamental difference between the way that Americans experienced the adversity of the Slave Power and the way that they experienced the adversities of Nazi and Soviet totalitarianism. First, the former was a domestic phenomenon and the latter was outside the American system. Totalitarianism elicited a response on the level of universal principle partly because it challenged Americans to find reasons why they could legitimately pass moral judgment against it. They required a principle or a set of principles derived from some grand premise of universal morality or human nature, not just passage of a law or change in a system of government, because the problem transcended their own political order. Second, among those Americans with direct experience of totalitarianism – i.e., mid-century immigrants from Europe – many of the most influential were intellectuals like Arendt and Strauss, and few were political figures of significant stature. The threat of totalitarianism thus tended to be more intellectualized than earlier, directly experienced threats had been, and it invited reaction on a more abstract plane. In Arendt's words, the search was on for a

itself as such. *Natural Right and History* argued against positivism and historicism and in favor of non-relative, *a priori* standards of right, and Jerome Kerwin's foreword (p. v) introduced the topic as follows:

For many years the political philosophy of responsible government has been a neglected field in American political science. Characteristic of this period was the complete rejection of natural law, the standard by which, traditionally, government relations were judged. Law and rights emanated from the states. Under democratic regimes it was held that majority will created law and granted rights. Beyond these, no restrictions of law could bind the sovereign state. In recent years that peculiar twentieth-century phenomenon – the totalitarian regime – revived among political philosophers the study of the traditionalist natural law doctrine, with its insistence upon limited state authority.

"new political principle," a foundational philosophy that would support the anti-Nazism and anti-Sovietism of post-war America.

"Human rights"

When the "new political principle" arose, a new vocabulary arose as well. People who wished to articulate the themes of universality, dignity, and so on that Arendt invoked in the quotation above began to speak of something called "human rights." Use of the modifier "human" before "rights" was a new development. The Founding and Reconstruction generations had commonly spoken of natural rights, civil rights, political rights, social rights, constitutional rights, and so on, but rarely of "human rights." A similar term, the "rights of man," had been known since the French Revolution and Thomas Paine, but even that phrase was largely absent from American rights discourse in the nineteenth and early twentieth centuries. After World War II, the term became nearly ubiquitous. Consider, as an index to this change in vocabulary, that during the hundred years prior to the Nazi Party's taking power in Germany, only six decisions of the Supreme Court contained the term "human rights," but thirteen Supreme Court decisions spoke of "human rights" between 1941 and 1949, and thirty-two more decisions used the term in the twenty years thereafter. When the United Nations, a coalition born of the struggle to defeat Nazism, specified the fundamental principles to be protected in the post-war world, it called the resulting document the Universal Declaration of Human Rights.[31]

Many post-war rights theorists have noted the rise of the term but without realizing that it represented the rise of a new concept, a new set of substantive commitments. Frequently, "human rights" was mistakenly taken as a new name for an old category. Ten years after the war, Maurice Cranston wrote that people in the 1950s meant by "human rights" "... what Locke and other theorists meant by 'natural rights,' but without any specific reference to a concept of

---

[31] In a move that signaled both the criticism of rights discourse that became fashionable late in the twentieth century and also the deep power that invocations of rights nevertheless continued to command, former West German Chancellor Helmut Schmidt in 1997 proposed that the nations of the world adopt a Universal Declaration of Human Responsibilities. The preamble to his draft echoed the communitarian critique of rights as overly individualist and divisive. Nevertheless, the nineteenth and final article of the draft declared that nothing in the proposed declaration may be interpreted to undermine the Universal Declaration of Human Rights of 1948.

nature."[32] More recently, John Finnis opened his discussion of rights in *Natural Law and Natural Rights* by saying that "human rights" is "a contemporary idiom for 'natural rights.'"[33] This tendency to equate human rights with natural rights has been widespread. The equation is not wholly specious: there are important similarities between twentieth-century conceptions of human rights and eighteenth-century conceptions of natural rights. For example, both categories of rights were considered inalienable from the people to whom they applied. Arendt said that a human right was something "which no tyrant could take away," language reminiscent of natural-rights argument two centuries earlier.[34]

Nevertheless, what modern Americans mean by "human rights" differs from what Locke and the Founders meant by "natural rights," and most contemporary theorists, by mistakenly equating human rights with natural rights, miss an opportunity to discover what distinctive set of commitments the newer vocabulary carries. Perhaps the most important of these commitments is that the rights so described attach to all human beings. Natural rights theorists often excluded non-whites, women, and other groups of people from the population of rights-bearers, but human rights theorists insist that all people everywhere bear the same rights. Cranston was correct that speaking of "human rights" instead of "natural rights" eliminates reference to a conception of nature, but he failed to note that it requires reference to a conception of humanity. And it was because of a particular conception of all humans as equally bearers of certain basic rights that people began to speak of those rights as "human" ones.

Thus, the vocabulary of "human rights" emerged during the 1940s as a way of articulating the anti-totalitarian political creed that all people had certain rights, no matter where or under what kind of law. Moreover, and in response chiefly to the Nazi face of totalitarianism, the idea of human rights insisted that certain basic rights attach to all people equally, regardless of race or religion, simply because they are human. Cranston wrote that "A human right *by definition is a universal moral right*, something which all men, everywhere, at all times, ought to have, something of which no one may be deprived without a grave affront to justice; something which is

---

[32] Maurice Cranston, *Human Rights Today* (Ampersand, 1st edn., 1955), p. 20.
[33] John Finnis, *Natural Law and Natural Rights* (Oxford University Press, 1980), p. 198.
[34] Arendt, *The Origins of Totalitarianism*, pp. 296–297.

owing to every human being simply because he is human."[35] That commitment has remained a dominant feature of the language of human rights. Feinberg, for example, defines human rights as absolute and unconditional, as "rights held by all human beings as such" and as those "which belong equally and unconditionally to all human beings, simply in virtue of their being human."[36] It is not difficult to see how a doctrine of rights operative for all people in all places would solve conceptual problems that Nazism posed for Americans: a human rights framework supplies an ostensibly universal and objective basis on which to condemn phenomena like Nazi Germany.

The commitments to universalism and anti-positivism implicit in "human rights" have been so strong in the post-war era that the vocabulary of human rights has often overwhelmed and substituted for earlier classifications of rights, as if "human rights" were not synonymous merely with "natural rights" but with "rights" itself. In some cases, the unmodified term "rights" is used to mean "human rights," that is, to refer to the legitimate claims that all human beings have, irrespective of location or political conditions.[37] The use of "rights" without a modifier to express the particular commitments of "human rights" attempts to establish, or, perhaps more commonly, reflects the establishment of those commitments as the best or true meaning of rights generally. Kinds of rights whose names require modifiers, like "legal rights" or "constitutional rights," are thus presented as variations from the central theme rather than as equally at the core of what it is to be a right. In other cases, rights that had previously been designated "constitutional rights," "legal rights," or any of many other kinds of rights have been subsumed under the heading of "human rights." In the 1950s, Harvard Law Professor Zechariah Chafee published three books titled *Three Human Rights in the Constitution of 1787*, *How Human Rights Got Into the Constitution*, and *Documents on Fundamental Human Rights*.[38] The "human rights" in these books include the right against bills of attainder and the right of petition, rights long present in American

---

[35] Cranston, *Human Rights Today* (Ampersand, 2nd edn., 1962), p. 40. Emphasis in the original.
[36] Feinberg, *Rights*, pp. 213, 225.
[37] See, e.g., Louis Henkin, "Rights: Here and There," *Columbia Law Review* 81, 1582, at 1582 (1981).
[38] Zechariah Chafee, *Three Human Rights in the Constitution of 1787* (University of Kansas Press, 1956); *How Human Rights Got Into the Constitution* (Boston University Press, 1952); *Documents on Fundamental Human Rights* (Harvard University Press, 1951).

law but not previously called "human rights." The pattern persists: John Finnis, for example, has identified property, contract, and assembly as "human rights."[39] These uses of the language of human rights to cover all sorts of rights illustrate how the commitments implicit in the human rights idea, including universalism and anti-positivism, have come to dominate rights discourse generally.

In discussions of human rights, the assertion that human beings have rights in virtue of their humanity often comes with no supporting argument, as if it were entirely self-evident. Sometimes a question-begging gesture toward explanation is made by saying that human rights derive from basic "human dignity."[40] As was the case in the rights discourse of both the Founding and Reconstruction, much rights discourse of the post-war era has been outcome-driven, less concerned with establishing a coherent account of the sources of rights and then deducing particular rights from those sources than with finding ways to secure the entitlements, liberties, powers, and immunities that seem most important and threatened at a given time. In the context of the confrontation with foreign totalitarianism, the claims that seemed most important were those that would attach to all human beings everywhere, not varying with the positive law of different regimes. The vocabulary of human rights helps advance that agenda, embedding in the nature of rights themselves a substantive point that anti-totalitarians wish to establish.

After World War II, the language of human rights began to figure prominently in both international and domestic politics. The basic United Nations document on political morality, adopted in 1948, is called the "Universal Declaration of Human Rights." In the *New York Times* on the day after the Supreme Court ruling in *Brown v. Board of Education*, both the official editorial commenting on the decision and private persons quoted for reaction explained the significance of desegregating the schools in terms of human rights.[41] Lyndon Johnson opened his speech in support of the Voting Rights Act by saying "I speak tonight for the dignity of man," later adding that "there is no issue of States rights or National rights. There is

---

[39] Finnis, *Natural Law*, p. 221.

[40] For typical uses of the "human dignity" theme in political discourse, see, e.g., Senator Hubert Humphrey on the Civil Rights Bill of 1964, *Congressional Record* for 24 March 1964, p. 6091; Lyndon Johnson's "Selma Speech" to Congress, 15 March 1965, in Friedman, *The Civil Rights Reader*, pp. 261, 263.

[41] *The New York Times*, 18 May 1954, editorial on p. 22; for private reaction, see, e.g., Harold Taylor, president of Sarah Lawrence College, quoted on p. 14.

only the struggle for human rights."[42] Senator Hubert Humphrey argued for civil rights legislation in terms of "individual dignity," saying that the "indignities" of being refused service at lunch counters or hotels violated "human rights."[43] Robert Kennedy, while Attorney General, spoke of the "human rights, human dignity, and human freedom which we have all inherited" and pledged that "No American will be denied his human rights or his Constitutional rights because of his race, creed, or religion."[44] These pronounce-ments seem almost banal today, but they simply would not have occurred in these terms before World War II. Franklin Roosevelt did not use the language of human rights to discuss the signature rights of the New Deal. After the war, his successors used the language of rights in a new form to give priority to a new set of political commitments. As those commitments have become standard, the associated language of human rights has become standard political rhetoric.

The term "human rights" appears nowhere in the American Constitution, of course, because the American Constitution was written long before the rise of "human rights" as a term and as a concept. Given that the 1940s and 1950s were not a constitution-making era in the United States, we cannot examine American constitutions to understand American conceptions of human rights at that time. Americans did, however, draft constitutions for other countries after the war, so it is possible to examine a non-American constitution for the same purpose. The original draft of the consti-tution of Japan, for example, was written by American occupation forces, and their draft is an example of how a constitution written by post-World War II Americans viewed the status of rights.

The first American draft of a Japanese constitution, written in February 1946, was in several respects closely patterned on the American Constitution. Its preamble, for example, contained di-rectly transplanted phrases: "We, the Japanese People," to "secure for ourselves and our posterity ... the blessings of liberty ... do ordain and establish this Constitution."[45] At the same time, the draft

[42] Lyndon Johnson, 15 March 1965, in Friedman, *The Civil Rights Reader*, pp. 261, 263.
[43] Hubert Humphrey, in the *Congressional Record*, 1964, p. 6091.
[44] Robert F. Kennedy, speech to the B'nai Brith, Chicago, 13 October 1963, in Thomas A. Hopkins, ed., *Rights for Americans: The Speeches of Robert F. Kennedy* (Bobbs-Merrill, 1964), p. 180; speech to the National Newspaper Publishers Association, Baltimore, 22 June 1962, in ibid., p. 85.
[45] For the text of the American draft of the Japanese constitution, see Kyoko Inoue,

differed in significant ways from the American Constitution, reflecting a concern with the universality of enforceable rights and indeed of political morality in general. For example, it declared "that laws of political morality are universal; and that obedience to such laws is incumbent upon all peoples." Chapter III of the draft constitution, titled "Rights and Duties of the People," asserted that "human rights" are fundamental, timeless, and inviolable:

Article IX. [First article of Chapter III] The people of Japan are entitled to the enjoyment without interference of all fundamental human rights.

Article X. The fundamental human rights by this Constitution guaranteed to the people of Japan ... are conferred upon this and future generations in sacred trust, to be held for all time inviolate.

Article XII. [A]ll Japanese by virtue of their humanity shall be respected as individuals ...

Article XIII. All natural persons are equal before the law. No discrimination shall be authorized or tolerated in political, economic, or social relations on account of race, creed, sex, social status, caste, or national origin.

The American Constitution contains no such language of universal rights. There is no explicit philosophy of universal rights even in the Bill of Rights or the Reconstruction amendments, which are restricted to narrower, more specific guarantees. "Congress shall make no law abridging the freedom of speech" is not the same as "All people have a fundamental human right to speak freely." Certainly, there is nothing in the American Constitution to compare with "All Japanese by virtue of their humanity shall be respected as individuals." In the American Founding period, one must look to the Declaration of Independence rather than the Constitution for such sweeping principles, and even in the Declaration there are but three general rights enunciated, with no explanatory detail given. Certainly, the Declaration says nothing about prohibiting discrimination "in political, economic, or social relations on account of race, creed, sex, social status, caste, or national origin." That is a substantive difference. "Fundamental human rights" could be taken to mean the same thing as "inalienable rights," but the "inalienable rights" of Americans in 1776 certainly did not include rights against racial or sexual discrimination. The Declaration is much better poetry, and

MacArthur's Japanese Constitution: A Linguistic and Cultural Study of its Making. (University of Chicago Press, 1991). I focus on the American draft rather than the constitution as finally approved because my purpose is to examine American and not Japanese conceptions of rights.

was of course not intended to operate as a legal code. The constitutional explication of universal human rights linked to a general ban on many kinds of discrimination was, however, an original feature of the 1940s, when the new language of human rights supplied a framework supportive of substantive commitments against discrimination.

APPLICATIONS OF RIGHTS: THE SUBSTANTIVE AGENDAS

Supreme Court decisions during the war years increasingly reflected substantive commitments associated with anti-Nazism. In each of the three examples given below, the Court in 1943 and 1944 reversed a position it had taken shortly before, twice by explicitly overruling earlier decisions. Each set of cases presented an issue that bore a relationship to American perceptions of Nazism, and each reversal showed how anti-Nazism fueled changes in the prevailing American conceptions of rights. The first example, the flag salute cases of 1940 and 1943, pitted the state's authority to compel demonstrations of loyalty against individual rights of free conscience and dissent. The second and third examples involved rights against racial discrimination, first as applied to Japanese Americans and then as applied to blacks. The commitment to opposing racial discrimination remained a strong element of American rights discourse in the 1950s and 1960s. In those decades, another face of anti-totalitarianism also informed the substance of rights discourse, this time in opposition to the Soviet Union. After I discuss these three examples of rights discourse changing in the 1940s in opposition to Nazism, I will discuss two areas in which anti-Sovietism played a similar role. The first of those two regards the rights of individuals in police custody, and the second regards the rights of free expression.

The flag-salute cases

In 1940, a brother and sister named William and Lillian Gobitis, members of the Jehovah's Witnesses religious sect, were expelled from a public school in Pennsylvania for refusing to salute the American flag and recite the Pledge of Allegiance during a daily ceremony at the school. The Gobitis children refused to salute on the grounds that their religious beliefs prohibited them from honoring graven images, flags included. The Supreme Court found that the right of free exercise of religion under the First Amendment did not protect the Gobitis children and that the school could constitutionally require their participation in the flag-salute ceremony. Most of the Court's opinion dealt with the tension between religious liberty and national cohesion, with the symbolic relationship between the flag and the rights being claimed against it, and with the rival rights of parents and the public at large to influence children's attitudes about the significance of the flag.[46] Three years later the Court reversed its decision. In *West Virginia State Board of Education v. Barnette*, a case presenting exactly the same circumstances as *Gobitis*, the Court held that First Amendment rights prohibited the state from requiring a salute to the flag and overruled *Gobitis* accordingly.[47] No one claimed that *Barnette* presented different facts or different questions from *Gobitis*. The Court simply ruled one way in 1940 and the other way in 1943.

The reversal was largely driven by the Court's desire to distinguish America from wartime Germany. As it happened, the flag-salute controversy manifested that desire in two different forms. One, arguably the more legally rational of the two, concerned the question of a government enforcing conformity of belief and action among citizens. That was what the flag-salute laws demanded, and, by 1943, such compelled regimentation was closely associated with the Nazi enemy, especially when it came at the expense of private religious beliefs. In his majority opinion, Justice Jackson followed this rationale explicitly:

Struggles to coerce uniformity of sentiment in support of some end thought essential to their time and country have been waged by many good as well as evil men ... Ultimate futility of such attempts to compel coherence is the lesson of every such effort from the Roman drive to stamp out Christianity as a disturber of its pagan unity, the Inquisition, as a means to religious and dynastic unity, the Siberian exiles as a means to Russian unity, down to the fast failing efforts of our present totalitarian enemies. Those who begin coercive elimination of dissent soon find themselves exterminating dissenters.[48]

A second way in which anti-Nazism contributed to the reversal in *Barnette* dealt with the mechanics of the salute itself. Unlike the

---

[46] *Minersville School District v. Gobitis*, 310 U.S. 586 (1940).
[47] *West Virginia State Board of Education v. Barnette*, 319 U.S. 624 (1943).
[48] Ibid., at 640–641. The mention of Siberian exiles suggests a contrast with Soviet as well as Nazi totalitarianism, even during the war.

practice familiar today, by which Americans salute the flag by placing their right hands over their hearts, the salute that the *Barnette* and *Gobitis* laws prescribed involved extending one's right arm forward from the shoulder, stiffly, in a manner reminiscent of the Roman Legion salute and the Nazi and Fascist salutes. In the *Barnette* case, several community organizations including the PTA, the Boy and Girl Scouts, and the Red Cross gave notice that they disapproved of the flag salute because it looked "too much like Hitler's."[49] The US Flag Association maintained that the salute was in fact different – the stiff right arm in the American salute was slightly raised and the palm of the hand turned up, and the stiff right arm in the Nazi salute was parallel to the ground and the palm of the hand turned down – but the difference was lost on non-specialists to whom a stiff-arm salute looked like a stiff-arm salute. In 1943, neither the community organizations mentioned nor the Supreme Court was favorably disposed toward compelling children to salute in a way that looked like the salute of the Nazi Party or the Hitler Youth. There is, of course, no way in which a stiff-arm salute is logically necessary to Nazi ideology or behavior. The link between those aspects of Nazism which made it objectionable and the stiff-arm salute was cultural rather than logical: it was a behavior associated with people who did objectionable things, not a behavior necessary to what was objectionable about their actions. That cultural adjacency, however, was enough to help reverse the way that the Supreme Court applied individual rights under the First Amendment.[50]

Issues of race

Many of the most significant changes in American rights discourse in the generation after the war came with regard to issues of race and especially issues of integration and black equality, as in the *Brown* decision. The reaction against Nazi racism did not, however, affect only blacks. Instead, the rights of American blacks after World War II advanced as part of a general advance in rights against racial discrimination. This was in contrast to the change in black rights during Reconstruction. The crisis preceding Reconstruction had

[49] Ibid., at 627.
[50] On the differences between logical and cultural adjacency, see Freeden, "Political Concepts," pp. 151–154.

focused specifically on blacks, and the reactive rights that followed attached to blacks before any other group. The reaction against Nazism, however, yielded a general right against racial discrimination. That right applied to blacks, the most obvious sufferers of racial discrimination in the United States, and to members of other racial groups as well.

The Japanese internment
Reaction against Nazi racism was a prominent undertone in the wartime matter of Japanese-Americans living on the West Coast. After the American entry into the war against Japan, the US military imposed curfews and other restrictions on persons of Japanese descent living on the West Coast, including both naturalized and native American citizens, and eventually "excluded" most Japanese-Americans from certain Western areas, interning those who lived there in military camps farther inland. Three cases alleging violations of the rights of American citizens in connection with these restrictions reached the Supreme Court. The changing way that the Court discussed and decided those cases, as well as contemporary commentary on the decisions, shows the influence of anti-Nazism on American conceptions of rights.

The first of the three cases, *Hirabayashi v. United States*, was decided in 1943. Claiming that a curfew for Japanese Americans and an order to register for forced relocation violated his rights as a citizen under the Fifth Amendment, an American-born resident of Seattle named George Hirabayashi refused to comply and was prosecuted and convicted for violating the curfew. The Supreme Court upheld the conviction without dissent. Writing for the Court, Chief Justice Harlan Stone wrote that the question to be decided was not whether the restrictions were racially discriminatory but merely whether "there was any substantial basis for the conclusion ... that the curfew as applied was a protective measure necessary to meet the threat of sabotage and espionage which would substantially affect the war effort."[51] Stone explicitly stated that although "racial discriminations are in most circumstances irrelevant and therefore prohibited," the government was entitled to "place citizens of one ancestry in a different category from others" when doing so was "relevant to measures for our national defense."[52] Racial discrimi-

---

[51] *Hirabayashi*, at 95.   [52] Ibid., at 100.

nation was not categorically unacceptable: "irrelevant and *therefore* prohibited" implies that such discrimination could, if relevant in a particular case, be legitimate. Stone thus held that the restrictions were not subject to strict scrutiny by the Court just because they were racially discriminatory. A finding that there was a rational basis for the classification, as the Court did find, would be sufficient to uphold the curfew.[53]

The Court ruled unanimously, but not all of the Justices were without reservations. Justice Murphy, deeply troubled by the racist content of the military restrictions, originally planned to dissent. Although his fellow justices ultimately cajoled him into concurring for the sake of unity on an important wartime issue, Murphy retained in his concurrence key passages from what was originally intended as a dissenting opinion.[54] He made clear what he found most troublesome about the military policy toward Japanese-Americans, calling it "a substantial restriction of the personal liberty of citizens of the United States based upon the accident of race or ancestry ... In this sense it bears a melancholy resemblance to the treatment accorded to members of the Jewish race in Germany and in other parts of Europe."[55] This explicit linkage between Japanese-American internment in the United States and Nazi treatment of Jews would persist and grow stronger among opponents of the military policy.

A year and a half later, in *Korematsu v. United States*, the Court upheld the conviction of an American citizen who had refused to report for relocation to a military internment center. Three Justices dissented this time, and their written opinions linked the case with Nazi policies. Justice Roberts, for example, wrote that Korematsu had been convicted "for not submitting to imprisonment in a concentration camp, based on his ancestry."[56] Even the majority upholding the restrictions evinced more discomfort than in *Hirabayashi*. Rejecting the *Hirabayashi* doctrine that racial classifications in the name of national defense need only pass a rational basis test to be upheld, Justice Black announced for the Court that "all legal restrictions which curtail the civil rights of a single racial group are immediately suspect ... [C]ourts must subject them to the most rigid

[53] Ibid., at 102.
[54] Peter Irons, *Justice at War* (Oxford University Press, 1983), pp. 245–247.
[55] *Hirabayashi*, Murphy concurring at 110–111.
[56] *Korematsu v. United States*, 323 U.S. 214, at 226 (1944) (Roberts, J., dissenting).

scrutiny."[57] He went to great lengths to try to distinguish the internment program from Nazi policies. Meeting Roberts's contention directly, Black insisted that *Korematsu* was not about "imprisonment of a citizen in a concentration camp solely because of his ancestry ... Our task would be simple, our duty clear, were this a case involving the imprisonment of a loyal citizen in a concentration camp because of racial prejudice."[58] In a truly incredible claim, he insisted that the internment had nothing to with "hostility to [Korematsu] or his race."[59] These protests show that Black wanted to deny the racist nature of the exclusion order, in contrast to the Court's earlier willingness to accept racial discrimination when rationally based in *Hirabayashi*. If the exclusion order were racially prejudicial, Black implied, it could not be sustained. Something else was even worse in Black's mind than racial prejudice: concentration camps. He went out of his way to engage in a terminological dispute with the dissent, writing of the relocation centers that "we deem it unjustifiable to call them concentration camps with all the ugly connotations that term implies."[60] In light of these exchanges between the majority opinion and the dissents, it seems that the case turned on two questions of definition, specifically, whether the exclusion order was racially prejudicial and whether the "relocation centers" were concentration camps. Racial prejudice and concentration camps were the trademarks of Nazi Germany, and the Japanese internment could not be upheld if it were of a kind with Nazism.

The final case in this series to reach the Court was *Ex Parte Mitsuye Endo*, decided in December 1944. Endo had been taken from Sacramento to a relocation center in Utah and had petitioned for a writ of habeas corpus to secure her release, claiming that she was a citizen detained without charge. The Supreme Court, acting unanimously, granted the writ. Writing for the Court, Justice Douglas used the Fifteenth Amendment's "race, creed or color" formula and declared that a citizen not individually suspected of disloyalty could not be detained because of membership in a racial group.[61] Some concurrences took even harder lines, denouncing the entire evacuation policy as unjustified racism.[62] Thus, the Court's attitude toward the military policy on Japanese-Americans evolved as the war went on, growing ever more sympathetic to the claims of members of a

---

[57] Ibid., at 216 (majority opinion).   [58] Ibid., at 223.   [59] Ibid.   [60] Ibid.
[61] *Ex Parte Mitsuye Endo*, 323 U.S. 283 (1944).   [62] Ibid., Murphy concurring.

minority race discriminated against by their government: the Court held unanimously for the discriminatory measures in the first case, divided in the second case, and in the third case held unanimously in favor of the victim of the discrimination.

The taint of association with Nazi racism surely contributed to the shift in American attitudes about the exclusion policy at the end of the war. The shift, after all, occurred at just the time when the extent of Nazi atrocities was becoming generally known.[63] Nor was it only in the judiciary that Americans saw the parallel. In a fiercely critical denouncement of the exclusion policy, Yale professor Eugene Rostow implicitly and explicitly linked the American military policy toward Japanese-Americans with Nazi policy toward Jews. Rostow propounded a charge that Black had specifically denied, writing that studies of relocation center conditions "make it plain that the camps were in fact concentration camps."[64] The military's claims about ingrained Japanese ethnic tendencies toward disloyalty were virtually indistinguishable, Rostow wrote, from "the pseudo-genetics of the Nazis."[65] Describing the congressional testimony of the military commander directly responsible for the internment, Rostow quoted several passages that seemed parallel to Nazi statements about Jews.[66] On the last page of his article, Rostow drew a deeper parallel, suggesting that Americans were publicly culpable for the Japanese internment in the same way that "the German people bear a common political responsibility for outrages secretly committed by the Gestapo and the SS."[67] Most revealingly, Rostow closed by expressing his hope that the Court would reconsider and repudiate *Hirabayashi* and *Korematsu*, explicitly invoking *Barnette*'s repudiation of *Gobitis* two years earlier.[68] This linkage of the Japanese internment cases to the flag-salute cases makes sense only as a linkage of cases influenced by the confrontation with Nazi Germany. The Supreme Court had overruled itself many times by 1945; it was not necessary for Rostow to cite any specific example in order to urge a repudiation of *Hirabayashi* and *Korematsu*. Had he wanted to cite a specific instance of repudiation, it might have seemed more sensible to cite

---

[63] The shift cannot be explained by a waning of anti-Japanese sentiment as the war neared a successful end, because anti-Japanese prejudice in America was at least as intense in the final stages of the war as it had been in previous periods. See John W. Dower, *War Without Mercy: Race and Power in the Pacific War* (Pantheon, 1986), pp. 51–55.

[64] Eugene V. Rostow, "The Japanese American Cases – A Disaster," *Yale Law Journal* 54, 489, at 502 (1945).

[65] Ibid., at 506.   [66] Ibid., at 531–532.   [67] Ibid., at 533.   [68] Ibid.

an example legally parallel to those cases, one that involved Fifth Amendment rights or the right of habeas corpus or rights against racial discrimination. Instead, he chose a First Amendment case having nothing to do with race. The link was not in a formal question of law but in the anti-Nazi orientation which framed both sets of cases.

State action and the rights of black Americans

The courts also displayed new enthusiasm for securing the rights of American blacks during the war. One striking set of cases involved problems of state action, the legal doctrine under which the guarantees of the Fourteenth and Fifteenth Amendments applied only in cases where government was an actor and which therefore meant that those amendments could not protect blacks from private discrimination. During Reconstruction, the courts had often taken an expansive view of the state action doctrine, thus substantially limiting the protection that the Fourteenth Amendment afforded to blacks. In the *Cruikshank* case, for example, the Supreme Court declined to find state action in Louisiana's failure to prosecute whites for the murder of blacks.[69] That decision typified nineteenth-century limitations on the judicial commitment to equal rights for black Americans. In the 1940s, however, the Supreme Court reversed its course. At a time when anti-Nazism fostered thicker rights against racial discrimination, the Court began construing the state action requirement extremely liberally when doing so was necessary to vindicating the equal rights of blacks.

The white primary: Smith v. Allwright

One prominent Supreme Court reversal on the state action issue concerned the "white primary," a Southern political institution in which blacks were prohibited from casting ballots in the primary elections that political parties used to select candidates for office. In 1935, the Supreme Court had ruled unanimously that white primaries were constitutional. Parties and party conventions, the Court had held, were private associations, and constitutional bans on racial discrimination in voting reached only public or "state" actors.[70] In 1944, the Court struck down exactly the same Texas white primary

---

[69] See discussion of *Cruikshank* in chapter 4, p. 148.
[70] *Grovey v. Townsend*, 295 U.S. 45 (1935).

that it had sustained before the war, ruling this time that a primary election is state action controlled by the Fifteenth Amendment.[71] Acquiescence in political racism was more difficult to sanction by that time. In an article reviewing the history of the Texas white primary and commenting on the Supreme Court's 1944 decision, Robert Cushman drew an explicit parallel between Germans and Southern whites in his very first sentence. He did not actually accuse Southerners of being Nazis, saying instead that they seemed to see the Fifteenth Amendment in the way that Germans saw the Treaty of Versailles, that is, as merely a compulsion imposed by the victors.[72] It is barely possible, however, to imagine that such a comparison written in 1945 did not invoke anti-Nazism against the white supremacism of the Texas white primary.[73]

Restrictive covenants: *Shelley v. Kraemer*

The most sweeping Supreme Court decision on state action and the rights of black Americans occurred three years after the war in the case of *Shelley v. Kraemer*. *Shelley* involved a restrictive covenant, a clause in the deed to a property that forbade the owner of the property to sell the property to a black buyer. Shelley, the owner of one such property in Missouri, tried to sell the property to a black family, and Kraemer sued to enforce the restrictive covenant and block the sale. Kraemer claimed that the Fourteenth Amendment did not forbid restrictive covenants, because the Fourteenth Amendment reached only state action and restrictive covenants were private agreements entered into by private parties. The Supreme Court agreed with Kraemer that restrictive covenants were private

---

[71] *Smith v. Allwright*, 321 U.S. 649 (1944).

[72] Robert Cushman, "The Texas 'White Primary' Case – *Smith v. Allwright*," *Cornell Law Quarterly* 30, 66 (1945).

[73] It is impossible to gauge the extent to which hints and allusions indicate a deeper role for anti-Nazism than that which actors of the time explicitly acknowledged, but it is reasonable to suspect that the anti-Nazi influence affected more people than openly acknowledged its role. Open discussion of Nazi atrocities and especially of the Holocaust was rare in the United States in the first twenty years after the war, as central aspects of the topic were widely considered unspeakable. See Robert Lane Fenrich, "Imagining Holocaust: Mass Death and American Consciousness at the End of World War II." Doctoral dissertation, Northwestern University, 1992. This is not to say that reaction against Nazism was not explicit in the rights theory and rights politics of the time. It was. As already illustrated, many people dealt explicitly with the Nazi theme. But given the well-known phenomenon from the 1940s through the 1960s of not discussing Nazi atrocities fully and openly, it is reasonable to suspect that those who made the connection explicit at that time were only a portion of those whose attitudes toward rights and especially minority rights had shifted in response to Nazism.

agreements but ruled without dissent for Shelley. Agreeing not to sell to blacks might be a private decision beyond the reach of the Fourteenth Amendment, Chief Justice Vinson wrote, but judicial enforcement of such a decision was state action, because the court that was asked to enforce the covenant was an arm of the state. Under the Fourteenth Amendment, no arm of the state could be involved in a racially discriminatory action. The covenants were therefore not invalid, but their enforcement was unconstitutional.[74]

It is easy to see that characterizing enforcement as state action greatly enhances the reach of the Fourteenth Amendment and therefore greatly expands constitutional protection of the rights of blacks and other minorities. Once enforcement of private agreements is state action, the power of the state can no longer stand behind private discriminations. Indeed, deeming state enforcement of private agreements "state action" is tantamount to eliminating much of the boundary between the public and private spheres, inasmuch as it makes every contractual agreement a public act subject, in principle, to constitutional limitations in its enforcement. The *Shelley* doctrine proved so expansive that later courts have largely tried to cabin its holding rather than following it to its logical conclusions. Nevertheless, it is not difficult to understand why the Court in 1948 took the extraordinary step of declaring enforcement of private agreements to be state action, even though so doing jeopardized a central doctrine of constitutional law. *Shelley* starkly posed the question of whether the government would support white supremacy, and it did so in the immediate aftermath of the war. Contemporaries knew that the case had symbolic importance: the United States took the then-unprecedented step in *Shelley* of intervening as an amicus in a civil rights case, even though the case involved no federal law and no federal agency.[75] Amicus briefs were also filed by groups such as the Non-Sectarian Anti-Nazi League to Champion Human Rights, a group with no obvious connection to issues of Missouri property law (and for whom *Shelley* was a once-and-only foray into the world of Supreme Court litigation) but whose very name bespeaks the set of commitments that makes the Court's attitude in this case comprehensible: in the wake of Nazism,

---

[74] *Shelley v. Kraemer*, 334 U.S. 1 (1948).
[75] Mary L. Dudziak, "Desegregation as a Cold War Imperative," *Stanford Law Review* 41, 61, at 105 (1988).

the ascendant doctrine of human rights called for strong commitments to oppose racial discrimination.[76]

The anti-Soviet influence

The differences between the influences of Soviet and Nazi totalitarianism on American rights discourse largely correlate with differences in the way that Americans understood those two foreign
political orders. Many of the substantive commitments inspired by
reaction against Nazism concerned the rights of members of racial
minority groups, and many of the Soviet-inspired commitments
involved protection against police power, including censorship. To
be sure, the American confrontation with the Soviet Union did not
always foster expanded rights of free expression. Sometimes, the
security fears that the Cold War engendered had the opposite effect.
In *Dennis v. United States*, for example, the Supreme Court upheld the
convictions of Communist Party leaders who had been convicted of
advocating the overthrow of the government of the United States. As
a case in which the right to free political speech clashed directly with
the desire to block the rise of communist power, *Dennis* provided a
perfect forum for different versions of anti-totalitarianism to struggle
with one another. Chief Justice Vinson wrote only a short opinion
for the Court, skirting the major issues, but the concurring and
dissenting opinions engaged in an extensive argument about the
relationship between communism and free speech in America.
Justice Jackson, for whom anti-totalitarianism had supported increased freedom for dissenters in *Barnette*, now reached the opposite
conclusion and concurred in the judgment. His major argument was
pragmatic. Implicitly acknowledging the tension with *Barnette*,
Jackson wrote that the problem in *Dennis* was not a "refusal of a
handful of school children to salute our flag" but a well-organized,
well-financed, highly disciplined political organization and a serious
threat to the American order.[77] Their superior organization and
coordination made the communists unlike the anarchist hotheads of
thirty years before, for whom Justice Holmes's clear-and-present-
danger test had been an adequate limitation on free speech. If things
progressed to the point where the communists presented a clear and

[76] *Shelley*, at 3.
[77] *Dennis v. United States*, 341 U.S. 494, at 568 (1951) (Jackson, J., concurring).

present danger of harm or violence, all would already be lost. Preventing the evils of totalitarianism thus required limiting free speech.[78]

Justice Douglas took precisely the opposite view. In a dissent whose spirit might have flowed directly from Jackson's *Barnette* opinion, Douglas argued that communists demanded conformity and that America must tolerate dissent in order not to be like the communists. He closed his opinion with a virtually paradigmatic statement of that argument: "Vishinsky wrote in 1930, in *The Law of the Soviet State*, 'In our state, naturally, there is and can be no place for freedom of speech, press, and so on for the foes of socialism.' Our concern should be that we accept no such standard for the United States."[79] A more clear statement of the anti-totalitarian argument for the right of free speech would be difficult to compose.

As the conflict between the different opinions in *Dennis* shows, anti-totalitarianism did not dictate a single answer to every question of rights. The construction of rights in reaction against totalitarianism was subject to a considerable amount of indeterminacy, and the project of negating totalitarianism could lead different people down different political paths. After all, the majority's position in *Dennis* was just as anti-totalitarian as the minority's. During the era of McCarthyism, decisions like *Dennis* were the rule rather than the exception. By the 1960s, however, the *Dennis* minority's version of anti-totalitarianism had gained significant strength. Morton Horwitz takes 1957 as the turning point in decisions in the Supreme Court, writing that until that date the Court deferred to Congress on Cold War measures to suppress political dissent but that thereafter the

[78] Ibid., at 567–570, 577.

[79] *Dennis*, at 591. Douglas consistently took this view of the relationship between totalitarianism and free speech. Consider his statement of the anti-Soviet, pro-free speech position in *Paris Adult Theatre*, an obscenity case arising more than twenty years after *Dennis*: "'Obscenity' at most is the expression of offensive ideas. There are regimes in the world where ideas 'offensive' to the majority (or at least to those who control the majority) are suppressed. There, life proceeds at a monotonous pace. Most of us would find that world offensive." *Paris Adult Theatre I v. Slaton*, 413 U.S. 49, at 71 (1973) (Douglas, J., dissenting). Douglas was frequently in the minority on obscenity issues, but his general anti-totalitarian argument for the right of free speech was often successful. A generation after *Dennis*, it prevailed in the controversy over a proposed Nazi march in Skokie, Illinois. The Skokie question was in some sense *Dennis* redux, pitting the anti-totalitarian right of free speech against the need to oppose actual advocates of a totalitarian regime. In upholding the right of the Nazi Party to march, a three-judge panel made precisely the argument that Douglas had made in his *Dennis* dissent, arguing that the right of free speech "distinguishes life in this country from life under the Third Reich." *Collin v. Smith*, 578 F.2d 1197, at 1201 (7th Cir. 1978).

Court intervened to protect the free expression of dissenters.[80] Anti-Soviet sentiment was then more likely to appear in arguments for expanded rights of free expression, portraying the United States as meaningfully different from and better than the Soviet Union because of the rights that Americans possessed. Robert Kennedy, once near the center of McCarthyism, declared in 1961 that America was winning the Cold War not because of its material wealth but because of the rights of the individual to free expression, free conscience, and political dissent.[81] It is also interesting to note that after the political pendulum swung against McCarthy, McCarthyism itself became something that advocates of the rights of free speech, free press, and free association would cite as a point of negative reference, in the way that Reconstruction-era abolitionists cited the Gag Rule and Founding-era advocates of free trade rights cited the Boston Port Bill. The model of adversity, reaction, and synthesis incorporated not just the struggle with the Soviet Union but also McCarthyism as an adverse circumstance. Since the 1960s, the memory of McCarthyism has itself supported a reactive right to free political speech.

The rights of criminal procedure

Anti-Sovietism also shaped a new commitment to protecting the rights of criminal defendants, persons held in police custody, and ordinary private citizens in their encounters with the police. Consider, for example, the development of Fourth Amendment doctrine in the first years of the Cold War. Today, every American knows that the police cannot search a private person's home without a warrant. That is the prevailing interpretation of the Fourth Amendment's provision that "The right of the people to be secure against … unreasonable searches and seizures, shall not be violated, and no warrants shall issue, but upon probable cause." As Akhil Amar has argued, however, the plain text of the Fourth Amendment does not actually require a warrant for every police search. It requires only that searches be "reasonable." The Amendment does say that

---

[80] Morton Horwitz, *The Transformation of American Law, 1870–1960* (Oxford University Press, 1992), p. 260.

[81] Robert F. Kennedy, speech to the 10th Anniversary Convocation Center for Study of Democratic Institutions of the Fund of the Republic, New York, 22 January 1963, in Hopkins, *Rights for Americans*, pp. 122–125.

warrants shall issue only on "probable cause," but it does not say that every search requires a warrant. Early in American history, Amar explains, there was no warrant requirement for police searches; the effect of a warrant was not to authorize a search but to insulate the searching officer from civil liability in a subsequent suit by the citizen whose home was searched. The police could search a person's house if the search was reasonable, and they were subject to civil liability if they guessed wrong about the reasonableness of the search, unless they secured a warrant in advance. No state constitution had a textual warrant requirement at the Founding, and state supreme courts routinely dismissed the idea that state constitutional language similar to that of the federal constitution implied a warrant requirement for all searches.[82]

The modern warrant requirement stems from the case of *Johnson v. United States*, which the Supreme Court decided in 1948. In *Johnson*, police officers of the state of Washington had entered and searched a hotel room after smelling opium from the hallway outside. The officers did not have a warrant. On a reasonableness test, the search would have been permissible: writing for the Court, Justice Jackson did not dispute that it would have been reasonable to infer the presence of illegal narcotics from the smell in the hallway. The Court decided, however, that reasonableness was not the proper test. In "a society which chooses to dwell in reasonable security and freedom from surveillance," Jackson wrote, the police cannot be permitted to draw such inferences themselves. They must instead present their information to a neutral judicial officer and secure his approval in the form of a warrant before they can search a person's private living area.[83] Jackson's evocation of a society that chose to dwell in freedom from surveillance was clearly meant to contrast with the alternative choice, which was totalitarian government. Any rule other than a strict warrant requirement, he wrote, "would obliterate one of the most fundamental distinctions between our form of government, where officers are under the law, and the police-state where they are the law."[84] Thus, in the year of *Shelley*, the Supreme Court worked another major transformation in a basic constitutional doctrine, again aggressively protecting rights that distinguished the United States from totalitarian regimes.

---

[82] Amar, *The Constitution and Criminal Procedure*, pp. 4–5.
[83] *Johnson v. United States*, 333 U.S. 10, at 14 (1948).   [84] Ibid., at 17.

One year later, when the Court took another step toward thickening individual rights against the police, Justice Frankfurter's opinion for the Court articulated a synthesis of the new anti-totalitarian Fourth Amendment with the older Fourth Amendment of the Founding. In *Wolf v. Colorado*, the Court unanimously agreed that the rights conferred by the Fourth Amendment applied against the states as well as the federal government. Echoing Jackson in *Johnson*, Frankfurter wrote that the security of an individual's privacy against arbitrary police intrusion was "basic to a free society." Then, fusing contemporary adversities with historical inheritances, he went on to say that "The knock at the door, whether by day or by night, as a prelude to a search, without authority of law but solely on the authority of the police, did not need the commentary of recent history to be condemned as inconsistent with the conception of human rights enshrined in the history and the basic constitutional documents of English-speaking peoples."[85] Frankfurter thus argued that unsanctioned police searches had always been prohibited in the American legal tradition and that contemporary conditions merely highlighted the wisdom of the pre-existing system of rights. In reality, of course, the system of rights was changing. The warrant requirement of *Johnson* a year before was a significant thickening of rights against police surveillance, not simply a reaffirmation of existing practices. The negation of contemporary totalitarianism, however, was grafted onto and synthesized with older elements of American rights discourse, each shaping how the Courts learned to view the other.

Jackson's language in *Johnson* did not differentiate between the Nazi and the Soviet faces of totalitarianism, but later developments in the rights of criminal defendants often did. One such case was *Gideon v. Wainwright*, in which the Supreme Court declared that a criminal defendant's right to legal counsel is "fundamental" and therefore applicable in state courts as well as federal ones. *Gideon* overruled *Betts v. Brady*, which was decided in 1942, the last year before anti-totalitarian agendas began to inspire decisions like *Barnette* and *Endo*. Writing for a unanimous Court in *Gideon*, Justice Black delivered a short opinion characterizing the right of counsel as "necessary to insure fundamental human rights of life and liberty." He then wrote that "The right of one charged with crime to counsel

---

[85] *Wolf v. Colorado*, 338 U.S. 25, at 27, 28 (1949).

may not be deemed fundamental and essential to fair trials in some countries, but it is in ours."[86] Any uncertainty about which countries were so invoked was eliminated one year later when the Court in another right-to-counsel case used the "other regimes" topos and spelled out the reference. Writing for the Court in *Escobedo v. Illinois*, which established the right of a defendant to confer with counsel when being questioned by police, Justice Arthur Goldberg cast the question in terms of the proper dynamics of a confrontation between the police and the citizen accused. "Our Constitution, unlike some others, strikes the balance in favor of the right of the accused," he wrote. He then footnoted a report on a 1956 congress of the Communist Party of the Soviet Union, discussing confessions obtained during Stalinist purges.[87] This reference to Soviet police practices reflected one of the influences underlying the Court's new commitment to the rights of defendants.[88]

Sometimes, opposition to the Soviet Union and opposition to Nazi Germany clashed in disputes over rights, as parties on two different sides of an issue would argue from opposition to two different forms of totalitarianism. The role of anti-totalitarianism in these conflicts was often rhetorical, but the instrumental value of anti-totalitarian rhetoric was necessarily predicated on totalitarianism's extensive contribution to shaping the discursive space of postwar political argument. Civil rights workers, for example, were frequently censured by people preoccupied with the threat of communism, and prominent Southern voices regularly argued against civil rights legislation by linking increases in federal power and curtailments of the rights of private property and free association with Soviet practices. The 1948 Dixiecrat platform denounced the Democratic innovations from which it dissented as "totalitarian

---

[86] *Gideon v. Wainright*, 372 U.S. 335, 343, 344 (1963), overruling *Betts v. Brady*, 316 U.S. 343 (1942).

[87] *Escobedo v. Illinois*, 378 U.S. 478, at 488–489 (1964).

[88] The influence on American rights discourse of opposition to the Soviet Union and everything associated with it extended beyond the issues of free expression and police procedure. The confrontation with the Soviet Union also encouraged advances in rights of racial equality, albeit not by the pattern of reaction I have described regarding other rights. Progress in civil rights in the United States served a public relations need for America during the Cold War. The Soviet Union could easily denounce the United States as undemocratic and point to the status of American blacks for support, and this attack found receptive audiences in many countries, particularly in non-white, non-aligned countries whose support the United States wished to enlist. During the 1950s and 1960s, many Americans were keenly aware that they needed to realize equal rights at home in order to serve foreign policy objectives. See Dudziak, "Desegregation."

government," and the governor of Georgia wrote in 1955 that the only group that stood to gain from the Supreme Court's *Brown* decision was the Communist Party.[89] Still at his post at the University of Chicago, Robert Hutchins commented on this pattern as early as 1949, noting with some dismay that "One who opposes racial discrimination or the Ku Klux Klan can be called a fellow traveler, for the Russians claim that they ought to be opposed."[90] Thus, anti-Sovietism as well as anti-Nazism played a role in shaping post-war American rights discourse, and each sometimes tempered or opposed arguments suggested by the other.

ANTI-POSITIVISM AND ITS CONTENT FROM NUREMBERG TO *GRISWOLD*

The anti-Soviet and anti-Nazi commitments that informed American rights discourse during and after World War II frequently found expression in the new vocabulary of "human rights" and, more generally, within the resurgent universalism and anti-positivism of the period. The relationship between form and content was not incidental. Universal and anti-positivist theories of rights gained strength at this time largely because they could advance substantive commitments whose primary targets were the policies of foreign regimes. In the first years after the war, the event that more than any other symbolized the administration of justice across national boundaries was the trial of major German war criminals at Nuremberg. Major themes of the trial, both formal and substantive, corresponded to major themes of post-war American rights discourse. As a legal event, Nuremberg elicited the attention of scholars concerned with the possibility of non-positive law. As a political symbol, Nuremberg represented the moral condemnation of Nazism and therefore the archetypal administration of justice in a world beginning to use Nazism as its touchstone for unacceptable conduct. Accordingly, Nuremberg as both symbol and event exercised a strong influence over subsequent American rights discourse. Nuremberg spawned a good deal of academic rights discussion as well as popular literature and film, placing before a wide variety of Americans the image of Nazis held accountable for crimes against abstract

---

[89] Dudziak, "Desegregation," at 79, 117.
[90] Quoted in Cushman, "American Civil Liberties in the Mid-Twentieth Century," *Annals of the American Academy of Political and Social Science* (May 1951), 1–8, at 6.

principles. Several influential American jurists of the period were affected in a much more direct way, by personal participation in the trial, including Herbert Wechsler, Telford Taylor, Francis Biddle, Edgar Bodenheimer, and of course, Justice Jackson, who served as lead prosecutor for the Allies.

The International Military Tribunal tried to confine the trial to issues of positive law, usually in the form of treaties and international conventions of warfare. As Judith Shklar has argued, however, the trial really turned on non-positive theories of justice.[91] Several contemporary commentators tried unsuccessfully to argue that the trial was conducted within the bounds of normal positivist jurisprudence. One argument held that the tribunal could not be accused of making new offenses and prosecuting people for them, because the tribunal was bound by the charter that had constituted it.[92] Of course, the question of that charter's authority to create offenses remained, because the charter was written by the Allies after the offenses had been committed. Another set of arguments maintained that international law was in an early stage of its development and therefore, as with early Roman law or early English common law, courts were necessarily lawmakers.[93] This argument, however, is not a denial but a justification of the trial's *ex post facto* nature. Another argument noted that the Allies had announced their intention to try and punish war criminals, thus giving the Germans adequate warning of the consequences of their actions.[94] Warnings, however, differ from threats only in being backed by legitimate authority: a thug who warns me that he will bash my head in if I walk down his street does not thereby acquire the sanction of justice for the bashing. The moral difference between the Allies and the thug depends not upon the issuance of a warning, which is common to both cases, but on the substantive justice of the consequences threatened. In the end, the propriety of Nuremberg rested on the distinctly non-positivist theory that some things were simply wrong, whether codified or not, and that justice sometimes calls upon courts to act even when lacking formal legal authorization.

The history of Nuremberg's symbolic significance provides an

---

[91] Judith N. Shklar, *Legalism: Law, Morals, and Political Trials* (Harvard University Press, 1986), pp. 146–190.
[92] Harold Leventhal et al., "The Nuernberg Verdict," *Harvard Law Review* 60, 857, at 858–859 (1947).
[93] Glueck, "The Nuernberg Trial," at 416–418.   [94] Ibid., at 440–442.

excellent illustration of the indeterminacy within American reactions against totalitarianism. A generation after the war, Nuremberg was best remembered as a trial about genocide. Its lessons foregrounded the evil of racism and the universality of individual rights. That view of Nuremberg, however, was substantially revisionist. The International Military Tribunal was conceived and implemented by people more concerned with the crime of aggressive war than with the ill-defined notion of "crimes against humanity": the roots of the Nuremberg trial lay in the War Department, whose top officials had confronted Nazism as a military enemy and who had never shown themselves particularly concerned by the fate of European Jews. Wechsler, Taylor, Jackson and others all the way up to Roosevelt discussed Nuremberg at the time chiefly in terms of the Nazi crime of aggression, that is, of war in violation of international treaties.[95] This is not to say that Nuremberg ignored the Holocaust – which it did not – but rather that the racism and genocide which have come to be remembered as the core of Nuremberg actually began as an ancillary matter. Later, when American rights discourse confronted issues of race, the aspects of Nuremberg that became most relevant were, obviously, those pertaining to race rather than those pertaining to aggressive war. The remembered vision of Nuremberg altered accordingly. The impulse to negate totalitarianism, then, did not mean only and necessarily the project of thickening the rights of racial equality. That result emerged from the confluence of recent adversities and long-standing issues within American rights discourse, each shaping the way that Americans perceived the other.

Edgar Bodenheimer and universal rights

In the years after the trial, Nuremberg's implications for positivism and universal rights became more and more accepted in American rights discourse. The work of one veteran of the trial, Edgar Bodenheimer, profoundly illustrates that shift. Bodenheimer was not the most influential jurisprude of his day, but he can be taken as a representative figure, suggestive of the ways in which mainstream American thinking about rights changed in response to events of World War II. Bodenheimer was a veteran of the prosecutor's office

---

[95] See Gary Jonathan Bass, "Judging War: The Politics of International War Crimes Tribunals" Ph.D. dissertation, Harvard University, 1998.

at Nuremberg, a longtime professor of law at the University of Utah, a sometime counsel for the federal government, and the author of several respected books on legal theory. He published the first edition of a treatise of legal philosophy, called *Jurisprudence*, in 1940 and a second, revised edition in 1962. Examining the two editions yields pictures of a mainstream legal theorist before and after the war, and patterns of change from the early edition to the later one chart his evolution. That evolution perfectly illustrates the shift from pre-war positivism to post-war universal rights.

Before the war, Bodenheimer argued that different views of natural law had arisen from different social or political conditions, ranging from the individualist Lockean law of nature to the Thomist Natural Law as an expression of Catholicism. In each case, he said, doctrines of supposedly "natural" law were produced by historical circumstances rather than derived from an immutable natural order. He further maintained that basing a system of enforceable law on a conception of natural law posed great dangers to a society, because many theories of nature and natural law would support pernicious political orders. Bodenheimer disapproved of the "Free Law" move-ment of early twentieth-century continental Europe, which encour-aged judges to look outside legal texts to other standards of justice.[96] After the war, however, Bodenheimer took the idea of a binding universal morality much more seriously and even argued that such a morality should be brought to bear on any system of law. The 1962 edition of *Jurisprudence* has chapters explicitly devoted to "non-formal" sources of law; the 1940 edition has none. In the 1940 edition, Bodenheimer explicitly avoided treating normative issues.[97] In the 1962 edition, he reversed, not only including normative issues but insisting that they must be included in any book in the genre. "No jurisprudential treatise should bypass or ignore the burning questions connected with the achievement of justice in human relations," he wrote. "Theory and philosophy of the law must remain sterile and arid if they fail to pay attention to the human values which it is the function of the law to promote."[98] The shift here is not just from one stance on a substantive issue within the law

---

[96] Edgar Bodenheimer, *Jurisprudence* (McGraw-Hill, 1940), pp. 166–168, 173–180, 183, 189–190.

[97] Ibid., pp. 191–192.

[98] Edgar Bodenheimer, *Jurisprudence: The Philosophy and Method of Law* (Harvard University Press, 1962), p. viii.

to another stance but from one to another conception of the nature and purpose of jurisprudence.

In 1940, Bodenheimer wrote that studies in anthropology and the history of law, using data from several continents, had shattered belief in an eternal natural law of reason, liberty, equality, and so on.[99] Ironically, this disposition to assess theories of justice in light of comparative anthropology left the door open for his later embrace of natural law. In the 1962 edition of *Jurisprudence*, Bodenheimer argued that discussion about justice was a universal phenomenon even if no single set of conclusions was, and he considered this social reality sufficient cause to investigate what some claimed was illusory. "So deeply is the evolution of human thought on justice embedded with speculation concerning the existence and significance of an assumed 'Law of Nature' that no adequate theory of justice can afford to ignore this enduring problem," he wrote.[100] After the war made him more inclined to seek principles of justice rooted in something other than positive law, Bodenheimer found a reason to look for those principles in data very much like the data he previously claimed precluded their existence.

In 1940, Bodenheimer wrote that ideas of equality always differ from society to society. As examples of varying classifications of people as equal and unequal at that time, he cited Jews in Germany and women in France, but, in keeping with his commitment to avoid normative judgments, he took no stand on the validity of the treatment of either of those groups.[101] In 1962, after the experience of the war, Bodenheimer gave telling examples of what he considered to lie beyond the diverse possibilities of justice, including laws "ordering the extermination or sterilization of an unpopular religion or national minority." In a little-needed footnote, Bodenheimer specified his reference to Jews and Poles under Nazi rule.[102] Equally transparent from this Nuremberg veteran was the declaration that "the exercise of critical judgment in carrying out monstrous commands ought to be required of a responsible human being."[103] In 1940, he had disparaged systems under which people gave their own consciences free play instead of seeking answers in positive law. In 1962, Bodenheimer discussed not only whether a judge can resort to

---

[99] Bodenheimer, *Jurisprudence* (1940), p. 286.
[100] Bodenheimer, *Jurisprudence* (1962), p. 186.
[101] Bodenheimer, *Jurisprudence* (1940), pp. 38–40.
[102] Bodenheimer, *Jurisprudence* (1962), p. 103.   [103] Ibid., p. 227.

principles of universal justice when the law is silent but also in what cases a judge can, and should, resort to universal justice *against* written positive law.[104] This endorsement of natural law jurisprudence by a former positivist was certainly prompted by the confrontation with Nazism.

The Hart–Fuller debate

Bodenheimer was far from the only theorist for whom the Nazi experience made legal positivism untenable. In the years and decades after World War II, the limits of positive law in a just political order were explored and re-explored, criticized and re-criticized. In 1958, Hart and Fuller debated the question of positivism in back-to-back essays in the *Harvard Law Review*, and their exchange is still considered the canonical statement of the debate between those positions.[105] I do not here intend to engage on their own terms the arguments that each put forward. Indeed, this chapter and in a sense this entire book attempts to outflank the argument between Hart and Fuller by placing it in a developmental context. Rather than try to show that Hart's or Fuller's argument is more analytically cogent, I am going to highlight what they have in common. Both essays took as their point of departure the question of how legal systems should deal with the problem of Nazism. (I will later make a similar claim about a more recent debate between Bruce Ackerman and Richard Posner.) At issue was whether natural law or positivism is the proper approach to law *in a post-Nazi world* and which is more likely to cause Nazi-style calamities in the future.

Hart, making the positivist case, recognized that the weight of the Nazi issue was mostly against him. His essay devoted considerable space to engaging that challenge directly, but his argument actually conceded most of the question. As part of his defense of positivism, Hart claimed that positive law, though the law, should not always be obeyed. Sometimes, a law is simply too unjust to command obedience. He portrayed his dispute with Fuller on this point as simply being about whether the unjust dictate being disobeyed is still worthy of being called a law.[106] Hart thus defended legal positivism after Nuremberg in part by emptying it of its normative significance:

---

[104] Ibid., p. 296.
[105] Hart, "Positivism"; Fuller, "A Reply."   [106] Hart, "Positivism," at 615–621.

a positivism that does not compel obedience to bad laws seems barely worth debating. A second part of Hart's defense of positivism was a historical claim, as Hart, anticipating one of Fuller's attacks, explicitly denied that German legal positivism helped the Nazi regime to rise. On the contrary, Hart alleged that Nazi jurisprudence had been insufficiently positivistic.[107] Arguing that judges should sentence convicted defendants only in accordance with predetermined rules rather than having discretion to shape sentences to individual cases, Hart alleged that Nazi judges used an "intelligent and purposive" method of sentencing.[108] Hart did not explain why intelligent or purposive sentencing was an evil. He seems to have assumed, perhaps correctly, that the simple fact of its association with Nazism would work condemnation. He was, in short, engaging in the *reductio ad Hitlerum*.

Fuller's essay was much more crowded with discussion of Nazism than was Hart's, and, given that Fuller was arguing the anti-positivist position, this added emphasis should come as no surprise.[109] Because Nazi Germany could have existed under a strictly positivist system, the Nazi example is usually invoked in support of the anti-positivist position (at least before audiences who take the

---

[107] Ibid., pp. 617–619. This point has itself been thoroughly debated. According to Ingo Muller, Nazi legal doctrines were "the exact opposite of legal positivism" (Ingo Muller, *Hitler's Justice* [Harvard University Press, 1991], p. 220). Others have argued that Nazi judges took liberties with pre-1933 laws but were strictly obedient positivists with Nazi-made laws. Arthur Kauffman, "National Socialism and German Jurisprudence from 1933 to 1945," *Cardozo Law Review* 9, 1629, at 1645 (1988). In a slightly different vein, Judith Shklar argued that German judges during the Nazi era regularly perverted Weimar laws but sometimes used positivist theory to rationalize their compliance with the Nazi regime. Shklar, *Legalism*, p. 72. Finally, Marcus Dubber points out that the relationship between Nazi jurisprudence and positivism depends largely on which of two understandings of "positivism" is in play. If "positivism" means "textualism," then positivism was indeed the strongest force in German jurisprudence at the time of Nazism. If, however, positivism means "the separation of law from morality as politics," then Nazism was entirely anti-positivist, because law, morality, and politics were all one in Nazi Germany. Marcus D. Dubber, "Judicial Positivism and Hitler's Injustice," *Columbia Law Review* 93, 1807, at 1820, 1822 (1993). Even on that last understanding, however, it would not necessarily be the case that German judges had been anti-positivist. It is also possible that judges who were not ideologically pro-Nazi could have complied with an anti-positivist regime for positivist reasons.

[108] Hart, "Positivism," at 613–614.

[109] It is indicative of the post-war climate in legal theory that Fuller, who argued the natural law position, was a leading legal realist. Realism and positivism were not necessarily aligned, so there was nothing remarkable about a realist critiquing positivism. What was remarkable, however, was that he should have chosen to make such a critique in the name of "natural law," a concept with which pre-war realists would have had little patience.

undesirability of Nazism as a given). Fuller took up the connection between positivism and Nazi Germany on the third page of his essay and kept the link in the foreground through the very end. At one point, as if about to broaden his base of evidence, he averred that "It is not necessary... to dwell on such moral upheavals as the Nazi regime" in order to show the flaws in positivism, but he returned to discussion of the Nazi regime only two pages later.[110] Suggesting that positivism aided the Nazi rise to power, Fuller noted that German legal scholars endorsed positivism in the decades before Hitler's rise to power and that natural law thinking was at that time disgraced both in the legal profession and in the academy.[111]

The Hart–Fuller debate over positivism and natural law, then, was largely a debate about which system was better suited to meet the challenges of Nazism. Both Hart and Fuller believed that a demonstration that positivism in fact led to Nazism would cripple positivism as a legal theory, which is why Hart explicitly denied the connection and Fuller pressed his attack at exactly that point. Conversely, Hart knew that he could support positivism if he could portray the Nazi judges as people who reached outside established legal norms and followed a private sense of justice. Hart's qualifications of his own position suggest that the spirit of natural law prevailed in his debate with Fuller: both sides agreed that there are sources outside the positive law which people must consult when deciding what to do in a given circumstance. That conclusion is unsurprising in a debate conducted in an era of natural law revival, only twelve years after Nuremberg.

---

[110] Fuller, "A Reply," at 646, 648.
[111] Ibid., at 657–660. In an ironic twist near the end of his essay (669–672), Fuller implied that reaction against the evils of Nazism was the primary motivation not for his own natural law position but for Hart's positivism. Nazism could easily make people afraid that the ideologies of a few powerful people will pervert the law, bringing injustice and destruction. Denying judges the discretion to convict, acquit, and sentence based on their own conceptions of justice is one possible protection against arbitrary power acting under color of law. Fuller's contention here raises the possibility that one of the most important and problematic features of post-war American constitutional philosophy – the concept of "neutrality" – is traceable to the fear of totalitarianism. Indeed, the foremost spokesman for neutrality in constitutional law, Herbert Wechsler, explicitly acknowledged that his concern for neutrality had roots in the confrontation with Nazism and specifically in his experience at Nuremberg. Norman Silber and Geoffrey Miller, "Toward 'Neutral Principles' in the Law: Selections from the Oral History of Herbert Wechsler," *Columbia Law Review* 93, 854, at 930 (1993).

Non-positive rights: applications

The shift away from positivism exhibited an interrelationship of form and content, as natural-law approaches to rights arose to serve substantive commitments. The shift also involved a connection between international and domestic politics, as Americans adopted non- and anti-positivist orientations not only because such attitudes could ground opposition to European totalitarianism but also in service of domestic political agendas. Frequently, those domestic agendas were bound up with other aspects of anti-Nazism, such as the commitment to racial equality. Consider a rhetorical formula that Dr. Martin Luther King, Jr., used to attack racially discriminatory laws. "Everything that Hitler did in Germany was legal," he said repeatedly.[112] Though more blunt – or perhaps simply more forthright – than Fuller's argument against Hart, King's formula made the post-war anti-positivist case clearly and directly: positivism and Nazism were compatible, so sources of enforceable justice must be located outside the positive law. Moreover, King's discursive use of Nazism involved the form and the substance of rights simultaneously: using a Nazi example to attack positivism in service of racial equality, his attack united two aspects of reaction to Nazism. Indeed, if we view the shift from positivism to non-positive rights as a formal one, we must also recognize that it was significantly driven by the desire to reach particular substantive outcomes, outcomes that were themselves encouraged by reactions against totalitarianism.

This trend toward natural law style thinking had important consequences in the courts in some of the most important legal cases of the post-war period. Consider, for example, the role of human rights and universal justice in the *Brown* decision. *Brown* was an epochal case, and this chapter cannot possibly explain or explore it fully. My present purpose is only to suggest that the methodological approach taken by one key justice in *Brown*, Felix Frankfurter, was influenced by the foundationalist, human-rights form of anti-totalitarianism. Frankfurter is a particularly good justice to examine for this purpose, because he was generally hostile to the idea that judges

---

[112] At least three instances are documented: to the Fellowship of the Concerned, 16 November 1961, in Martin Luther King, Jr., *A Testament Of Hope: The Essential Writings of Martin Luther King, Jr.*, ed. James Melvin Washington, (Harper & Row, 1986), p. 50; in the Letter from Birmingham City Jail, 16 April 1963, ibid., pp. 294–295; and in a *Playboy* interview, ibid., p. 356.

should enforce their own visions of justice. He had been on the Supreme Court for fifteen years before *Brown* and had consistently deemed text, precedent, and history the only legitimate means of deciding cases. When *Brown* came before the Court, Frankfurter assigned a law clerk to research the legislative history of the Fourteenth Amendment to determine its true intended meaning. The clerk was Alexander Bickel, later professor of law at Yale and one of the most important constitutional theorists of his generation.[113] A year after the *Brown* decision, Bickel published the results of his research and the rationale on which Frankfurter had decided for desegregation. According to the Bickel–Frankfurter analysis, nothing in the text or the legislative history of the Fourteenth Amendment mandated the desegregation of public schools. The Fourteenth Amendment did, however, contain language broad enough to allow some future generation to use it to prohibit segregation. No matter what the Reconstruction Congress might have thought, the Fourteenth Amendment "left the way open to, in fact invited, a decision based on the moral and material state of the nation in 1954, not 1866."[114] The argument, in other words, was that the Court could find against segregation in *Brown* even though the Constitution and its legislative history were inconclusive on the point. That argument, however, was in tension with Frankfurter's usual approach to jurisprudence. When the Constitution was inconclusive, Frankfurter generally located discretion not in the courts but in the legislatures. Nevertheless, Frankfurter decided in *Brown* to strike down racial segregation. He seems to have been aware that he was deciding on an abstract sense of justice and in so doing violating his own ideals of judicial review.[115] His decision is thus comprehensible as a convergence of methodological and substantive aspects of the anti-totalitarian influence. Even if the positive law might say otherwise, Frankfurter concluded, justice required prohibiting racial discrimination.

Willingness to decide cases on the basis of a sense of justice outside the law produced other seminal decisions on issues of constitutional rights. Two features of the decision in *Griswold v.*

---

[113] Richard Kluger, *Simple Justice: The History of Brown v. Board of Education and Black America's Struggle for Equality* (André Deutsch, 1977), p. 653.

[114] Alexander M. Bickel, "The Original Understanding and the Segregation Decision," *Harvard Law Review* 69, 1, at 56, 58, 63–65 (1955).

[115] Horwitz, *Transformation*, pp. 259–260, describes Frankfurter's correspondence with Learned Hand and Benjamin Cardozo about the impossibility of resisting the moral imperative to desegregate.

Connecticut, decided eleven years after *Brown*, illustrate this point. At issue in *Griswold* was whether a state could prohibit married people from using contraception. Answering in the negative, the Supreme Court established a right to privacy, a right not explicitly recognized in the Constitution. Douglas's opinion for the Court hinted that the necessary alternative to a state that recognized a right to privacy was a Soviet-style police state. Early in his opinion, Douglas discussed censorship and discrimination on the basis of political views, matters of questionable logical relevance to a contraceptives case. In conclusion, he raised the specter of a police force that would monitor all aspects of citizens' lives, their bedrooms included, if the law in *Griswold* were allowed to stand.[116] Censorship, discrimination on the basis of political views, and constant police surveillance were all aspects of Soviet totalitarianism, and that association helps to explain the linkage of those three concepts in this judicial opinion.

Establishing a right that protected the relevant set of substantive commitments required reliance on the ascendant anti-positivism. Noting that the Constitution guaranteed no right to privacy as such, Douglas famously announced that constitutional rights had "penumbras" and "emanations" within which the privacy right was contained. One could argue that penumbras and emanations of a constitution are bound up with positive law, because it is the positive law that produces the penumbras and the emanations. Nevertheless, locating individual rights in the penumbras and emanations of positive law implies that non-positive aspects of justice are as enforceable as positive ones. More important still in *Griswold* was a revival of the Ninth Amendment, long a moribund provision of the Constitution. The Ninth Amendment's statement that the rights of the people are not limited to those explicitly stated in the Constitution had long been considered toothless. On the theory that such a guarantee could be used to justify anything, it was used to justify nothing. Indeed, as Justice Goldberg noted in his concurring opinion in *Griswold*, the Court had previously referred to that Amendment in only three previous cases in history.[117] In *Griswold*, however, Gold-

---

[116] *Griswold v. Connecticut*, 381 U.S. 479, 482–483, 485–486 (1965).
[117] *Griswold*, at 486–493 (Goldberg, J., concurring). The three cases were *Ashwander v. TVA*, 297 U.S. 288 (1936), *Tennessee Electric Power Co. v. TVA*, 306 U.S. 118 (1939), and *United Public Workers v. Mitchell*, 330 U.S. 75 (1947). See also Bennet B. Patterson, *The Forgotten Ninth Amendment* (Bobbs-Merrill, 1955); John Hart Ely, *Democracy and Distrust* (Harvard University Press, 1980), pp. 34–40.

berg rested his finding of a privacy right on Ninth Amendment grounds, declaring explicitly that people have certain judicially enforceable rights whether the law mentions those rights or not. In all, five justices – Douglas, Goldberg, Warren, Brennan, and Clark – invoked Ninth Amendment authority for their stance on the privacy right. Thus, a majority of the Supreme Court believed that people had certain rights not mentioned in the written law and, in contrast to the Court's attitude for almost all of its history to that point, that those rights could be enforced by the courts.

In the years following World War II, then, American approaches to rights underwent a pronounced shift from positivism to universal or human rights. Needing to articulate a basis on which Nazism could be condemned as morally wrong, Americans revived the concept of enforceable rights prior to the written law. There is a binding law superior to any written law, this line of thinking went, and it confers upon all human beings in virtue of their humanity certain rights which must be protected. This was an implicit message of Nuremberg, the articulated position of Fuller and of the post-war Bodenheimer and eventually of the Supreme Court. Furthermore, the rise of universal or human rights was more than formal. It was linked to certain substantive ideas about the content of rights, many of which were themselves informed by aspects of the confrontation with European totalitarianism. Formal ideas about universal or non-positive rights helped support rights of privacy, racial equality, and so forth beyond the extent to which those rights were protected in the positive law, and substantive commitments to the importance of those rights helped support formal ideas about the universal or non-positive nature of rights.

ANTI-TOTALITARIANISM AND POST-WAR POLITICAL PHILOSOPHY

Throughout this book, I have argued that rights discourse generally involves discussants who advance some set of substantive commitments through the claims, formal or substantive, that they make about rights. I have also argued that that characterization applies not only to political and judicial discourse but to the rights discourse of academic political philosophy as well. Academic rights discourse is usually more careful, better reasoned, and more reflective than political or even judicial rights discourse, but academic rights discourse also shares important traits with the rights discourses of law and politics. In chapter 1, I showed how the substantive commitments of theorists like Dworkin, Sunstein, Raz, and Feinberg shape their formal approaches to rights. Earlier in this chapter, with reference to theorists like Hart, Fuller, and Bodenheimer, I showed that the substantive commitments of academic rights discourse overlap substantially with those driving political and legal rights discourse: mid-century academics as well as non-academics adjusted their conceptions of rights in order to cope with the problem of totalitarianism.

When considering the influence that reaction against totalitarianism and especially Nazism has had on academic rights theory, it is important to recognize that academic political philosophy as a discipline, including the philosophy of rights, enjoyed a striking revival after World War II. The degree to which interest in academic political philosophy increased during the post-war decades is difficult to overestimate. At Harvard in 1938, the only theoretical work in the introductory political science course consisted of selections from Blackstone.[118] That was before Arendt's call for a "new political principle," before attention to foundational normative issues became a pressing contemporary need. The reawakening of natural law thinking discussed earlier is part of the revival of normative political philosophy. The languages of human rights, universal rights, and human dignity provide first principles from which political philosophers attempt to derive comprehensive theories of political morality. Increased judicial willingness to find rights outside the legal text also testifies to the risen relevance of abstract moral theorizing. This trend, I have argued, is partly a result of confrontations with totalitarianism, which created a need for general and even universal moral principles among Americans who wished to articulate their opposition.

Many prominent contemporary political philosophers operate within the discursive space shaped by that anti-totalitarian agenda, but fewer acknowledge the constitutive role that totalitarianism has played in their enterprise. One notable exception is Michael Walzer, who argues that his theory of "complex equality" has precisely the merit of opposing modern totalitarianism. By "complex equality," Walzer means a system in which social goods such as money, office,

---

[118] Richter, *Essays in Theory and History*, p. 6.

education, divine grace, recognition, and political power are rele-
gated to separate spheres and in which a person's dominant position
in one sphere is not permitted to purchase an improved position in
another. The virtue of complex equality is that it impedes an
individual or a small group from becoming dominant over all
spheres of society. The rich cannot use their wealth to monopolize
higher learning, nor can the educated use their learning to monopolize political power, nor can the politically powerful use the state
to direct the saving and damning of souls. Walzer says that
"Complex equality is the opposite of totalitarianism: maximum
differentiation as against maximum coordination." As such, it
"speaks ... to the most terrifying experiences of the twentieth
century [and] protects us against the modern tyranny of politics,
against the domination of the party/state."[119]

Ackerman and Posner

The anti-totalitarian influence is clearly visible in a book I have
made periodic reference to thus far: Bruce Ackerman's *We the People:
Foundations.* In *We the People,* Ackerman argues that the key to
understanding constitutional doctrine in the middle of the twentieth
century lies in recognizing the New Deal as a revolution which
changed the rules of constitutional interpretation. To support that
claim, he describes a process of constitutional amendment that he
argues is controlling even though it does not abide by the formal
amending procedures laid down in Article Five. The non-formal
amending process Ackerman describes works as follows: one of the
"political" branches of the federal government has a new vision of
American politics that conflicts with the prevailing reading of the
Constitution. The actions it takes under this new vision are duly
invalidated as unconstitutional by the Supreme Court. Then, in a
series of elections where the conflicting constitutional visions are
clearly at issue, the innovating branch is returned to power by the
voters. The Court should then understand that the people have
endorsed the new constitutional vision. As the people are the
ultimate source of authority, the Court is now obligated to construe
the Constitution in a way compatible with their will, that is, in a way
compatible with the innovations. Armed with this understanding of

---

[119] Michael Walzer, *Spheres of Justice* (Basic Books, 1983), p. 316.

constitutional amendment, Ackerman argues that the New Deal worked a constitutional shift in much the same way that Reconstruction and the Founding did. Since the late 1930s, he concludes, a vision born of the New Deal – properly synthesized with elements of the previous "revolutions" – is the dominant and legitimating force in constitutional law.[120]

At the end of the book, however, Ackerman announces his dissatisfaction with the amending process he describes. He recommends that Americans "entrench fundamental rights against constitutional revision" by declaring certain constitutionally guaranteed rights to be unamendable, neither by the formal procedures of Article Five nor by the alternate process discussed above. To show that such entrenchment is plausible, he notes that "In the aftermath of Hitler's defeat, the German people made it unconstitutional for subsequent majorities to weaken their commitment to a host of fundamental freedoms. The text's guarantees of basic human dignity were proclaimed unamendable."[121]

This proposal of unamendability is in tension with the book's basic point about popular authority over the Constitution. The stronger the argument that the people are the source of constitutional legitimacy, the more difficult it is to argue that constitutional provisions should be entrenched and unrevisable. Ackerman is aware of the tension between these two arguments, and he addresses that tension by placing them in two different spheres. He characterizes his theory of "dualist" popular sovereignty as a descriptive account, not a prescriptive argument for how things should be. His prescriptive argument recommends entrenchment.[122] It would be difficult, however, to separate the two arguments completely, because legitimacy is itself a normative concern. Even an argument of second-order legitimacy, according to which whatever the people believe to be legitimate is legitimate, contains a normative component, because it takes a position on the source of legitimate value by locating it in the beliefs of the people. Moreover, even if the descriptive and normative arguments could be separated, the basic tension would remain: If the people are sovereign over the Constitution, it is not clear how the Constitution can be placed beyond the people's power.

[120] Ackerman, *We the People: Foundations*, pp. 131–162.
[121] Ibid., p. 320.   [122] Ibid., pp. 15–16.

In a critique of Ackerman's model of informal amendment, Richard Posner presents a hypothetical situation that hints at the connection between anti-totalitarianism and the tension within *We the People*. "Suppose," Posner writes, that "a Hitler-style demagogue is elected president and persuades Congress to enact plainly unconstitutional statutes sweeping away basic civil liberties." The courts "duly invalidate these statutes but the demagogue is reelected anyway" in elections in which the invalidation of those statutes is clearly at issue. According to Posner, Ackerman would be committed by his dualist theory to holding that the courts should then uphold the demagogue's agenda, "even though it entailed their disregarding the written Constitution, which had never been amended." It is in order to prevent such a situation from arising that Ackerman recommends placing some constitutional provisions beyond the reach of amendment. "In short," Posner concludes, Ackerman aims "to 'entrench' the Bill of Rights against a future Hitler."[123]

Posner's assessment seems correct. Indeed, it does no more than accord with Ackerman's own stated motive for entrenchment: *We the People* first introduces the idea by saying that "it would be a good idea to entrench the Bill of Rights against subsequent revision by some future American majority caught up in some awful neo-Nazi paroxysm."[124] Seen in that context, Ackerman's use of the post-war German Constitution to demonstrate the possibility of entrenchment emerges as more than an arbitrarily chosen example. It is a hint that the problem of Nazism is a specific influence shaping his call for entrenched rights.

The essence of Posner's critique of Ackerman's non-formal amending procedure is that it would not prevent a Nazi regime from gaining power in America. Ackerman, by making the prescriptive argument for entrenchment, agrees that the critique has force. Neither theorist explains why the argument from Nazism is a good test of a legal theory,[125] but both accept that to show that Nazism could come to power within a given legal order is to present a

---

[123] Richard A. Posner, "Democracy and Dualism," *Transition* 56, 68, at 72 (1992) (emphasis in original).

[124] Ackerman, *We the People: Foundations*, p. 16.

[125] In another place, Posner explicitly refuses to make such an argument. Having denounced the Nazis as "monsters," Posner notes: "I have not thought it necessary to pause to explain why I called the Nazis 'monsters'; indeed the explanation would have added nothing interesting to the bare statement." Richard A. Posner, *The Problems of Jurisprudence* (Harvard University Press, 1990), pp. 229, 237.

compelling case against it. In using the problem of Nazism as an implicit touchstone for legal theory, Ackerman and Posner follow in the tradition of Fuller and Hart.[126]

Liberal neutrality

One of the most important elements of the anti-Nazism that has shaped recent political theory is, as discussed throughout this chapter, a strong commitment that traits such as race and religion can never be valid grounds for discrimination. When Ackerman and Posner discuss the possibility that a system of constitutional amendment could sweep away fundamental rights, the rights against such discrimination are implicitly in the foreground. The centerpiece of English-speaking political philosophy in the past generation, Rawls's *A Theory of Justice*, is a paradigmatic example of an argument against such discrimination. It is also a paradigmatic example of an argument for what is often called "liberal neutrality," the idea that government should be neutral among competing visions of the good. Indeed, neutrality and nondiscrimination, as two related and yet differentiable ideas, have been central themes of American legal and political theory since World War II.

According to Sunstein, these ideas lie at the core of the American constitutional order. The principle of neutrality, or, as he sometimes puts it, "impartiality," forbids the government from acting simply out of "naked preference" for one vision or another. In keeping with his general argument about deliberative democracy, Sunstein argues that government must instead give reasons for what it does, and "We like this better" is not a valid reason. He describes this neutrality or impartiality principle as part of an "antiauthoritarian impulse":

---

[126] Posner, it should be noted, operates within the anti-totalitarian framework as much as Ackerman does. In his parting shot at Ackerman, Posner calls the informal amendment model "[d]angerous, because it invites judges to treat the popular will as a form of higher law entitling them to disregard ordinary concepts of legality. That is what Hitler's judges did" ("Democracy and Dualism," at 79). This argument is recognizably the *reductio ad Hitlerum*. Moreover, other leading legal theorists also operate within the same framework. Consider, as another example, John Hart Ely's landmark work *Democracy and Distrust*. At the very end of the book, Ely defends his theory against the charge that it could be compatible with a repetition of the Holocaust. Ely deflects the criticism, but he first acknowledges its force: "It's not good enough to answer that the Holocaust couldn't happen here. We can pray it couldn't, I believe it couldn't, but nonetheless *we should plan our institutions on the assumption that it could*" (Ely, *Democracy and Distrust*, p. 181, emphasis added).

government cannot justify its actions by mere will or preference. It thus cannot establish one creed at the expense of others, nor can it privilege one class of persons at the expense of others. It must be neutral among visions of the good and among its citizens. Sandel, as a leading critic of the neutrality idea, writes that the commitment to neutrality is a twentieth-century innovation. He sees the flag-salute cases as a turning point when liberal neutrality triumphed over earlier, republican visions of the relationship between government and the good life, substituting a regime of rights neutral among competing conceptions of the good for a regime in which government educated and guided citizens toward a certain vision of the good.[127] The idea that the Constitution provides a system of rights that is neutral among ends, he argues, is a post-war development.[128]

What Sandel does not do, however, is explain why the neutral, liberal vision of constitutional rights arose when it did. He identifies when it arose, and his work as a whole is dedicated to showing the weaknesses of liberal neutrality as a theory of politics. He and other critics of the neutral idea, including MacIntyre and Raz, have argued persuasively that thoroughgoing liberal neutrality is impossible, because any state necessarily encourages some ways of life and discourages others.[129] Liberalism, too, is a way of life. But simply ignoring the desire for liberal neutrality because of its logical impossibility would miss an opportunity to discover one of the underlying motivations behind much of contemporary political philosophy. Instead of dismissing the theory entirely, we should use it

---

[127] On this point, Justice Jackson would probably have agreed with Sandel. In the 1947 case of *Everson v. Board of Education* (330 U.S. 1), the Supreme Court made one of its seminal statements of support for liberal neutrality, writing that states must be neutral toward religion, meaning both that they must be neutral among religions and that they must be neutral between religion and irreligion. Religions, after all, are classic institutionalizations of competing visions of the good. Four justices dissented in *Everson*, but not because they disputed the neutralist proposition. On the contrary, they maintained that the majority's position, which permitted the state of New Jersey to provide transportation to religious schools as well as public schools, was not neutral enough. Dissenting in the name of a stronger neutrality, Justice Jackson began by citing *Barnette* for the proposition that school policies may not invade constitutional rights (ibid. at 21–22). It would seem that that proposition needs no authorities for support; obviously school policies may not invade constitutional rights. But the citation to *Barnette* was not merely establishing authority for a legal doctrine. It was, as Sandel would recognize, establishing a lineage and underscoring the importance of liberal neutrality.

[128] Sandel, *Democracy's Discontent*, pp. 39–54, 279.

[129] MacIntyre, *After Virtue*; Raz, *The Morality of Freedom*; Michael Sandel, *Liberalism and the Limits of Justice* (Cambridge University Press, 1982). See also William Galston, *Liberal Purposes: Goods, Values, and Diversity in the Liberal State* (Johns Hopkins University Press, 1969).

to tell us something about the commitments of the theorist. Why is neutrality attractive, indeed attractive enough to pursue despite its tenuous claim to existence? Ian Shapiro suggests one good answer in his analysis of the role of neutrality in Rawls and Nozick, and that answer can be expanded to encompass partisans of neutrality generally. They value neutrality, Shapiro argues, because of their deep fear of paternalism and teleology, which they see as the necessary alternatives.[130] Paternalism and teleology were frightening to late twentieth-century theorists, because they were intimately familiar with the destruction those forces could unleash. Thus, when Fuller spotted the impulse toward liberal neutrality in his debate with Hart, he described it as the desire to exclude morals or concepts of the good generally from politics out of a fear that such ideals in control of state machinery will persecute people who differ from the relevant ideal.

If correct, theories of neutralist liberalism would pass a basic test of post-war American political morality. They would provide a universally true grounding for the belief that totalitarianism is to be condemned. Indeed, even if these theories are not descriptively true, they provide powerful arguments for the anti-totalitarian camp. Perhaps, then, the enduring appeal of certain theories of abstract, neutral liberalism derives largely from their being excellent expositions of positions that many contemporary Americans – and their English-speaking peers generally – would like to believe true. Even many modern American theorists who find fault with liberal neutrality nevertheless have political commitments that liberal theory captures admirably. Those commitments regard some of the most important tenets of belief about rights after the conflict with Nazi Germany and the Soviet Union. No one shall be discriminated against on the basis of accidents of birth such as race or religion; indeed, we will declare those factors to be morally irrelevant so as to prevent their being used against people in the terrible ways we have witnessed. Everyone must therefore have the right to treatment as an equal. No state shall promote one conception of the good life to the exclusion of all others; we have seen that perfectionism becomes totalitarianism and that totalitarianism brings suffering, destruction, and death. Everyone must therefore have the right to pursue his own conception of the good life. These rules shall apply everywhere,

---

[130] Shapiro, *The Evolution of Rights in Liberal Theory*, pp. 283–284.

irrespective of local law or custom, irrespective even of the will of the majority. Everyone must therefore be guaranteed the enjoyment of his rights, no matter where and among whom he lives. Those are the central themes of American rights discourse after World War II.

Dworkin and the rights of individuals

Those themes bring us, finally, back to Ronald Dworkin and rights as trumps. Dworkin is a paradigmatic liberal. Central themes of post-war American rights discourse such as neutrality, universality, and individual dignity are central to Dworkin's image of rights and the rights-bearing individual, whose core rights include the rights of nondiscrimination, equality, and free choice of visions of the good life. Indeed, in an admiring reflection on Rawls, Dworkin hailed Rawls's original position, an archetype of liberal neutrality, as a proper way to think intuitively about justice.[131] Probing deeper, Dworkin argues that the original position presupposes a deep theory of rights. After all, the parties in the original position each have a veto power over the arrangements of their society.[132] Each can stand in the way of the interests of the others, even of all of the others. That vision of veto power recapitulates Dworkin's metaphor of rights as trumps, trumps which block society from harming an individual even if doing so is to the advantage of everyone else.

In a careful analysis, Dworkin argues that the right that must finally be fundamental to Rawls is the individual's right to equal concern and respect.[133] That right is the core of Dworkin's theory of rights, the principle to which Dworkin repeatedly argues all rights can be reduced.[134] Drawing on the post-war language of human rights, Dworkin declares that the right to equal concern and respect is something that all men and women have "simply as human beings."[135] Who would oppose that right to equal concern and respect? "Those who believe that some goal, like utility or the triumph of a class or the flowering of some conception of how men should live, is more fundamental than any individual right."[136] Here again is the core notion of Dworkin's formal definition of rights. Rights, he says, are held by individuals, and they prevent society from harming individuals in the pursuit of some greater societal

[131] Dworkin, *Taking Rights Seriously*, p. 159.
[132] Ibid., pp. 176–177.   [133] Ibid., p. 181.
[134] E.g., Ibid., pp. 272–278.   [135] Ibid., p. 182.   [136] Ibid.

good. Every individual has these rights, regardless of who or where they are, simply by virtue of being human. The substantive commitments that bring Dworkin to this definition are the commitments to oppose discrimination, repression, and injury based on some pernicious goal that a society might choose to pursue, such as the triumph of a class or a race. The commitments are universal, prior to any positive law. They are, in short, the commitments of anti-Nazism and anti-Sovietism, and they inform Dworkin's definition of rights. Having defined rights in a way that opposes totalitarianism, Dworkin can use the discursive power of rights language to advance his political commitments.

Conclusion: rights and reasons

"To have a right," wrote John Stuart Mill, is "... to have something which society ought to defend me in the possession of."[1] The word "possession" makes this statement most easily applicable to the kind of rights that I have called "entitlements," but we can easily imagine how the thought might be extended to the whole range of rights. All that is required is that we allow the things possessed to include liberties, powers, and immunities, and that for "possession" we read "exercise" or "enjoyment" as appropriate. In the spirit of Mill's dictum, we could then say that to have a right is to have an entitlement, liberty, power, or immunity, the possession, exercise, or enjoyment of which society should defend. But why, exactly, should society defend it? One possibility is that the existence of a right is an independent justification for requiring that defense. Another is that to classify something as a right is to state in a shorthand way that such defense is normatively required but without explaining that requirement's normative underpinnings. Throughout this book, I have argued for the second possibility.

Mill would have agreed. Immediately following the sentence quoted above, he wrote that if asked why society should defend the possession (or enjoyment, or exercise) of things recognized as rights, he would reply that the general utility required it.[2] Mill, of course, was a utilitarian, believing that the general utility was the ultimate justification for all things. In conceiving of rights as grounded in and only in the general utility, he built his underlying normative commitments into his theory of rights. He thereby followed a pattern in rights argument that I have illustrated throughout this book; most practitioners of rights discourse build their normative commitments

---

[1] John Stuart Mill, *Utilitarianism*, ed. George Sher (Hackett, 1979), p. 52.   [2] Ibid.

into their theories of rights, albeit not always as cogently and self-consciously as did Mill.

The practice of rights discourse is a normative enterprise, and Mill's theory of rights was an overtly normative theory. In that respect, it differs in kind from the theory I have been explicating. Mill specified an exclusive justification for rights because his interest in rights was to construct the category in a way compatible with his normative project. Because my concern is not to identify what propositions really should be classified as rights, either in an ontological sense or in reflective equilibrium, but rather to understand what practitioners of rights discourse are doing when they advance theories of rights, my approach does not discriminate among different normative sources alleged to justify claims of rights. A right, I have argued, is a creature of a social practice by which people endow certain entitlements, liberties, powers, and immunities with special protection. I have not engaged the moral question of which propositions deserve such protection.

Nevertheless, there is an important area of overlap and agreement between my approach and Mill's. Mill recognized that a right is not itself a normative ground. The fact that we classify some proposition as a right is not a justification for that proposition, nor does it indicate that the proposition can be or has been justified. It does indicate that whoever did the classifying would like the proposition to be justified and even prioritized and defended, but that is not the same thing. Sometimes, calling something a right is shorthand for invoking some other justificatory ground. Mill believed that other ground to be the general utility; other theorists locate it elsewhere. Locke and Jefferson grounded rights in the law of nature, Dickinson in reason, Moses Mather in God, John Quincy Adams and Jefferson Davis in the Declaration, Arendt in human dignity, Dworkin in the principle of equal concern and respect for all individuals. I have not tried to decide which among those grounds are normatively valid, but I have tried to show that rights themselves are not the grounds of normative arguments. Moreover, if rights themselves are not the grounds, neither, in an ultimate sense, are the other normative sources like nature or dignity for which claims of rights operate as placeholders or waystations. One could require a theorist to give reasons why nature is normatively binding, too, and that investigation could suggest that something else must underlie nature, just as nature underlies rights. One turtle stands on another.

This book has been about rights and reasons. In part it has been about the reasons why certain propositions are regarded as rights, and in part it has been about the status that rights have as reasons in political and moral arguments. I have argued that the agreed existence of a right, except in the context of legal positivism, is not an independent reason for action or moral judgment. It is a reflection of some prior attitude about what action or judgment is appropriate in a given circumstance. The question I have asked, therefore, is not what a right is in some ontological sense but rather what people do in saying that something is a right. It is a question about the use of language in normative debate. Calling something a right announces both its importance and the imperative that it be protected. It is, however, an announcement, not a reason why someone inclined to contest the normative proposition asserted should accept that norm. To be sure, people often do treat rights as reasons, assenting to propositions because of demonstrated or agreed-upon rights. When the rights in question clearly derive from some normative source that the people concerned do regard as binding, treating rights as reasons in this way makes sense. Rights are then a kind of shorthand for an accepted normative idea. But it is that underlying norm and not the shorthand that is a good reason for assent, and where the shorthand is used without an underlying norm, no good reason has been given.

The practice of calling things "rights" to claim priority and protection regardless of the kind of normative ground offered, and indeed regardless of whether any underlying norm is articulated, has been characteristic of rights discourse throughout American history. During the Founding, American rebels used the language of rights to assert all manner of grievances against British rule; loyalists used the same language to defend the British administration. Both sides argued from a wide range of ostensible normative grounds, including God, nature, right reason, the ancient constitution, and the common law. What the various claims of rights had in common was simply the attitude that each one announced about priority and protection. In the middle of the nineteenth century, Americans in the North and the South pressed rival agendas with rights language rooted in common sources, such as the Declaration of Independence and the Constitution. During Reconstruction, the Republican Congress and the federal judiciary articulated a formal scheme of rights that advanced a sectional or partisan agenda, dismantling the "Slave

Power" and preserving Republican control of the national government without requiring full equality of white and non-white citizens. Then, when circumstances made it necessary, they modified that formal scheme so as better to serve those substantive aims. In the twentieth century, the confrontation with totalitarianism prompted Americans to use the language of rights to protect individuals against racial discrimination, oppressive police powers, censorship, enforced political conformity, and so on. Courts revived the possibility of guaranteeing rights not specified by the positive law, and academic philosophers made the leading tenets of anti-totalitarianism central to their theories of rights.

At all these times, the reasons why certain propositions were called "rights" were bound up with prevailing circumstances and substantive political commitments. New circumstances and new commitments begot new rights, and, in extreme cases, new terminologies for describing rights generally. That was the process at work in the rise of the typology of "civil," "political," and "social" rights during Reconstruction and again with the rise of "human rights" in the middle of the twentieth century. As Skinner and Rorty have argued, the substitution of one vocabulary for another reflects shifts in political and moral attitudes. Changes in the basic ways of structuring normative discourse do not occur except under significant pressure, because it is generally easier to modify an existing structure than to reform the entire conceptual scheme. Taking the easier route of modification is, for example, what Reconstruction Republicans did when they reclassified voting, the paradigmatic "political right," as a "civil right." Sometimes, however, the substantive changes in the commitments that rights discourse is meant to serve are sweeping enough to require a new scheme and a new set of terms. Even then, though, the old conceptions of rights do not completely disappear, because much of the old structure is likely to be assimilated within the new. This process of merging old rights with new theories is part of what I have called synthesis. Such synthesis has occurred whenever Americans have modified or replaced formal theories to accommodate the changing set of propositions they wanted to call "rights."[3]

---

[3] The ideas of several theorists whom I discussed early in this book are present in this view of how, when, and with what limitations a new way of structuring rights discourse replaces an old one. James, Quine, and Kuhn all discuss the interaction between an existing system of ideas and a new idea with which it may not be compatible. The influence of the existing

Because rights are creatures of a linguistically constituted social practice, for some proposition to be generally *called* a right is the same as for that proposition to *be* a right, as long as the act of naming obeys the rules of the governing practice. That last qualification is critical. Without it, my characterization of what it means for something to be a right would be simple nominalism. As part of a practice, however, the naming of rights is much more. Just as a soccer goal is only a goal if it is scored according to the rules of soccer, a right is only a right if it is invoked according to the rules of the relevant political discourse. Not only is a person's kicking a ball into a net not sufficient for the scoring of a goal, but it makes no difference if he cries out "Goal!" as he watches the ball fly. Beyond an action, beyond an isolated act of labeling, the existence of a goal requires the context of a constituent practice. In that context, an action and a labeling (perhaps by a referee) in accordance with a set of meaning-imparting rules do constitute a goal. Similarly, calling something a right is sufficient for that thing to be a right only if the act of calling occurs within the proper constitutive practice. The "rules" of political discourse are, of course, less defined than those of soccer, and the possible indeterminacy of rights is broader than that of goals. Nevertheless, we are not entirely without guidance. For example, the thing claimed as a right must be an entitlement, liberty, power, or immunity, as those concepts were described in chapter 1. Something not describable in at least one of those four ways – such as a color or a physical object – cannot be a right, even if it is named as one.[4] Theoretically, the practice could evolve in some way compatible with this new kind of right. The rules of the practice are constantly open to revision. Thus far in American history, however, the rules of the practice have remained remarkably stable. The entitlements-liberties-powers-immunities rule is one persistent characteristic of rights discourse, and the important-and-should-be-protected rule is another.

At the same time, American rights discourse has not been static.

---

system, they argue, is sufficiently powerful to confine acceptance of a new, contradictory belief to exceptional circumstances. When a new idea is adopted, people will try to preserve as much of the old system as possible intact. This is a second meaning of what I earlier called the principle of "nonviolence," specifically, in Quine's words, the tendency "to disturb the system as little as possible." James, *Pragmatism*, esp. pp. 31–32; Quine, "Two Dogmas," esp. p. 44; Kuhn, *Scientific Revolutions*, esp. pp. 76–77. The idea also draws on Gadamer's idea of fusing historical horizons and Ackerman's notion of constitutional synthesis.

[4] There can, of course, be a right *to* a physical object, but a physical object cannot *be* a right.

The operation of the practice I have described has varied with different personalities, historical periods, and conversational contexts. For example, the kinds of substantive commitments that people have advanced with general theories or specific claims of rights have ranged from explicit moral philosophy to inchoately held senses of justice to purely partisan advantage. The rights discourses of different historical periods have advanced different kinds of commitments, as have different participants within the discourse of a given time. For Reconstruction Republicans more interested in electoral control than in racial equality, a change in rights theory reflected less a changed conception of political morality than a changed assessment of the necessary means to a pragmatic end. For other Reconstruction Republicans, racial equality had a greater independent value, and changes in the prevailing theory of rights served both their commitment to egalitarianism and their practical political interests.

Similarly, rights theorists recognize the link between their theories of rights and their substantive commitments only to varying degrees. Arendt's explicit call for a "new political principle" that would perform a certain function suggests that she knew that new theoretical principles took shape as they did in order to serve certain ends. Otis, Mather, and Adams may have understood themselves differently. Their conceptions of rights served, and were probably shaped by, their political cause, but they do not seem to have knowingly tailored theories of rights to fit their rebellion. Arendt was a professional philosopher: it cannot be said, therefore, that political figures but not academics allow the normative content they wish to defend to structure their theories of rights. What can be said about the difference between academic and non-academic rights discourse, however, is that academics, including Arendt, generally tend to fashion the interrelationship between the form and the content of their rights theories more reflectively. That Arendt and others know that their theories must exhibit certain characteristics and do certain kinds of work merely means that they craft their thought with a degree of self-consciousness. It does not mean that their theories are underhanded or invalid. Indeed, it could only mean those things if the only kind of valid academic theory were one that deduced consequences from *a priori* and perhaps ontological principles. But when people theorize in reflective equilibrium, or when the relevant mode of theorizing is interpretive in Dworkin's sense, there is no reason why principles that define rights must be prior to the content of certain rights that a theory of rights must encompass. Indeed, deliberately moving back and forth between form and content, principle and instantiation, revising each in turn, is then much of what it means to formulate a real theory of rights.

I have been arguing that conceptions of rights respond to changing historical circumstances, and, more broadly, for the relevance of history to political thought. Historical events and circumstances are complex and contingent, and an investigation of the historical development of rights theories should note the differences as well as the similarities among the rights discourse of different times. Accordingly, I tried in chapter 2 to paint in broad strokes when describing the process by which people facing new historical circumstances transform conceptions of rights. Some of the historical transformations discussed in chapters 3, 4, and 5 fit the pattern described in chapter 2 more closely than others. That is as it should be. To undertake an analysis of the role historical circumstances play in shaping conceptions of rights and then to overlook the diversity of those circumstances would be, as West said of Rorty, "to promote an ahistorical approach in the name of history."[5]

Diversity of circumstances should not, however, obscure fundamental commonalities that pervade most rights reasoning. No matter what the degree of strategic action involved, arguments about rights tend to privilege the concrete negation of adversity. Sometimes a politician, lawyer, or philosopher knows himself to be using rights language in that way, and sometimes that self-awareness is absent, but substantive and above all reactive commitments shape conceptions of rights whether or not their influence is recognized. This aspect of American rights discourse is common across historical periods and professional categories, just like the aspects that I earlier called the "important-and-should-be-protected rule" and the "entitlements-liberties-powers-immunities rule."[6] Founding-era political activists in New York created America's only unqualified right

---

[5] West, *American Evasion*, p. 208.
[6] Those two rules have a different status in rights discourse than does the tendency to outcome-driven reasoning. Outcome-driven reasoning is characteristic of rights discourse; the two rules named above are constitutive of the practice. Consistent with the understanding of rights presented in this thesis, there could be a rights-related argument that was not outcome-driven, but there could not be a right not classifiable as an entitlement, liberty, power, or immunity, nor could a claim of a right carry no normative implications about priority and protection of the thing claimed.

against the domestic quartering of soldiers not because they reasoned differently from people in Pennsylvania and Connecticut but because the long-term British occupation of New York left them with a heightened distaste for quartering. The Supreme Court in the 1940s recognized new rights of dissent and political participation in the flag-salute and white primary cases because new political commitments demanded new judicial outcomes. Ackerman, Posner, and Dworkin know before they begin to articulate a system of rights that certain substantive results must be guaranteed and others must be avoided. In some of these cases, the actors believe or believed themselves to be deliberately tailoring theories of rights to produce desired outcomes, and in some cases they believe or believed themselves to be following the true nature of rights to a coincidentally happy conclusion, and sometimes a reflective theorist sees and avoids the problems of both extremes. No matter what the level of self-consciousness of a particular rights theorist, however, a "conclusion" is usually more than the last step of his argument. Sometimes it is the first step, as the commitment to prioritize and protect some substantive proposition underlies the argument from its inception. And sometimes "conclusions" and "premises" arise and develop in tandem, each conditioning the other.

THE CASE OF ACADEMIC THEORY

The academic and the political discourses of rights are interconnected. Political philosophy is not just philosophical but also political, and one of its political elements is the attempt to promote substantive agendas in the social world. Among academic theorists, my argument is most unfriendly to two groups. The first includes those who believe that their definitions of rights capture the inherent features of an ontological category, uninformed by particular linguistic practices or political commitments.[7] I have not argued that it is impossible to produce an ontological theory of rights, though my argument as a whole could be read as making alternatives to

---

[7] This group includes absolute rights skeptics as well as other kinds of rights absolutists. To insist that there are no such things as rights, period, is to argue from ontology as surely as it is to insist that rights exist and have a given set of inherent formal features. Against the absolute rights skeptic, this thesis argues that rights do exist, as creatures of a social practice. To say that rights exist because of a social practice is to argue for their reality, not their unreality.

ontology more plausible. Philosophers of rights can produce abstract accounts of rights that are internally consistent, but their claims must always remain as contestable as their metaphysics. Moreover, the more abstract their theories, the more difficult it is for those theories to illuminate the concrete worlds of politics and law. For that purpose, which I suspect is the purpose that makes rights philosophy most valuable to begin with, I suggest that it is more interesting and more fruitful to view rights as creatures of a social practice than as members of an ontological category.

The second group of theorists to whom my argument is unfriendly includes those who believe that their arguments about rights have no political or moral implications, as Feinberg asserted in the example I discussed in chapter 1. Normativity is built into the concept of rights, and to affirm or deny the rights-status of a proposition is inescapably – though not exclusively – a normative act. That is why people bother to contest the concept of rights in the first place. To be sure, it is logically possible for someone to construct a theory about rights with no intention whatsoever of its having any normative implications, and it is even possible in principle for that person to discuss his theory with an audience, presumably small, of people as rigorously committed to the non-normative status of the theory as he. There is nothing inherent in the nature of language that prevents someone from using the word "rights" in that way. The same is true, however, for any other word: all that I have acknowledged in the last few sentences is that people can use language idiosyncratically. My project has been to show that the actual discourse of rights does not function in that non-normative way, and the illustrations of the history of rights discourse from the Founding through the twentieth century are meant to demonstrate just how alien to the mainstream practice of rights discourse such a non-normative usage would be.

Some academic philosophers might be tempted to argue that the kind of historical analysis I have presented has no bearing on the kind of rights philosophy they practice. Such an objector could make two related arguments. The first is that the way that other people in generations past used a term should not limit current usage, especially if living people have discovered a usage that better maps the relevant concept. The second is that it is a mistake to muddle the technical discourse of academic political theory with the differently technical discourse of the law and the manifestly non-technical discourse of politics. These two arguments are both versions of the claim that academic theorists can define and use terms independently of the role those terms play in non-professional language. As a conceptual matter, that claim is not implausible. There could be topics in legal and political philosophy where the discussion among academics was so different from the discussion among non-academics that it would not make sense to analyze the two conversations as parts of a single practice. The claim cannot, however, be successfully applied to the actual discourse of rights, because the way that academics have discussed rights has not been independent of the way that rights language has been used outside the academy. Academic and non-academic rights discourse follow the two rules of the social practice, the entitlements-liberties-powers-immunities rule and the important-and-to-be-protected rule, and academic and non-academic rights discourse share a common set of political commitments, commitments largely shaped by the process of adversity, reaction, and synthesis. The academic and the political discourses of rights have been interrelated, and the analysis of those discourses may safely regard them as such.

A further note bears mention about the claim that political theorists can conduct their conversation in ways completely independent of non-academic political discourse. Were we to accept any form of that claim as strong enough to license political philosophers to disregard the present analysis, it would be appropriate to wonder why the technical discourse of academic political theory warranted attention. The theorist who protests that his use of language and concepts is distinct from political usage risks suggesting that he is too far removed from real politics for his ideas to have normative relevance. At the very least, he concedes that there is another way of talking about rights which probably takes no account of his way. Furthermore, that other way is more directly tied to the adjudication of substantive issues. Not only would academic philosophy have to give up all claims of producing an exclusive account of rights, it would have to admit that the account it did offer illuminated the political world less well than would a different kind of account. The attempt to create a separate space for academic discourse insulates politics from philosophy, not just philosophy from politics. And the less that philosophy speaks the language of politics, the less that people who care about politics will find reason to listen to philosophy.

If my account of rights is correct, we should be skeptical about the ways in which some rights theorists, whether in law, politics, or academia, present rights as reasons in normative argument. The normative questions that those arguments address, however, still call for answers, and those questions remain open at the end of this book. I have not tried to identify the best moral responses to questions currently conceived as questions of rights, nor have I provided criteria that would direct such identification. Indeed, I have been more concerned to explain why some methods are *not* good ways to make normative arguments.

My analysis also raises further questions, and I will mention two of them here. One is a conundrum of American jurisprudence, and the other is a broader question about the construction of concepts in political philosophy. Taking the two in that order, let us first return briefly to a topic mentioned in chapters 3 and 5: the Ninth Amendment to the United States Constitution. Of all American constitutional provisions, this one provides the most basic challenge to theorists of rights. It reads, "The enumeration in the Constitution, of certain rights, shall not be construed to deny or disparage others retained by the people." The Founders included this amendment because they believed it impossible to specify in writing all the rights that people had, down, in the words of one legislator, to the right to wear one's hat. This rationale is generally taken to mean that rights are so numerous that listing them all would be impractical to the point of impossibility. One imagines that only a committee of constitution-writers magically empowered to stop time while they wrote could, in theory, compile a complete list of rights. The understanding of rights for which I have argued, however, suggests another aspect to the impossibility of writing a comprehensive list of rights. The problem is not merely that a complete list would be long. That view of the problem implies that the full catalog of rights, though extremely long, is fixed. But if rights are the products of a social practice by which people protect propositions that they consider important and under threat, and if perceptions of threat and importance change as circumstances change, then the corpus of rights itself changes through time. The impossibility of writing a complete catalog is thus conceptual, not just practical. The founders could not possibly have known what Americans of later generations would regard as important and in need of protection. Thus, the Framers of the Constitution could not have compiled an exhaustive list of rights not only because their time was finite but also because a list of rights exhaustive in 1791 might be woefully imperfect a generation later. The Ninth Amendment can be read as a way of coping not only with extant unenumerated rights but with not-yet-existing rights as well.

The Ninth Amendment has been ignored for most of American history, as few legal theorists have taken seriously the idea that it can be used to support constitutional arguments.[8] Perhaps that disparagement is a mistake. To the Ninth Amendment's declaration that there are rights beyond those enumerated in the Constitution, this book adds that new rights arise in new circumstances and that such development is inherent in the nature of rights. If rights are features of a social practice in the way I have described, then changed circumstances and attitudes engender new rights. Those new rights may not be specified in the Constitution. But the Constitution, through the Ninth Amendment, provides a mechanism for recognition and enforcement of unenumerated rights. Presumably, that mechanism could extend to new unenumerated rights as well as old ones. If new rights arise with new circumstances and new attitudes, and if the Constitution prohibits the disparagement of unenumerated rights, judges and legal theorists should give more credence to the possibility, and indeed the requirement, of enforcing rights not specified in the positive law. Perhaps this suggestion is unworkable: how will judges know when a new right exists? Perhaps it is dangerous: what if a judge decides to invoke the Ninth Amendment and the inherent dynamism of rights to enforce a right of hotel operators to deny accommodation on the basis of race? These questions are open and must be addressed. But they should be addressed as serious questions, not as rhetorical ones, and certainly not as knock-down arguments against Ninth Amendment jurisprudence.

TURTLES ALL THE WAY DOWN

A second question raised by this analysis concerns the status of other concepts in political philosophy that are related to the concept of

---

[8] See Ely, *Democracy and Distrust*, pp. 33–34.

rights. Part of my argument about rights has been that arguments from rights do not supply ultimate normative grounds. Despite the common discussion in contemporary political theory of something called "rights-based" morality, rights themselves are not sources of justification.[9] Frequently, arguments about rights acknowledge deeper grounds, such as nature, reason, or the positive law. Frequently, such deeper grounds underlie arguments about rights even when they are not explicitly invoked. On the understanding of rights that I have offered, it would seem salutary for normative arguments to be conducted in such a way that the intermediate level of "rights" did not distort what is, at a deeper level, an argument about some other source of normative authority.

At this point, however, we should wonder whether those other sources really do provide justificatory groundings for normative argument or whether they, too, are surrogates for other grounds of decision. Perhaps an analysis of the language of nature would uncover a social practice analogous to the one that underlies the language of rights. If so, it might conclude that settling normative questions by reference to conceptions of nature makes no sense, either. The possibility that rights are a discursive waystation one step short of the true grounds of political morality would thus slip away, and those true grounds – wherever they were – would recede farther into the distance. At the extreme, one might wonder whether there are any fixed grounds at all or whether the search for normative anchors is doomed to an endless regress, foundational arguments shifting from ground to ground as each one dissolves under scrutiny in turn. Perhaps these concerns lead to sheer relativism. I would prefer to say, with both Rorty and Dworkin, that normative positions can be sound even if there comes a point in debate at which no further arguments can be offered on their behalf.[10] Whether and how that preference is defensible is a question for a different book, or perhaps for many different books.

What I hope this study has established is the practice-dependent nature of rights and the historical contours of the relevant practice. That a right exists means that someone has established as normative that some substantive commitment is important and should be

---

[9] For the term and concept of "rights-based" theories, see Dworkin, *Taking Rights Seriously*, p. 171 and generally pp. 150–183; Joseph Raz, "Right-Based Moralities," in Waldron, *Theories of Rights*, pp. 182–200.

[10] Rorty, *Consequences of Pragmatism*, pp. 160–175; Dworkin, *Law's Empire*, pp. 80–86.

protected. Why it is important and why it should be protected are not thereby explained. We should be skeptical of arguments that establish or deny the existence of rights on formal grounds, skirting the substantive issues that are inextricable from all questions of rights. Similarly, we should beware of arguing questions of rights in a way limited by inherited typologies. Formal conceptions of rights generally carry the substantive commitments of the historical circumstances from which they arose, and those may not be the circumstances relevant to later discussions. Legal and political theorists should take note of old ways of thinking about rights not only to discover wise arguments, as many philosophers do, but also to learn how historical circumstances shape legal and political discourse. Understanding the formative influences on political discourse is an important part of self-knowledge for the political theorist. And political theorists who pay insufficient attention to the role of historical circumstance are likely to underestimate their own historicity.

Bibliography

BOOKS AND ARTICLES

Ackerman, Bruce. *We The People: Foundations.* Cambridge, MA: Harvard University Press, 1991

Adams, Charles Francis. *What Makes Slavery a Question of National Concern? A Lecture, Delivered, by Invitation, at New York, January 30, and at Syracuse, February 1, 1855.* Boston: Little, Brown, 1855

Adams, John. *The Works of John Adams, Second President of the United States,* Charles Frances Adams, ed. Boston: Little, Brown, 1850–1856

Papers of John Adams, Robert J. Taylor, ed. Cambridge, MA: Harvard University Press, 1977

Adams, Samuel. *The Writings of Samuel Adams.* Harry Alonzo Cushing, ed. New York: G. P. Putnam's Sons, 1904–1908

Amar, Akhil. "Philadelphia Revisited: Amending the Constitution Outside Article V." *University of Chicago Law Review* 55 (1988): 1043–1104

"The Bill of Rights as a Constitution." *Yale Law Journal* 100 (1991): 1131–1210

"The Bill of Rights and the Fourteenth Amendment." *Yale Law Journal* 101 (1992): 1193–1284

"The Fifteenth Amendment and 'Political Rights'." *Cardozo Law Review* 17 (1996): 2225–2229

The Constitution and Criminal Procedure: First Principles. New Haven: Yale University Press, 1997

The Bill of Rights: Creation and Reconstruction. New Haven: Yale University Press, 1998

American Jewish Committee. *On Three Fronts: Thirty-ninth Annual Report, 1945.* New York: American Jewish Committee, 1946

Anderson, David. "The Origins of the Press Clause." *UCLA Law Review* 30 (1983): 455–541

Annals of the Congress of the United States, 1789–1824 (42 vols.). Washington, DC: Gales & Seaton, 1834–56

Arendt, Hannah. *The Origins of Totalitarianism,* 2nd edn. San Diego: Harcourt Brace Jovanovich, 1968

Bailyn, Bernard. *Pamphlets of the American Revolution.* Cambridge, MA: Harvard University Press, 1965
   The Ideological Origins of the American Revolution. Cambridge, MA: Harvard University Press, 1967
Ball, Terence, James Farr, and Russell L. Hanson, eds. *Political Innovation and Conceptual Change.* Cambridge: Cambridge University Press, 1989
Barnes, Barry and David Bloor. "Relativism, Rationalism, and the Sociology of Knowledge," in Hollis and Lukes, 1982, pp. 21–47
Bass, Gary Jonathan. "Judging War: The Politics of International War Crimes Tribunals." Ph.D. dissertation, Harvard, 1998
Benedict, Michael Les. *A Compromise of Principle: Congressional Republicans and Reconstruction, 1863–1869.* New York: Norton, 1974
Berger, Monroe. "The Supreme Court and Group Discrimination." *Columbia Law Review* 49 (1949): 201–230
Berlin, Isaiah. *Two Concepts of Liberty.* Oxford: Clarendon Press, 1958
Berman, William C. *The Politics of Civil Rights in the Truman Administration.* Columbus, OH: The Ohio State University Press, 1970
Bickel, Alexander M. "The Original Understanding and the Segregation Decision." *Harvard Law Review* 69 (1955): 1–65
Bland, Richard. *The Colonel Dismounted.* Williamsburg: Joseph Royle, 1764
   An Inquiry into the Rights of the British Colonies. Williamsburg: Alexander Purdie & Co., 1766
Bloom, Harold. *The Anxiety of Influence.* Oxford: Oxford University Press, 1973
Bloor, David, *Knowledge and Social Imagery.* Chicago: University of Chicago Press, 1976
Bodenheimer, Edgar. *Jurisprudence.* New York: McGraw-Hill, 1940
   Jurisprudence: The Philosophy and Method of Law. Cambridge, MA: Harvard University Press, 1962
Bohman, James. *New Philosophy of Social Science.* Cambridge: Polity Press, 1991
Branyan, Robert L., and Lawrence H. Larsen, eds. *The Eisenhower Administration, 1953–1961: A Documentary History.* New York: Random House, 1971
Brock, William R. *An American Crisis: Congress and Reconstruction, 1865–1867.* London: Macmillan, 1963
Brown, Brendan F. "Racialism and the Rights of Nations." *Notre Dame Lawyer* 21 (1945): 1–16
Burke, Edmund. *The Works of Edmund Burke.* Boston: Little Brown, 1881
Cahn, Edmond N. "Justice, Power, and Law." *Yale Law Journal* 55 (1946): 336–364
Cavell, Stanley. *Must We Mean What We Say?* Cambridge: Cambridge University Press, 1976
Chafee, Zachariah. *Documents on Fundamental Human Rights.* Cambridge, MA: Harvard University Press, 1951

How Human Rights Got Into the Constitution. Boston: Boston University Press, 1952

Three Human Rights in the Constitution of 1787. Lawrence: University of Kansas Press, 1956

Chandler, Thomas. *A Friendly Address to all Reasonable Americans, on the Subject of our Political Confusions,* New York: Rivington, 1774

Clark, Jonathan. *The Language of Liberty, 1660–1832.* Cambridge: Cambridge University Press, 1994

Congressional Globe (46 vols.). Washington, DC, 1834–73

Connolly, William. *The Terms of Political Discourse,* 3rd edn. Oxford: Basil Blackwell, 1993

Continental Congress. *A Declaration by the Representatives of the United Colonies of North America, Now Met in General Congress in Philadelphia, Setting forth the Causes and Necessity of their taking up Arms.* Newbury-Port, 1775

Cox, LaWanda, and John H. Cox. "Negro Suffrage and Republican Politics: The Problem of Motivation in Reconstruction Historiography." *Journal of Southern History* 33 (1967): 303–330

Cranston, Maurice. *Human Rights Today,* 1st edn. London: Ampersand, 1955
Human Rights Today, 2nd edn. London: Ampersand, 1962

Cress, Lawrence. "An Armed Community: The Origins and Meaning of the Right to Bear Arms." *Journal of American History* 71 (1984): 22–40

Curry, Thomas J. *The First Freedoms: Church and State in America to the Passage of the First Amendment.* New York: Oxford University Press, 1986

Cushman, Robert. "The Texas 'White Primary' Case – *Smith v. Allwright.*" *Cornell Law Quarterly* 30 (1945): 66–76

"American Civil Liberties in the Mid-Twentieth Century." *Annals of the American Academy of Political and Social Science* (May 1951): 1–8

Dagger, Richard, "Rights," in Ball, Farr, and Hanson, 1989, pp. 292–308

Dalfiume, Richard M. *Desegregation of the U.S. Armed Forces: Fighting on Two Fronts, 1919–1953.* Columbia, MO: University of Missouri Press, 1969

Dalrymple, John. *The Rights of Great Britain Asserted against the Claims of America.* Philadelphia, 1776

Davidson, Donald. *Inquiries into Truth and Interpretation.* Oxford: Oxford University Press, 1984

Davis, David. *The Slave Power Conspiracy and the Paranoid Style.* Baton Rouge: Louisiana State University Press, 1969
The Problem of Slavery in the Age of Revolution, 1770–1823. Ithaca: Cornell University Press, 1975

Davis, Jefferson. *The Rise and Fall of the Confederate Government.* New York: Thomas Yoseloff, 1958

Dewey, John. *Reconstruction in Philosophy.* Boston: Beacon Press, 1948
The Public and its Problems. Athens, OH: Swallow, 1954
"The Need for a Recovery of Philosophy," in *John Dewey: The Middle Works, 1899–1924,* vol. X. Carbondale: Southern Illinois University Press, 1980

Dickinson, John. *Writings of John Dickinson*, Paul L. Ford, ed. Philadelphia: The Historical Society of Pennsylvania, 1895

Dower, John W. *War Without Mercy: Race and Power in the Pacific War*. New York: Pantheon Books, 1986

Downer, Silas. *A Discourse, Delivered in Providence, in the Colony of Rhode-Island, upon the 25th Day of July, 1768, at the Dedication of the Tree of Liberty from the Summer House in the Tree, By a Son of Liberty*. Providence: John Waterman, 1768

Dubber, Marcus D. "Judicial Positivism and Hitler's Injustice." *Columbia Law Review* 93 (1993): 1807–1831

Dudziak, Mary L. "Desegregation as a Cold War Imperative." *Stanford Law Review* 41 (1988): 61–120

Dulany, Daniel. *Considerations of the Propriety of Imposing Taxes in the British Colonies*. Annapolis: Jonas Green, 1765

Dumbauld, Edward. *The Bill of Rights and What it Means Today*. Norman, OK: University of Oklahoma Press, 1957

Dworkin, Ronald. *Taking Rights Seriously*. London: Duckworth, 1977, repr. 1991

A Matter of Principle. Oxford: Oxford University Press, 1985

Law's Empire. Cambridge, MA: Harvard University Press, 1986

Elliot, Jonathan. *Debates in the Several State Conventions on the Adoption of the Federal Constitution*. Philadelphia: J. B. Lippincott & Co., 1901

Elster, Jon. "Bias, Belief, and Ideology," in Hollis and Lukes, 1982, pp. 123–148

Making Sense of Marx. Cambridge: Cambridge University Press, 1985

Ely, John Hart. *Democracy and Distrust*. Cambridge, MA: Harvard University Press, 1980

Evans, Charles. *American Bibliography: A Chronological Dictionary of all Books, Pamphlets, and Periodical Publications Printed in the United States of America*. New York: Peter Smith, 1941

Farr, James. "Conceptual Change and Constitutional Innovation," in Terrence Ball and J. G. A. Pocock, eds., *Conceptual Change and the Constitution*. Lawrence: The University Press of Kansas, 1988

Farrand, Max, ed. *The Records of the Federal Convention of 1787*, revised edn. New Haven: Yale University Press, 1966

Federalist Papers, Clinton Rossiter, ed. New York: Penguin, 1961

Fehrenbacher, Don E., ed. *Abraham Lincoln: A Documentary Portrait Through His Speeches and Writings*. Stanford, CA: Stanford University Press, 1964

Feinberg, Joel. *Rights, Justice, and the Bounds of Liberty*. Princeton: Princeton University Press, 1980

Fenrich, Robert Lane. "Imagining Holocaust: Mass Death and American Consciousness at the End of World War II." Ph.D. dissertation, Northwestern University, 1992

Fitch, Thomas. *Reasons Why the British Colonies, in America, Should Not be*

Charged with Internal Taxes, by Authority of Parliament. New Haven: B. Mecom., 1764

Foner, Eric. *Free Soil, Free Labor, Free Men: The Ideology of the Republican Party Before the Civil War.* Oxford: Oxford University Press, 1970

Reconstruction: America's Unfinished Revolution, 1863–1877. New York: Harper & Row, 1988

Freeden, Michael. *Rights.* Milton Keynes: Open University Press, 1991

"Political Concepts and Ideological Morphology." *Journal of Political Philosophy* 2(2) (1994): 140–164

Freehling, William. *The Road to Disunion.* New York: Oxford University Press, 1990

Friedman, Leon, ed. *The Civil Rights Reader: Basic Documents of the Civil Rights Movement.* New York: Walker and Co., 1968

Fuller, Lon. "Positivism and Fidelity to Law – A Reply to Professor Hart." *Harvard Law Review* 71 (1958): 630–672

Gadamer, Hans-Georg. *Truth and Method*, 2nd edn., Joel Weinsheimer and Donald G. Marshall, eds. and trans. London: Sheed and Ward, 1993

Galston, William. *Liberal Purposes: Goods, Values, and Diversity in the Liberal State.* Cambridge: Cambridge University Press, 1991

Gillete, William. *The Right to Vote.* Baltimore: Johns Hopkins University Press, 1969

Glendon, Mary Ann. *Rights Talk: The Impoverishment of Political Discourse.* New York: Free Press, 1991.

Glueck, Sheldon. "The Nuernberg Trial and Aggressive War." *Harvard Law Review* 59 (1946): 396–456

Goodman, Nelson. *Fact, Fiction, and Forecast.* Cambridge, MA: Harvard University Press, 1955

Ways of Worldmaking. Indianapolis: Hackett, 1978

Habermas, Jürgen. *Between Facts and Norms: Contributions to a Discourse Theory of Law and Democracy.* Cambridge, MA: MIT Press, 1996

Hamilton, Alexander. *A Full Vindication of the Measures of the Congress, from the Calumnies of their Enemies.* New York: James Rivington, 1774

The Papers of Alexander Hamilton, Harold C. Syrett and Jacob E. Cooke, eds. New York: Columbia University Press, 1961

Handlin, Oscar and Lillian Handlin. *Liberty in America: 1600 to the Present*, vol. II, *Liberty in Expansion, 1760–1850.* New York: Harper & Row, 1989

Harris, Angela. "Foreword: The Jurisprudence of Reconstruction." *California Law Review* 82 (1994): 741–785

Hart, H. L. A. "Positivism and the Separation of Law and Morals." *Harvard Law Review* 71 (1958): 593–629

Essays in Jurisprudence and Philosophy. New York: Oxford University Press, 1983

"Are There Any Natural Rights?" in Waldron, 1984, pp. 77–90

The Concept of Law, Oxford: Oxford University Press, 1994
Hartz, Louis. *The Liberal Tradition in America.* New York: Harcourt Brace and
World, 1955
Heimert, Alan. *Religion and the American Mind from the Great Awakening to the
Revolution.* Cambridge, MA: Harvard University Press, 1966
Henkin, Louis. "Rights: Here and There." *Columbia Law Review* 81 (1981):
1582–1610
Hofstadter, Richard. *The American Political Tradition.* New York: Knopf, 1973
Hohfeld, Wesley. *Fundamental Legal Conceptions as Applied in Judicial Reasoning.*
Westport, CT: Greenwood Press, 1978
Hollis, Martin. "The Social Destruction of Reality," in Hollis and Lukes,
1982, pp. 67–86
Hollis, Martin, and Steven Lukes, eds. *Rationality and Relativism.* Oxford:
Blackwell, 1982
Holly, Israel. *God Brings About his Holy and Wise Purpose or Decree, Concerning
Many Particular Events, by Using and Improving the Wicked Dispositions of
Mankind in Order Thereto.* Hartford: Eben, Watson, 1774
Hopkins, Thomas A., ed. *Rights for Americans: The Speeches of Robert F. Kennedy.*
Indianapolis: Bobbs-Merrill, 1964
Horwitz, Morton. *The Transformation of American Law, 1870–1960.* New York:
Oxford University Press, 1992
Hyman, Harold, ed. *The Radical Republicans and Reconstruction, 1861–1870.*
Indianapolis: Bobbs-Merrill, 1967
Hyman, Harold, and William Wiecek. *Equal Justice Under Law: Constitutional
Development 1835–1875.* New York: Harper & Row, 1982
Inoue, Kyoko. *MacArthur's Japanese Constitution: A Linguistic and Cultural Study
of its Making.* Chicago: University of Chicago Press, 1991
Irons, Peter. *Justice at War.* New York: Oxford University Press, 1983
James, William. *Pragmatism,* Bruce Kuklick, ed. Indianapolis: Hackett, 1981
Jaspers, Karl. "The Nuremberg Trials," William B. Ball, trans. *Notre Dame
Lawyer* 22 (1947): 150–160
Jefferson, Thomas. *A Summary View of the Rights of British America.* Williams-
burg: Clementina Rind, 1774
Basic Writings of Thomas Jefferson, Philip Foner, ed. New York: Wiley, 1944
Papers of Thomas Jefferson, Julian P. Boyd, ed. Princeton: Princeton
University Press, 1950
Jensen, Merrill. *The New Nation.* New York: Knopf, 1950
Journal of the Joint Committee of Fifteen on Reconstruction, Benjamin B. Kedrick,
ed. New York: Columbia, 1914
Kauffman, Arthur. "National Socialism and German Jurisprudence from
1933 to 1945." *Cardozo Law Review* 9 (1988): 1629–1649
King, Martin Luther, Jr. *A Testament of Hope: The Essential Writings of Martin
Luther King, Jr.,* James Melvin Washington, ed. San Francisco: Harper
& Row, 1986

Kluger, Richard. *Simple Justice: The History of Brown v. Board of Education and Black America's Struggle for Equality.* London: André Deutsch, 1977

Konop, Thomas F. "The Fundamental Rights of Man." *Notre Dame Lawyer* (1935) 10: 341–348

Koselleck, Reinhart. *Futures Past: On the Semantics of Historical Time,* Keith Tribe, trans. Cambridge, MA: MIT Press, 1985

Kuhn, Thomas. *The Structure of Scientific Revolutions.* Chicago: University of Chicago Press, 1962

Kurland, Phillip, and Ralph Lerner, eds. *The Founders' Constitution.* Chicago: University of Chicago Press, 1987

Lee, Richard Henry. *The Letters of Richard Henry Lee,* James Curtis Ballagh, ed. New York: Macmillan, 1914

Leventhal, Harold, Sam Harris, John M. Woolsey, Jr., and Warren F. Farr. "The Nuernberg Verdict." *Harvard Law Review* 60 (1947): 857–907

Levinson, Sanford. "The Embarrassing Second Amendment." *Yale Law Journal* 99 (1989): 637–659

Levy, Leonard. *Constitutional Opinions.* New York: Oxford University Press, 1986

Livingston, Philip. *The Other Side of the Question: or, A Defense of the Liberties of North America.* New York: Rivington, 1774

Llewellyn, Karl. "On Reading and Using the Newer Jurisprudence." *Columbia Law Review* 40 (1940): 581–614

Locke, John. *Second Treatise of Government,* C. B. Macpherson, ed. Indianapolis: Hackett, 1980

Lusky, Louis. "Footnote Redux: A *Carolene Products* Reminiscence." *Columbia Law Review* 82 (1982): 1093–1109

Lutz, Donald. "The Relative Influence of European Writers on Late Eighteenth-Century American Political Thought." *American Political Science Review* 78 (1984): 189–197

MacCormick, Neil. *Legal Right and Social Democracy.* Oxford: Clarendon Press, 1982

MacIntyre, Alisdair. *After Virtue.* Notre Dame, IN: University of Notre Dame Press, 1981

MacKinnon, Harold. "Natural Law and Positive Law." *Notre Dame Lawyer* 23 (1948): 125–139

MacPherson, James. *Battle Cry of Freedom.* New York: Oxford University Press, 1988

Madison, James. *The Papers of James Madison,* Charles F. Hobson and Robert A. Rutland, eds. Charlottesville, VA: University Press of Virginia, 1984

Malcolm, Joyce Lee. *To Keep and Bear Arms: The Origin of an Anglo-American Right.* Cambridge, MA: Harvard University Press, 1994

Marshall, T. H. *Citizenship and Social Class.* Cambridge: Cambridge University Press, 1950

Marx, Karl. *The Eighteenth Brumaire of Louis Bonaparte,* Eden and Cedar Paul, trans. New York: International Publishers, 1926

Mather, Moses. *America's Appeal to the Impartial World*. Hartford: Ebenezer Watson, 1775

Mayhew, Jonathan. *Observations on the Charter and Conduct of the Society for the Propagation of the Gospel in Foreign Parts*. Boston: Richard and Samuel Draper, Newbury-Street, Edes and Gill, 1763

McCoy, Donald R., and Richard T. Ruetten. *Quest and Response: Minority Rights and the Truman Administration*. Lawrence: The University Press of Kansas, 1973

McDougal, Myers S., and Gertrude C. K. Leighton. "The Rights of Man in the World Community." *Yale Law Journal* 59 (1949): 60–115

McLoughlin, William G., ed. *Isaac Backus on Church, State, and Calvinism: Pamphlets, 1754–1789*. Cambridge, MA: Harvard University Press, 1968

Middlekauff, Robert. *The Glorious Cause*. New York: Oxford University Press, 1982

Mill, John Stuart. *Utilitarianism*, George Sher, ed. Indianapolis: Hackett, 1979
Principles of Political Economy. Fairfield, NJ: Augustus M. Kelley, 1987

Miller, John. "The Militia and the Army in the Reign of James II." *Historical Journal* 16 (1973): 659–679

Morgan, Edmund S. *Inventing the People: The Rise of Popular Sovereignty in England and America*. New York: Norton, 1988

Morris, Thomas. *Free Men All: The Personal Liberty Laws of the North, 1780–1861*. Baltimore: Johns Hopkins University Press, 1974

Morrison, Samuel Eliot. *Sources and Documents Illustrating the American Revolution 1764–1788 and the Formation of the Federal Constitution*. New York: Oxford University Press, 1965

Muller, Ingo. *Hitler's Justice*. Cambridge, MA: Harvard University Press, 1991

Noble, Oliver. *Some Strictures upon the Sacred Story Recorded in the Book of Esther, Shewing the Power and Oppression of State Ministers tending to the Ruin and Destruction of God's People*. Newbury-Port: E. Luntt and H. W. Tinges, 1775

Novick, Peter. *That Noble Dream: The "Objectivity Question" and the American Historical Profession*. Cambridge: Cambridge University Press, 1988

Nye, Russel B. *Fettered Freedom: Civil Liberties and the Slavery Controversy, 1830–1860*. East Lansing: Michigan State College Press, 1949

Old South Leaflets. Boston: Directors of the Old South Work, 1896–1909

Otis, James. *Rights of the British Colonies Asserted and Proved*. Boston: Edes and Gill, 1764
Vindication of the British Colonies against the Aspersions of the Halifax Gentleman, in His Letter to a Rhode Island Friend. Boston: Edes and Gill, 1765

Paine, Thomas. *Rights of Man*, Henry Collin, ed. New York: Penguin, 1969

Palmer, Ben. "The Natural Law and Pragmatism." *Notre Dame Lawyer* 23 (1948): 313–341

Patterson, Bennet B. *The Forgotten Ninth Amendment*. Indianapolis: Bobbs-Merrill, 1955

Pocock, J. G. A. "Machiavelli, Harrington, and English Political Ideologies in the Eighteenth Century." *William and Mary Quarterly*, 3rd series, 22 (1965)

The Machiavellian Moment: Florentine Political Thought and the Atlantic Republican Tradition. Princeton: Princeton University Press, 1975.

Popper, Karl. *The Poverty of Historicism.* London: Routledge and Kegan Paul, 1957

Posner, Richard A. *The Problems of Jurisprudence.* Cambridge, MA: Harvard University Press, 1990

"Democracy and Dualism." *Transition*, 56 (1992): 68–79

Powell, Lewis F., Jr. "*Carolene Products* Revisited." *Columbia Law Review* 82 (1982): 1087–1092

Purcell, Edward A., Jr. *The Crisis of Democratic Theory: Scientific Naturalism and the Problem of Value.* Lexington: The University Press of Kentucky, 1973

Quincy, Josiah, Jr. *Observations on the Act of Parliament Commonly Called the Boston Port Bill; with Thoughts on Civil Society and Standing Armies.* Boston: Edes and Gill, 1774

Quine, W. V. O. *Word and Object.* Cambridge, MA: MIT Press, 1960

From a Logical Point of View, 2nd edn. Cambridge, MA: Harvard University Press, 1980

"Two Dogmas of Empiricism," in Quine, 1980, pp. 20–47

Rabban, David. "The Emergence of Modern First Amendment Doctrine." *University of Chicago Law Review* 50 (1983): 1205–1355

"Free Speech in Progressive Social Thought." *Texas Law Review* 74 (1996): 951–1038

Radin, Max. "War Crimes and the Crime of War." *Virginia Law Quarterly* 21 (1945): 497–516

"Natural Law and Natural Rights." *Yale Law Journal* 59 (1950): 214–237

Rakove, Jack N. *Original Meanings: Politics and Ideas in the Making of the Constitution.* New York: Vintage Books, 1996

Rawls, John. *A Theory of Justice.* Cambridge, MA: Harvard University Press, 1971

Political Liberalism. New York: Columbia University Press, 1993

Raz, Joseph. "Rights Based Moralities," in Waldron, 1984, pp. 182–200

The Morality of Freedom. Oxford: Oxford University Press, 1986

Reuter, Paul. "Nurnberg 1946 – The Trial." *Notre Dame Lawyer* 23 (1948): 76–97

Richards, David A. J. *Conscience and the Constitution: History, Theory, and Law of the Reconstruction Amendments.* Princeton: Princeton University Press, 1993

Richter, Melvin, ed. *Essays in Theory and History.* Cambridge, MA: Harvard University Press, 1970

Ricoeur, Paul. *Hermeneutics and the Human Sciences,* John B. Thompson, ed. and trans. Cambridge: Cambridge University Press, 1981

Rooney, Miriam Theresa. "Law Without Justice." *Notre Dame Lawyer* 23 (1948): 140–172

Rorty, Richard. *Philosophy and the Mirror of Nature*. Oxford: Blackwell, 1980
Consequences of Pragmatism. Minneapolis: University of Minnesota Press, 1982
Contingency, Irony, and Solidarity. Cambridge: Cambridge University Press, 1989

Rostow, Eugene. "The Japanese American Cases – A Disaster." *Yale Law Journal* (1945) 54: 489–533

Sandel, Michael. *Liberalism and the Limits of Justice*. Cambridge: Cambridge University Press, 1982
Democracy's Discontent: America in Search of a Public Philosophy. Cambridge, MA: Harvard University Press, 1996

Schlesinger, Arthur M., Jr. *The Vital Center*. Boston: Houghton Mifflin, 1949

Searle, John. *Speech Acts: An Essay in the Philosophy of Language*. Cambridge: Cambridge University Press, 1969

A Serious Address to the Inhabitants of the Colony of New York, Containing a full and minute Survey of the Boston-Port Act. New York: Holt, 1774

Shapiro, Fred R. "The Most-Cited Law Review Articles." *California Law Review* 73 (1985): 1540–1554

Shapiro, Ian. *The Evolution of Rights in Liberal Theory*. Cambridge: Cambridge University Press, 1986

Shklar, Judith N. *Ordinary Vices*. Cambridge, MA: Harvard University Press, 1984
Legalism: Law, Morals, and Political Trials. Cambridge, MA: Harvard University Press, 1986
"The Liberalism of Fear," in Nancy Rosenblum, ed., *Liberalism and the Moral Life*. Cambridge, MA: Harvard University Press, 1989
American Citizenship: The Quest for Inclusion. Cambridge, MA: Harvard University Press, 1991

Silber, Norman, and Geoffrey Miller. "Toward 'Neutral Principles' in the Law: Selections from the Oral History of Herbert Wechsler." *Columbia Law Review* 93 (1993): 854–931

Skinner, Quentin. *The Foundations of Modern Political Thought*. Cambridge: Cambridge University Press, 1978
"Language and Political Change," in Ball, Farr, and Hanson, 1989, pp. 6–23

Smith, Rogers. *Liberalism and American Constitutional Law*. Cambridge, MA: Harvard University Press, 1985

Stampp, Kenneth. *The Era of Reconstruction, 1865–1877*. New York: Knopf, 1965

Steiner, Hillel. *An Essay on Rights*. Oxford: Blackwell, 1994

Sternberg, William P. "Natural Law in American Jurisprudence." *Notre Dame Lawyer* 13 (1938): 89–100

Stokes, Anson Phelps. *Church and State in the United States.* New York: Harper
 & Brothers, 1950
Stoljar, Samuel. *An Analysis of Rights.* London: Macmillan, 1984
Storing, Herbert J., ed. *The Complete Anti-Federalist.* Chicago: University of
 Chicago Press, 1981
Strauss, Leo. *Natural Right and History.* Chicago: University of Chicago Press,
 1950
Sunstein, Cass. *The Partial Constitution.* Cambridge, MA: Harvard University
 Press, 1993
Sutherland, Elizabeth, ed. *Letters from Mississippi.* New York: McGraw-Hill,
 1965
Taylor, Charles. "Interpretation and the Sciences of Man," in Taylor, 1985,
 vol. II, pp. 15–57
  Philosophy and the Human Sciences, Philosophical Papers. Cambridge: Cam-
  bridge University Press, 1985
tenBroek, Jacobus. *Equal Under Law.* New York: Collier, 1965
Thacher, Oxenbridge. *The Sentiments of a British American.* Boston: Edes and
 Gill, 1764
Thompson, E. P. *Whigs and Hunters: The Origin of the Black Act.* Harmonds-
 worth: Penguin, 1990
Thorpe, Francis Newton, ed. *The Federal and State Constitutions, Colonial
 Charters, and other Organic Laws of the States, Territories, and Colonies Now or
 Heretofore Forming the United States of America.* Washington, DC: US
 Government Printing Office, 1909
Tuck, Richard. *Natural Rights Theories.* Cambridge: Cambridge University
 Press, 1979
Tully, James. *A Discourse on Property: John Locke and his Adversaries.* Cambridge:
 Cambridge University Press, 1980
Tully, James, ed. *Meaning and Context: Quentin Skinner and his Critics.* Cam-
 bridge: Polity Press, 1988
Vamberry, Rustem. "Law and Legalism." *The Nation* 161 (1945):
 573–575
Waldron, Jeremy, ed. *Theories of Rights.* Oxford: Oxford University Press,
 1984
Walzer, Michael. *Spheres of Justice.* New York: Basic Books, 1983
  Interpretation and Social Criticism. Cambridge, MA: Harvard University
  Press, 1987
Warren, Robert Penn. *The Legacy of the Civil War.* New York: Random
 House, 1961
Weber, Max. *The Methodology of the Social Sciences,* Edward A. Shils and
 Henry A. Finch, trans. and ed. Glencoe, IL: The Free Press, 1949
Wechsler, Herbert. "The Issues of the Nuremberg Trial." *Political Science
 Quarterly* 62 (1947): 11–26
  "Toward Neutral Principles in Constitutional Law." *Harvard Law Review*
  73 (1959): 1–35

West, Cornel. *The American Evasion of Philosophy: A Genealogy of Pragmatism.* Madison: University of Wisconsin Press, 1989

Western, J. R. *The English Militia in the Eighteenth Century: The Story of a Political Issue, 1660–1802.* London: Routledge and Kegan Paul, 1965

Wiecek, William. *Liberty Under Law: The Supreme Court in American Life.* Baltimore: Johns Hopkins University Press, 1988

Williams, Elisha. *The Essential Rights and Liberties of Protestants.* Boston: S. Kneeland and T. Green, 1744

Wills, Gary. *Lincoln at Gettysburg: The Words that Remade America.* New York: Simon & Schuster, 1992

Wilson, James. "Considerations on the Authority of Parliament," in Morrison, 1965, pp. 105–114

Wittgenstein, Ludwig. *Philosophical Investigations,* G. E. M. Anscombe, trans. Oxford: Blackwell, 1958

The Blue and Brown Books, 2nd edn. Oxford: Basil Blackwell, 1969

Wood, Gordon S. *The Creation of the American Republic, 1776–1787.* New York: Norton, 1972

Woodward, C. Vann. *The Strange Career of Jim Crow.* New York: Oxford University Press, 1955

Zevin, B. D., ed. *Nothing to Fear: The Selected Addresses of Franklin Delano Roosevelt, 1932–1945.* London: Hodder & Stoughton, 1947

CASES

Abrams v. United States, 250 U.S. 616 (1919)

Adamson v. California, 332 U.S. 46 (1947)

Ashwander v. TVA, 297 U.S. 288 (1936)

Batson v. Kentucky, 476 U.S. 79 (1986)

Benton v. Maryland, 395 U.S. 784 (1969)

Betts v. Brady 316 U.S. 343 (1942)

Blylew v. United States, 80 U.S. 581 (1873)

Bradwell v. Illinois, 83 U.S. 130 (1873)

Brandenburg v. Ohio, 395 U.S. 444 (1969)

Brown v. Board of Education of Topeka, 347 U.S. 483 (1954)

Carter v. Carter Coal Co., 298 U..S 238 (1936)

Civil Rights Cases, 109 U.S. 3 (1883)

Collin v. Smith, 578 F.2d 1197 (7th Cir. 1978)

Dennis v. United States, 341 U.S. 494 (1951)

Dred Scott v. Stanford, 160 U.S. 393 (1857)

Dubolcet v. Louisiana, 103 U.S. 550 (1880)

Duncan v. Louisiana, 391 U.S. 145 (1968)

Escobedo v. Illinois, 378 U.S. 478 (1964)

Ex Parte Mitsuye Endo, 323 U.S. 283 (1944)

Ex Parte Virginia, 100 U.S. 339 (1880)

Everson v. Board of Education, 330 U.S. 1 (1947)

Gideon v. Wainright, 372 U.S. 335 (1963)
Griswold v. Connecticut, 381 U.S. 479 (1965)
Grovey v. Townsend, 295 U.S. 45 (1935)
Hirabayashi v. United States, 320 U.S. 81 (1943)
Hornbuckle v. Toombs, 85 U.S. 648 (1873)
In Re Oliver, 333 U.S. 257 (1948)
In re Turner, 24 F. Cas. 337 (1867)
J. E. B. v. Alabama, 511 U.S. 127 (1994)
Johnson v. Louisiana, 406 U.S. 256 (1972)
Johnson v. United States, 333 U.S. 10 (1948)
Klopfer v. North Carolina, 386 U.S. 213 (1967)
Korematsu v. United States, 323 U.S. 214 (1944)
Lemmon v. People, 20 N.Y. 562 (1860)
Lochner v. New York, 198 U.S. 45 (1905)
Malloy v. Hogan, 378 U.S. 1 (1964)
Map v. Ohio, 367 U.S. 463 (1961)
Minersville School District v. Gobitis, 310 U.S. 586 (1940)
Morgan v. Virginia, 328 U.S. 373 (1946)
Neal v. Delaware, 103 U.S. 370 (1880)
Nebbia v. New York, 291 U.S. 502 (1934)
Paris Adult Theatre I v. Slaton, 413 U.S. 49 (1973)
People v. Washington, 36 Cal. 658 (1869)
Plessy v. Ferguson, 163 U.S. 544 (1896)
Pointer v. Texas, 380 U.S. 400 (1965)
Robinson v. California, 370 U.S. 660 (1962)
Roe v. Wade, 410 U.S. 113 (1973)
Schechter Poultry Corp. v. United States, 295 U.S. 495 (1935)
Shanks v. DuPont, 28 U.S. 242 (1830)
Shelley v. Kraemer, 334 U.S. 1 (1948)
Slaughterhouse Cases, 83 U.S. 36 (1873)
Smith v. Allwright, 321 U.S. 649 (1944)
Strauder v. West Virginia, 100 U.S. 303 (1880)
Tennessee Electric Power Co. v. TVA, 306 U.S. 118 (1939)
United Public Workers v. Mitchell, 330 U.S. 75 (1947)
United States v. Carolene Products Co., 304 U.S. 144 (1938)
United States v. Cruikshank, 92 U.S. 542 (1875)
United States v. Joseph, 94 U.S. 614 (1876)
United States v. Reese, 92 U.S. 214 (1876)
Virginia v. Rives, 100 U.S. 313 (1880)
Washington v. Texas, 388 U.S. 14 (1967)
West Coast Hotel Co. v. Parrish, 300 U.S. 379 (1937)
West Virginia State Board of Education v. Barnette, 319 U.S. 624 (1943)
Williams v. Florida, 399 U.S. 78 (1970)
Wolf v. Colorado, 338 U.S. 25 (1949)
Yick Wo v. Hopkins, 118 U.S. 356 (1886)

Index

IDEAS IN CONTEXT

Edited by QUENTIN SKINNER (*General Editor*),
LORRAINE DASTON and JAMES TULLY

Titles marked with an asterisk are also available in paperback